THE NEW FOLGER LIBRARY SHAKESPEARE

Designed to make Shakespeare's great plays available to all readers, the New Folger Library edition of Shakespeare's plays provides accurate texts in modern spelling and punctuation, as well as scene-by-scene action summaries, full explanatory notes, many pictures clarifying Shakespeare's language, and notes recording all significant departures from the early printed versions. Each play is prefaced by a brief introduction, by a guide to reading Shakespeare's language, and by accounts of his life and theater. Each play is followed by an annotated list of further readings and by a "Modern Perspective" written by an expert on that particular play.

Barbara A. Mowat is Director of Research *emerita* at the Folger Shakespeare Library, Consulting Editor of *Shakespeare Quarterly*, and author of *The Dramaturgy of Shakespeare's Romances* and of essays on Shakespeare's plays and their editing.

Paul Werstine is Professor of English in the Graduate School and at King's University College at Western University. He is a general editor of the New Variorum Shakespeare and author of *Early Modern Playhouse Manuscripts and the Editing of Shakespeare*, as well as many papers and essays on the printing and editing of Shakespeare's plays.

Folger Shakespeare Library

The Folger Shakespeare Library in Washington, D.C., is a privately funded research library dedicated to Shakespeare and the civilization of early modern Europe. It was founded in 1932 by Henry Clay and Emily Jordan Folger, and incorporated as part of Amherst College in Amherst, Massachusetts, one of the nation's oldest liberal arts colleges, from which Henry Folger had graduated in 1879. In addition to its role as the world's preeminent Shakespeare collection and its emergence as a leading center for Renaissance studies, the Folger Shakespeare Library offers a wide array of cultural and educational programs and services for the general public.

EDITORS

BARBARA A. MOWAT
Director of Research emerita
Folger Shakespeare Library

PAUL WERSTINE
Professor of English
King's University College at the University of Western Ontario, Canada

FOLGER SHAKESPEARE LIBRARY

The Two Noble Kinsmen

By WILLIAM SHAKESPEARE
and JOHN FLETCHER

EDITED BY BARBARA A. MOWAT
AND PAUL WERSTINE

SIMON & SCHUSTER PAPERBACKS
NEW YORK LONDON TORONTO SYDNEY

Simon & Schuster Paperbacks
A Division of Simon & Schuster, Inc.
1230 Avenue of the Americas
New York, NY 10020

Copyright © 2010 by The Folger Shakespeare Library

This Simon & Schuster paperback edition April 2010

SIMON & SCHUSTER PAPERBACKS and colophon are
registered trademarks of Simon & Schuster, Inc.

For information regarding special discounts for bulk purchases,
please contact Simon & Schuster Special Sales at 1-866-506-1949
or business@simonandschuster.com.

The Simon & Schuster Speakers Bureau can bring authors
to your live event. For more information or to book an
event, contact the Simon & Schuster Speakers Bureau at
1-866-248-3049 or visit our website at www.simonspeakers.com.

Manufactured in the United States of America

10   9   8   7   6   5

ISBN 978-0-671-72296-8

From the Director of the Folger Shakespeare Library

It is hard to imagine a world without Shakespeare. Since their composition four hundred years ago, Shakespeare's plays and poems have traveled the globe, inviting those who see and read his works to make them their own.

Readers of the New Folger Editions are part of this ongoing process of "taking up Shakespeare," finding our own thoughts and feelings in language that strikes us as old or unusual and, for that very reason, new. We still struggle to keep up with a writer who could think a mile a minute, whose words paint pictures that shift like clouds. These expertly edited texts, presented here with accompanying explanatory notes and up-to-date critical essays, are distinctive because of what they do: they allow readers not simply to keep up, but to engage deeply with a writer whose works invite us to think, and think again.

These New Folger Editions of Shakespeare's plays are also special because of where they come from. The Folger Shakespeare Library in Washington, DC, where the Editions are produced, is the single greatest documentary source of Shakespeare's works. An unparalleled collection of early modern books, manuscripts, and artwork connected to Shakespeare, the Folger's holdings have been consulted extensively in the preparation of these texts. The Editions also reflect the expertise gained through the regular performance of Shakespeare's works in the Folger's Elizabethan Theater.

I want to express my deep thanks to editors Barbara Mowat and Paul Werstine for creating these indispensable editions of Shakespeare's works, which incorporate the best of textual scholarship with a richness of commentary that is both inspired and engaging. Readers who want to know more about Shakespeare and his plays can follow the paths these distinguished scholars have tread by visiting the Folger itself, where a range of physical and digital resources (available online) exist to supplement the material in these texts. I commend to you these words, and hope that they inspire.

Michael Witmore
Director, Folger Shakespeare Library

Contents

Editors' Preface

In recent years, ways of dealing with Shakespeare's texts and with the interpretation of his plays have been undergoing significant change. This edition, while retaining many of the features that have always made the Folger Shakespeare so attractive to the general reader, at the same time reflects these current ways of thinking about Shakespeare and his contemporaries. For example, modern readers, actors, and teachers have become interested in the differences between, on the one hand, the early forms in which Shakespeare's plays were first published and, on the other hand, the forms in which editors through the centuries have presented them. In response to this interest, we have based our edition on what we consider the best early printed version of a particular play (explaining our rationale in a section called "An Introduction to This Text") and have marked our changes in the text—unobtrusively, we hope, but in such a way that the curious reader can be aware that a change has been made and can consult the "Textual Notes" to discover what appeared in the early printed version.

Current ways of looking at the plays are reflected in our brief introductions, in many of the commentary notes, in the annotated lists of "Further Reading," and especially in each play's "Modern Perspective," an essay written by an outstanding scholar who brings to the reader his or her fresh assessment of the play in the light of today's interests and concerns.

As in the Folger Library General Readers' Shakespeare, which this edition replaces, we include explanatory notes designed to make Shakespeare's language clearer to a modern reader, and we place the notes on the page facing the text that they explain. We also follow the earlier edition in including illustrations— of objects, of clothing, of mythological figures—from books and manuscripts in the Folger Shakespeare Library collection. We provide fresh accounts of the life of Shakespeare, of the publishing of his plays, and of the theaters in which his plays were performed, as well as an introduction to the text itself. We also include a section called "Reading Shakespeare's Language," in which we try to help readers learn to "break the code" of Elizabethan poetic language. (For this play, which was coauthored by John Fletcher, we call this section "Reading the Language of *The Two Noble Kinsmen*.")

For each section of each volume, we are indebted to a host of generous experts and fellow scholars. The "Reading Shakespeare's Language" sections, for example, could not have been written had not Arthur King, of Brigham Young University, and Randall Robinson, author of *Unlocking Shakespeare's Language*, led the way in untangling Shakespearean language puzzles and shared their insights and methodologies generously with us. "Shakespeare's Life" profited by the careful reading given it by the late S. Schoenbaum; "Shakespeare's Theater" was read and strengthened by Andrew Gurr, John Astington, and William Ingram; and "The Publication of Shakespeare's Plays" is indebted to the comments of Peter W. M. Blayney. We, as editors, take sole responsibility for any errors in our editions.

We are grateful to the authors of the "Modern Perspectives"; to Leeds Barroll and David Bevington for their generous encouragement; to the Huntington and Newberry Libraries for fellowship support; to King's University College for the grants it has provided to Paul Werstine; to the Social Sciences and Humanities Research Council of Canada, which has provided him with Research Time Stipends; to R. J. Shroyer of the

University of Western Ontario for essential computer support; to the Folger Institute's Center for Shakespeare Studies for its sponsorship of a workshop on "Shakespeare's Texts for Students and Teachers" (funded by the National Endowment for the Humanities and led by Richard Knowles of the University of Wisconsin), a workshop from which we learned an enormous amount about what is wanted by college and high school teachers of Shakespeare today; to Alice Falk for her expert copyediting; and especially to Stephen Llano, our production editor at Simon & Schuster, whose expertise and attention to detail are essential to this project. Our special thanks to Stanley Curtis for sharing his expertise on, and directing us to a picture of, early modern cornets (see page 70) and to Sarah Weiner for putting us in touch with him. Of the editions we consulted, we found Lois Potter's 1997 Arden 3 edition especially useful.

Our biggest debt is to the Folger Shakespeare Library—to Gail Kern Paster, Director of the Library, whose interest and support are unfailing (and whose scholarly expertise is an invaluable resource) and to Werner Gundersheimer, the Library's Director from 1984 to 2002, who made possible our edition; to Deborah Curren-Aquino, who provides extensive editorial and production support; to Jean Miller, the Library's former Art Curator, who combs the Library holdings for illustrations, and to Julie Ainsworth, Head of the Photography Department, who carefully photographs them; to Peggy O'Brien, former Director of Education at the Folger and now Chief of Family and Public Engagement for the District of Columbia Public Schools, who gave us expert advice about the needs being expressed by Shakespeare teachers and students (and to Martha Christian and other "master teachers" who used our texts in manuscript in their classrooms); to Mary Bloodworth and Michael Poston for their

Shakespeare and Fletcher's
The Two Noble Kinsmen

This play tells the story of a very typical love triangle—
best friends swear devotion to each other until they
both fall in love with the same girl. It's an age-old story
that continues to intrigue us, whether we find it in a
novel or a movie or a play. Here, though, it manages
to seem both familiar and strange. Written (according
to the title page of its 1634 printing) by Shakespeare
and John Fletcher (Shakespeare's replacement as principal dramatist for the King's players), the play is based
on the first story in Chaucer's *Canterbury Tales*, "The
Knight's Tale." There the dramatists found the love triangle consisting of the two Theban knights Arcite and
Palamon and their beloved Emelye, sister of Hippolyta
the Duchess of Athens. Chaucer had in turn found the
story in a yet earlier Italian narrative poem by Boccaccio. Thus in *The Two Noble Kinsmen* we have a late
medieval narrative transformed into a seventeenth-
century play—a familiar kind of story, but a fascinat-
ingly distant and strange work of art.

Initially in "The Knight's Tale" and in *The Two Noble
Kinsmen*, Arcite and Palamon are completely devoted
to each other's interests, bound together as kinsmen
and as knights in the service of the same king, Creon,
who, early in the play, is defeated by Theseus, Duke
of Athens; Arcite and Palamon are captured and sen-
tenced to perpetual imprisonment in Athens. Once
they see from their prison window the beautiful Emilia
(as Shakespeare and Fletcher rename her) in a garden
below, they immediately become rivals for her love,
eager to fight to the death for sole possession of her.

Part of the strangeness of the play is that in their pursuit of Emilia, they give no thought to the fact that she is ignorant of their existence, that she is a member of the royal family that just defeated their city, and that they, as her brother-in-law's prisoners of war, are powerless over their own fates.

Still more strange, though, is the play's celebration of the nobility of Arcite and Palamon as fighters and of the magnificence of their desire for Emilia—a desire so consuming that their lives seem to them worthless without her. Arcite is suddenly pardoned and released, banished from Athens; then Palamon escapes. Neither will leave the country where death hangs over their heads but where Emilia lives. Encountering each other in a wood outside Athens, they manage, with armor and weapons stolen by Arcite from Theseus, and with the elaborate courtesy and ceremony befitting noble kinsmen, to begin their fight to the death for Emilia. Theseus, happening on them and impetuously sentencing both to die, then reverses his judgment out of admiration for the nobility of their violent longing. He decrees that the rivals must fight in a tournament under his auspices and persuades Emilia to accept the victor in marriage. Theseus will execute the loser—just as the loser would wish.

Although Emilia can be made to marry the winner, she is no willing bride. She has been in love before, in her girlhood, with Flavina, who has died, and she wishes to be spared from marriage. As the fateful tournament approaches, she repeatedly tries to avert it by choosing in advance between Arcite and Palamon, but while she admires both as far more worthy than herself, she cannot choose. (In this way, perhaps, Shakespeare and Fletcher exploit one of the famous features of Chaucer's "Knight's Tale," the virtual impossibility of distinguishing between Arcite and Palamon.) Emilia eventually prays to be allowed to remain a virgin.

The play's simultaneous familiarity and strangeness continue with an intriguing character that Shakespeare and Fletcher add on to Chaucer's love triangle: the impressionable late adolescent daughter of the Athenian jailor. She can see a difference between the Theban knights and becomes so infatuated with Palamon that she helps him escape from her father's jail in the hope that he will love her, even though she thereby risks her own life and her father's. If Palamon were to return her love, *The Two Noble Kinsmen* would have the necessary ingredients for a comedy, with both knights finding love and marriage; such a comic resolution of a love triangle is a familiar one. However, in the seventeenth century the social gulf between the royal Theban knight Palamon and the Athenian commoner is unimaginably wide—so much so that he cannot even recognize her affection for him. So fraught are the human relations of the play that only the gods can eventually bring them to their resolution.

After you have read the play, we invite you to turn to the essay printed after it, "*The Two Noble Kinsmen:* A Modern Perspective," written by Professor Dieter Mehl of the University of Bonn.

Phoebus Apollo driving the horses of the sun.
From Vincenzo Cartari, *Le vere e noue imagini . . .* (1615).

Hercules. (1.1.73–77; 2.5.2; 3.6.224–25; 5.3.143)
From Vincenzo Cartari, *Le vere e noue imagini* . . . (1615).

The goddess Diana. (2.5.71; 4.2.65; 5.1.100–102)
From Robert Whitcombe, *Janua divorum* . . . (1678).

Reading the Language of
The Two Noble Kinsmen

For many people today, reading the language of seventeenth-century drama can be a problem—but it is a problem that can be solved. Those who have studied Latin (or even French or German or Spanish), and those who are used to reading poetry, will have little difficulty understanding the language of *The Two Noble Kinsmen*. Others, though, need to develop the skills of untangling unusual sentence structures and of recognizing and understanding poetic compressions, omissions, and wordplay. And even those skilled in reading unusual sentence structures may have occasional trouble with the words in the play. Four hundred years of "static" intervene between its speaking and our hearing. Most of its vocabulary is still in use, but some of its words are no longer used, and many now have meanings quite different from those they had in the seventeenth century. In the theater, most of these difficulties are solved for us by actors who study the language and articulate it for us so that the essential meaning is heard—or, when combined with stage action, is at least *felt*. When we are reading on our own, we must do what each actor does: go over the lines (often with a dictionary close at hand) until the puzzles are solved, the characters speak in words and phrases that are, suddenly, understandable and meaningful, and we find ourselves caught up in the story being dramatized.

Words

As you begin to read the opening scenes of a seventeenth-century poetic drama, you may notice unfamiliar words. Some are simply no longer in use. In the early scenes of *The Two Noble Kinsmen*, for example, we find the words *meditance* (i.e., meditation), *visitating* (i.e., visiting), *unpanged* (i.e., not afflicted with mental or physical anguish), and *futurely* (i.e., hereafter). More problematic are the words that are still in use but that now have different meanings. In the opening scenes of this play, for example, the word *undertaker* is used where we would say "supporter, helper," *respect* where we would say "pay attention to," *quaint* where we would say "pretty," and *pretended* where we would say "intended" or "planned." Such words will be explained in the notes to the text, but they will become familiar as you continue to read seventeenth-century drama.

Some words found in seventeenth-century poetic drama are strange not because of the "static" introduced by changes in language over the past centuries but because these are words that the writer is using to build a dramatic world that has its own space, time, and history. In the opening scene of *The Two Noble Kinsmen*, for example, the playwrights construct a vivid confrontation between a royal Athenian wedding party with its "maiden pinks" and "oxlips" and "lark's-heels trim," on the one hand, and, on the other, three weeping queens whose language makes vivid the devastated world of Thebes from which they come, with its unburied corpses lying "swoll'n" in "th' blood-sized field," "blist'ring 'fore the visitating sun" and attacked by "beaks of ravens, talons of the kites," their skulls "grinning at the moon." The language of this dramatic world fills it not only with such "mortal loathsomeness" but also with mythological gods and heroes—with "Mars's altar," "Juno's mantle," "holy Phoebus," "helmeted Bellona," and "Hercules" tumbling down upon "his Nemean hide"—as well as with allusions to a familiar mythological past: to Hippolyta's former life as the "dreaded Amazonian" who killed "the scythe-tusked boar," to the renown of Theseus, whose "fame / Knolls in the ear o' th' world," to (in scene 2) Juno's "ancient fit of jealousy," and to Phoebus Apollo's past rage against "the horses of the sun." Such language builds the world in which the adventures of "two noble kinsmen" are played out.

Sentences

In an English sentence, meaning is quite dependent on the place given each word. "The dog bit the boy" and "The boy bit the dog" mean very different things, even though the individual words are the same. Because English places such importance on the positions of words in sentences, unusual arrangements can puzzle a reader. Seventeenth-century poetic drama frequently shifts sentences away from "normal" English arrangements—often to create the rhythm that is sought, sometimes to emphasize a particular word, sometimes to give a character his or her own speech patterns, or to allow the character to speak in a special way. When we attend a good performance of such a play, the actors will have worked out the sentence structures and will articulate the sentences so that the meaning is clear. When reading the play, we need to do as the actor does: that is, when puzzled by a character's speech, check to see if words are being presented in an unusual sequence.

Sometimes such dramas rearrange subjects and

verbs (i.e., instead of "He goes" we find "Goes he"). In *The Two Noble Kinsmen*, when Hippolyta explains that she never before followed a path so willingly ("never yet / *Went I* so willing way"), she uses such a construction (1.1.114–15). So does Theseus when he later says "Now *turn we* towards your comforts" (1.1.275). The "normal" order would be "I went" and "we turn." These dramas also frequently place the object or the predicate adjective before the subject and verb (i.e., instead of "I hit him," we might find "Him I hit," or, instead of "It is black," we might find "Black it is"). Theseus provides an example of this kind of inversion when he says "But those we will depute" (1.4.12), and another example when he says "Troubled I am" (1.1.86). The "normal" order would be "we will depute those" and "I am troubled."

Often *The Two Noble Kinsmen* uses inverted sentences that fall outside these categories. Such sentences must be studied individually until their structure can be perceived. Theseus's comment, "Fortune at you / Dimpled her cheek with smiles" (1.1.72–73), is a relatively simple example of such an inversion. Its "normal" order would be "Fortune dimpled her cheek with smiles at you." Arcite's "[H]ere to keep in abstinence we shame / As in incontinence" (1.2.6–7) is more complicated. Its "normal" order would be, approximately, "We shame to keep in abstinence here as [much] as in incontinence."

Inversions are not the only unusual sentence structures in plays of this period. Often words that would normally appear together are separated from each other. Like inversions, separations—of subjects and verbs, for example—frequently create a particular rhythm or stress a particular word, or else draw attention to a particular piece of information. Take, for example, Theseus's "*Hercules*, our kinsman, / Then weaker than your eyes, *laid by his club*" (1.1.73–75). Here the subject ("Hercules") is separated from its verb ("laid by") by the subject's two modifiers, "our kinsman" and "Then weaker than your eyes." The first modifier provides a piece of information that contributes to the play's mythological background; the second, extolling the First Queen's youthful eyes as more powerful than legend's strongest man, makes vivid Theseus's memory of her when young. By allowing these modifiers briefly to shoulder aside the verb, the sentence calls attention to a bit of mythological context and to the contrast between the remembered powerful eyes of the young queen and the present "blubbered" eyes (1.1.208) of the widow. Or take the Second Queen's

> this *thy lord,*
> Born to uphold creation in that honor
> First nature styled it in, *shrunk* thee into
> The bound thou wast o'erflowing[.]
>
> (1.1.91–94)

Here the subject and verb ("thy lord . . . shrunk") are separated by a truncated clause ("[who was] born to uphold creation in that honor first nature styled it in"), a clause that justifies the Second Queen's affirmation of Theseus's conquest of Hippolyta: Theseus, she claims, was born to preserve intact the superiority of the male, to uphold that which is right and proper in the natural world. By inserting this metaphysical clause between "thy lord" and "shrunk," the queen presents this world-view as self-evident, not a point to be argued. On a first reading of sentences such as these, it is helpful to locate the basic sentence elements and mentally rearrange the words into a more familiar order; on later readings, or when attending a good performance of the play, we can fully enjoy the sentences' complexity and subtlety.

Locating and rearranging words that "belong together" is especially necessary in passages in which long interruptions separate basic sentence elements. When the Second Queen begs Hippolyta, as "soldieress," to entreat Theseus to protect her and the other queens ("Bid him that we . . . Under the shadow of his sword may cool us"), she uses such a construction:

> *soldieress*
> That equally canst poise sternness with pity,
> Whom now I know hast much more power on him
> Than ever he had on thee, who ow'st his strength
> And his love too, who is a servant for
> The tenor of thy speech, dear glass of ladies,
> *Bid* him that we, whom flaming war doth scorch,
> Under the shadow of his sword may cool us[.]
> (1.1.95–102)

Here, the separation between "soldieress" and "bid" is extensive and complex, made up of four clauses, three modifying "soldieress" and one modifying "he" (i.e., Theseus)—so complex that Hippolyta is addressed again ("dear glass of ladies") before the verb ("Bid"). And at this point, the subject-verb sequence ("we . . . may cool us") is interrupted for a second time, here by a clause and two prepositional phrases.

In *The Two Noble Kinsmen*, sentences often combine unusual structures in complicated configurations. Consider the Third Queen's protest against the unfairness of the edict forbidding the burial of her dead husband, who died valiantly in battle. Even suicides, she argues, are allowed burial:

> Those that with cords, knives, drams, precipitance,
> Weary of this world's light, have to themselves
> Been death's most horrid agents, human grace
> Affords them dust and shadow.
> (1.1.162–65)

What initially may appear to be the elements of this sentence's structure ("Those that . . . have . . . been . . . agents") are separated by three phrases ("with cords, knives, drams, precipitance," "weary of this world's light," "to themselves"). Only in the third line, with the introduction of a new subject ("human grace") and its verb ("affords"), do we discover that the long opening clause is, in effect, the indirect object of "affords," an expansion of the "them" who are afforded "dust and shadow." It is almost impossible to rearrange the words of these lines into a "normal," straightforward sentence; however, once one untangles the structures and understands the function of the basic sentence elements and the interrupting words and phrases, the lines become a powerful, angry plea for the queen's cause.

Wordplay

The Two Noble Kinsmen depends heavily on wordplay, especially on metaphors and on puns. A metaphor is a play on words in which one object or idea is expressed as if it were something else, something with which the metaphor suggests it shares common features. The Third Queen, when begging Emilia to take her part, uses a metaphor to express the reward that will be in store for Emilia: "This good deed," she says, "Shall raze you out o' th' book of trespasses / All you are set down there" (1.1.34–36). Emilia's life is here imaged as a written record of her sins; the "good deed" here becomes a kind of eraser that will obliterate that record. Later, when the First Queen wants to suggest that Theseus is powerful enough to redeem from King Creon of Thebes the rotting corpses of her husband and his fellow kings for proper burial, she calls Theseus "Thou purger of the earth" (1.1.52), thereby through metaphor making him into war itself, whose act of destruction was often compared to a cleansing of the earth. The Third Queen also resorts to metaphor when she apologizes for not being able to achieve eloquence because she is weeping: "O, my petition was / Set down in ice, which by hot grief uncandied / Melts into drops" (1.1.118–20). She thus compares the fixed state of the speech she had prepared in her mind to ice that her grief has melted ("uncandied") into tears.

In this play, metaphors tend to follow each other in rapid succession. Note, for example, Emilia's description of the love between Theseus and Pirithous as contrasted with her youthful love for "the maid Flavina" (1.3.96):

> Theirs has more ground, is more maturely seasoned,
> More buckled with strong judgment, and their
>   needs
> The one of th' other may be said to water
> Their intertangled roots of love.
>
>   (1.3.66–69)

In these four lines, the love of Theseus and Pirithous is, first, an edifice or structure on a larger foundation or base ("more ground"); it becomes "more maturely seasoned" timber, then a body more strongly armored (i.e., its body armor fastened "with strong judgment"), and, finally, a set of intertwined roots watered by "their needs / The one of th' other."

Only occasionally, as in the following example, does a single metaphor dominate many successive poetic lines:

>   not to swim
> I' th' aid o' th' current were almost to sink,
> At least to frustrate striving; and to follow

> The common stream, 'twould bring us to an eddy
> Where we should turn or drown; if labor through,
> Our gain but life and weakness.
>
> (1.2.7–12)

Here, Arcite urges Palamon to join him in leaving Thebes, which he considers corrupt and therefore dangerous for the two of them, whether they refuse to go along with the city's corruption or accept it and attempt to fit in. His argument is presented in the form of an extended metaphor in which they are swimmers in a strong current. If they attempt to go against the current in which they find themselves, they will come close to sinking or be frustrated and defeated; if, on the other hand, they choose to go with the current, they will be trapped and spun around in an eddy and either drown, or, if they escape the whirlpool, will be left barely alive, weakened and debilitated.

Because in this play metaphors are used so frequently and (whether in rapid succession or extended over many lines) written in such highly compressed language, they require, on first reading, an untangling similar to that recommended for the play's complex sentence structures. But, as with the complex structures, the untangling is worth the effort. In Arcite's speech quoted above, for instance, the image of the swimmers in the stream, struggling against the current or hurled around in the whirlpool, is remarkably vivid and is captured in a mere handful of lines of poetry.

A pun is a play on words that sound the same but that have different meanings (or on a single word that has more than one meaning). *The Two Noble Kinsmen* uses both kinds of puns, and uses them often. In the play's first scene, for example, Theseus responds to the pleas of the three queens that he forgo his wedding in order to battle Creon by saying

> Why, good ladies,
> This is a service whereto I am going
> Greater than any was; it more imports me
> Than all the actions that I have foregone,
> Or futurely can cope.
>
> (1.1.197–201)

In these lines, he puns first on the word *service*, which means both "duty of a soldier" and "ceremony" (here, of marriage). This is meaningful wordplay, in that it brings together in a single word his commitment to his military duty and to Hippolyta. He then puns on the word *actions* as "military engagements" and as "acts or deeds." Here, the primary meaning is military, but once again he nicely joins the deeds of his life with his military feats in a single word. *Service* and *actions* each play on a single word that has more than one meaning. Another example of the many such puns in this play is Arcite's "We shall know nothing here but one another, / Hear nothing but the clock that tells our woes" (where *tells* means both "counts" and "reports" [2.2.45–46]); yet another is the Woman's response to Emilia's likening of a virgin to a rose: "Sometimes her modesty will blow [blossom, flourish] so far / She falls for 't" (where "she falls" means simultaneously "the rose falls off the stem" and "the virgin surrenders her chastity" [2.2.177–78]).

When Theseus, later in the first scene, says farewell to Hippolyta with the words "I stamp this kiss upon thy currant lip; / Sweet, keep it as my token" (1.1.253–54), he puns on the words *currant* and *current*, words that sound the same but have different meanings. In this interesting example of wordplay, the primary meaning, *currant*, "red, like the fruit," applies most immediately and naturally to Hippolyta's lips; the secondary meaning, *current*, "sterling, genuine, having the quality of current coin," is emphasized by the words *stamp* and *token*, terms related to the stamping of coins and to tokens as stamped pieces of metal used like coins (another bit of wordplay, since this meaning of *token* is secondary to Theseus's primary meaning of "keepsake" or "love token"). The same type of pun is found in Act 3, scene 1, when, in response to Arcite's "Dear cousin Palamon—," Palamon replies "Cozener Arcite" (46–47). A *cozener* is a cheater or deceiver, and play on these similar-sounding words was common. In our commentary notes on the text, we have noted many examples of such wordplay, but a careful reader will discover many that we failed to see or that we had insufficient space to mention—some of them trivial, but many of them interesting and sometimes significant.

Implied Stage Action

Finally, in reading seventeenth-century poetic drama—indeed, in reading any drama—we should always remember that what we are reading is a performance script. The dialogue is written to be spoken by actors who, at the same time, are moving, gesturing, picking up objects, weeping, shaking their fists. Some stage action is described in what are called "stage directions"; some is signaled within the dialogue itself. We must learn to be alert to such signals as we stage the play in our imaginations.

Sometimes the dialogue offers an immediately clear indication of the action that is to accompany it. In *The Two Noble Kinsmen* 2.5, for example, Pirithous takes the disguised Arcite to Emilia, saying to him "Kiss her fair hand, sir." When Arcite then says to Emilia, "Dearest beauty, / Thus let me seal my vowed faith" (53–55), it is clear that he kisses her hand. Again, in 3.5, when the Jailer's Daughter says to the Schoolmaster "Give me your hand. . . . I can tell your fortune" and then says "You are a fool" (90–93), we can feel certain that between her promise to tell his fortune and her reading of his character as that of "a fool," she has looked at his hand. (In each of these cases, we have added the appropriate stage direction marked in brackets to indicate that it is our addition.)

Often in this play, though, signals to the reader (and to the director, actor, and editor) are not at all clear. In the opening scene, for instance, even though the early text provides extremely clear directions for the opening action, specifying which queen kneels to which member of the Athenian nobility, it gives almost no guidance as to when they stand; thus, our bracketed stage directions raising the queens from their knees are placed where it seems to us to make most sense for them to stand. We put these directions for the queens to rise, one by one, at the points where each is explicitly instructed to rise by the Athenian she is supplicating, or when, in the case of the Second Queen, Hippolyta grants what is being begged of her. Conversely, later in the scene, it is made clear that at some point, Hippolyta and Emilia kneel to Theseus; the evidence is at line 240, when he says to them "Pray stand up," and then adds "I am entreating of myself to do / That which you kneel to have me" (241–42). Here, the point at which they stand is specified in this dialogue, but the play leaves much less clear the moment when each of them should kneel. In this passage, we locate our directions for them to kneel at the points at which each begins explicitly to petition Theseus, again putting the directions in brackets. However, we would not argue that our edited version is the only possible alternative.

In *The Two Noble Kinsmen*, then, readers are often given the opportunity to practice the skill of reading the language of stage action, of imagining the move-ment or gesture that should—or, at least, that *might*—accompany a given bit of dialogue. That practice repays us many times over when we reach scenes heavily dependent on stage business. Act 3, scene 5, for instance, fills the stage with action and spectacle, from the gathering of the countrymen and -women, dressed in costumes appropriate for the morris dance to follow, to the entrance of the mad young woman (the Jailer's Daughter), who then joins the dancers, to the arrival of the court party and the setting out of chairs, to the morris dance itself, and then the formal exit of Theseus and his court. For a reader, this scene requires a vivid stage-related imagination. But with such an imagination, scenes like this one—along with, for example, the scene of the interrupted trial by combat (3.6) and the scene in which the two knights and Emilia each pray before the altar of their chosen god (5.1)—may come to life much as they do on the stage.

CATECHISMVS

paruus pueris primùm Latinè
qui ediscatur , proponendus
in Scholis.

LONDINI
Apud Iohannem Dayum Typo-
graphum. An. 1573.

Cum Priuilegio Regiæ Maiestatis.

Title page of a 1573 Latin and Greek catechism for children.

Shakespeare's Life

Surviving documents that give us glimpses into the life of William Shakespeare show us a playwright, poet, and actor who grew up in the market town of Stratford-upon-Avon, spent his professional life in London, and returned to Stratford a wealthy land-owner. He was born in April 1564, died in April 1616, and is buried inside the chancel of Holy Trinity Church in Stratford.

We wish we could know more about the life of the world's greatest dramatist. His plays and poems are testaments to his wide reading—especially to his knowledge of Virgil, Ovid, Plutarch, Holinshed's *Chronicles*, and the Bible—and to his mastery of the English language, but we can only speculate about his education. We know that the King's New School in Stratford-upon-Avon was considered excellent. The school was one of the English "grammar schools" established to educate young men, primarily in Latin grammar and literature. As in other schools of the time, students began their studies at the age of four or five in the attached "petty school," and there learned to read and write in English, studying primarily the catechism from the Book of Common Prayer. After two years in the petty school, students entered the lower form (grade) of the grammar school, where they began the serious study of Latin grammar and Latin texts that would occupy most of the remainder of their school days. (Several Latin texts that Shakespeare used repeatedly in writing his plays and poems were texts that schoolboys memorized and recited.) Latin comedies were introduced early in the lower form; in the upper form, which the boys entered at age ten or eleven, students wrote their own Latin orations and declamations, studied Latin historians and rhetoricians, and began the study of Greek using the Greek New Testament.

Since the records of the Stratford "grammar school" do not survive, we cannot prove that William Shakespeare attended the school; however, every indication (his father's position as an alderman and bailiff of Stratford, the playwright's own knowledge of the Latin classics, scenes in the plays that recall grammar-school experiences—for example, *The Merry Wives of Windsor*, 4.1) suggests that he did. We also lack generally accepted documentation about Shakespeare's life after his schooling ended and his professional life in London began. His marriage in 1582 (at age eighteen) to Anne Hathaway and the subsequent births of his daughter Susanna (1583) and the twins Judith and Hamnet (1585) are recorded, but how he supported himself and where he lived are not known. Nor do we know when and why he left Stratford for the London theatrical world, nor how he rose to be the important figure in that world that he had become by the early 1590s.

We do know that by 1592 he had achieved some prominence in London as both an actor and a playwright. In that year was published a book by the playwright Robert Greene attacking an actor who had the audacity to write blank-verse drama and who was "in his own conceit [i.e., opinion] the only Shakescene in a country." Since Greene's attack includes a parody of a line from one of Shakespeare's early plays, there is little doubt that it is Shakespeare to whom he refers, a "Shake-scene" who had aroused Greene's fury by successfully competing with university-educated dramatists like Greene himself. It was in 1593 that Shakespeare became a published poet. In that year he published his long narrative poem *Venus and Adonis;*

in 1594, he followed it with *Lucrece*. Both poems were dedicated to the young earl of Southampton (Henry Wriothesley), who may have become Shakespeare's patron.

It seems no coincidence that Shakespeare wrote these narrative poems at a time when the theaters were closed because of the plague, a contagious epidemic disease that devastated the population of London. When the theaters reopened in 1594, Shakespeare apparently resumed his double career of actor and playwright and began his long (and seemingly profitable) service as an acting-company shareholder. Records for December of 1594 show him to be a leading member of the Lord Chamberlain's Men. It was this company of actors, later named the King's Men, for whom he would be a principal actor, dramatist, and shareholder for the rest of his career.

So far as we can tell, that career spanned about twenty years. In the 1590s, he wrote his plays on English history as well as several comedies and at least two tragedies (*Titus Andronicus* and *Romeo and Juliet*). These histories, comedies, and tragedies are the plays credited to him in 1598 in a work, *Palladis Tamia*, that in one chapter compares English writers with "Greek, Latin, and Italian Poets." There the author, Francis Meres, claims that Shakespeare is comparable to the Latin dramatists Seneca for tragedy and Plautus for comedy, and calls him "the most excellent in both kinds for the stage." He also names him "Mellifluous and honey-tongued Shakespeare": "I say," writes Meres, "that the Muses would speak with Shakespeare's fine filed phrase, if they would speak English." Since Meres also mentions Shakespeare's "sugared sonnets among his private friends," it is assumed that many of Shakespeare's sonnets (not published until 1609) were also written in the 1590s.

The Globe

A stylized representation of the Globe theater.
From Claes Jansz Visscher, *Londinum florentissima
Britanniae urbs . . .* [c. 1625].

In 1599, Shakespeare's company built a theater for themselves across the river from London, naming it the Globe. The plays that are considered by many to be Shakespeare's major tragedies (*Hamlet, Othello, King Lear,* and *Macbeth*) were written while the company was resident in this theater, as were such comedies as *Twelfth Night* and *Measure for Measure.* Many of Shakespeare's plays were performed at court (both for Queen Elizabeth I and, after her death in 1603, for King James I), some were presented at the Inns of Court (the residences of London's legal societies), and some were doubtless performed in other towns, at the universities, and at great houses when the King's Men went on tour; otherwise, his plays from 1599 to 1608 were, so far as we know, performed only at the Globe. Between 1608 and 1612, Shakespeare wrote several plays—among them *The Winter's Tale* and *The Tempest*—presumably for the company's new indoor Blackfriars theater, though the plays seem to have been performed also at the Globe and at court. Surviving documents describe a performance of *The Winter's Tale* in 1611 at the Globe, for example, and performances of *The Tempest* in 1611 and 1613 at the royal palace of Whitehall.

Shakespeare wrote very little after 1612, the year in which he probably wrote *King Henry VIII.* (It was at a performance of *Henry VIII* in 1613 that the Globe caught fire and burned to the ground.) Sometime between 1610 and 1613 he seems to have returned to live in Stratford-upon-Avon, where he owned a large house and considerable property, and where his wife and his two daughters and their husbands lived. (His son Hamnet had died in 1596.) During his professional years in London, Shakespeare had presumably derived income from the acting company's profits as well as from his own career as an actor, from the sale of his play manuscripts to the acting company, and, after 1599, from his shares as an owner of the Globe. It was presumably that income, carefully invested in land and other property, which made him the wealthy man that surviving documents show him to have become. It is also assumed that William Shakespeare's growing wealth and reputation played some part in inclining the crown, in 1596, to grant John Shakespeare, William's father, the coat of arms that he had so long sought. William Shakespeare died in Stratford-upon-Avon on April 23, 1616 (according to the epitaph carved under his bust in Holy Trinity Church) and was buried on April 25. Seven years after his death, his collected plays were published as *Mr. William Shakespeares Comedies, Histories, & Tragedies* (the work now known as the First Folio).

The years in which Shakespeare wrote were among the most exciting in English history. Intellectually, the discovery, translation, and printing of Greek and Roman classics were making available a set of works and worldviews that interacted complexly with Christian texts and beliefs. The result was a questioning, a vital intellectual ferment, that provided energy for the period's amazing dramatic and literary output and that fed directly into Shakespeare's plays. The Ghost in *Hamlet*, for example, is wonderfully complicated in part because he is a figure from Roman tragedy— the spirit of the dead returning to seek revenge—who at the same time inhabits a Christian hell (or purgatory); Hamlet's description of humankind reflects at one moment the Neoplatonic wonderment at mankind ("What a piece of work is a man!") and, at the next, the Christian disparagement of human sinners ("And yet, to me, what is this quintessence of dust?").

As intellectual horizons expanded, so also did geographical and cosmological horizons. New worlds— both North and South America—were explored, and

in them were found human beings who lived and wor-
shiped in ways radically different from those of Renaissance Europeans and Englishmen. The universe during
these years also seemed to shift and expand. Copernicus had earlier theorized that the earth was not the
center of the cosmos but revolved as a planet around
the sun. Galileo's telescope, created in 1609, allowed
scientists to see that Copernicus had been correct: the
universe was not organized with the earth at the center,
nor was it so nicely circumscribed as people had, until
that time, thought. In terms of expanding horizons,
the impact of these discoveries on people's beliefs—
religious, scientific, and philosophical—cannot be over-
stated.

London, too, rapidly expanded and changed during the years (from the early 1590s to around 1610)
that Shakespeare lived there. London—the center of
England's government, its economy, its royal court, its
overseas trade—was, during these years, becoming an
exciting metropolis, drawing to it thousands of new
citizens every year. Troubled by overcrowding, by poverty, by recurring epidemics of the plague, London was
also a mecca for the wealthy and the aristocratic, and
for those who sought advancement at court, or power
in government or finance or trade. One hears in Shakespeare's plays the voices of London—the struggles
for power, the fear of venereal disease, the language
of buying and selling. One hears as well the voices of
Stratford-upon-Avon—references to the nearby Forest
of Arden, to sheepherding, to small-town gossip, to vil-
lage fairs and markets. Part of the richness of Shakespeare's work is the influence felt there of the various
worlds in which he lived: the world of metropolitan
London, the world of small-town and rural England,
the world of the theater, and the worlds of craftsmen
and shepherds.

That Shakespeare inhabited such worlds we know from surviving London and Stratford documents, as well as from the evidence of the plays and poems themselves. From such records we can sketch the dramatist's life. We know from his works that he was a voracious reader. We know from legal and business documents that he was a multifaceted theater man who became a wealthy landowner. We know a bit about his family life and a fair amount about his legal and financial dealings. Most scholars today depend upon such evidence as they draw their picture of the world's greatest playwright. Such, however, has not always been the case. Until the late eighteenth century, the William Shakespeare who lived in most biographies was the creation of legend and tradition. This was the Shakespeare who was supposedly caught poaching deer at Charlecote, the estate of Sir Thomas Lucy close by Stratford-upon-Avon; this was the Shakespeare who fled from Sir Thomas's vengeance and made his way in London by taking care of horses outside a playhouse; this was the Shakespeare who reportedly could barely read but whose natural gifts were extraordinary, whose father was a butcher who allowed his gifted son sometimes to help in the butcher shop, where William supposedly killed calves "in a high style," making a speech for the occasion. It was this legendary William Shakespeare whose Falstaff (in *1* and *2 Henry IV*) so pleased Queen Elizabeth that she demanded a play about Falstaff in love, and demanded that it be written in fourteen days (hence the existence of *The Merry Wives of Windsor*). It was this legendary Shakespeare who reached the top of his acting career in the roles of the Ghost in *Hamlet* and old Adam in *As You Like It*—and who died of a fever contracted by drinking too hard at "a merry meeting" with the poets Michael Drayton and Ben Jonson. This legendary Shakespeare is a rambunctious, undisciplined man, as attractively "wild" as his plays were seen by earlier generations to be. Unfortunately, there is no trace of evidence to support these wonderful stories.

Perhaps in response to the disreputable Shakespeare of legend—or perhaps in response to the fragmentary and, for some, all-too-ordinary Shakespeare documented by surviving records—some people since the mid–nineteenth century have argued that William Shakespeare could not have written the plays that bear his name. These persons have put forward some dozen names as more likely authors, among them Queen Elizabeth, Sir Francis Bacon, Edward de Vere (earl of Oxford), and Christopher Marlowe. Such attempts to find what for these people is a more believable author of the plays is a tribute to the regard in which the plays are held. Unfortunately for their claims, the documents that exist that provide evidence for the facts of Shakespeare's life tie him inextricably to the body of plays and poems that bear his name. Unlikely as it seems to those who want the works to have been written by an aristocrat, a university graduate, or an "important" person, the plays and poems seem clearly to have been produced by a man from Stratford-upon-Avon with a very good "grammar school" education and a life of experience in London and in the world of the London theater. How this particular man produced the works that dominate the cultures of much of the world almost four hundred years after his death is one of life's mysteries—and one that will continue to tease our imaginations as we continue to delight in his plays and poems.

Shakespeare's Theater

The actors of Shakespeare's time performed plays in a great variety of locations. They played at court (that is, in the great halls of such royal residences as Whitehall, Hampton Court, and Greenwich); they played in halls at the universities of Oxford and Cambridge, and at the Inns of Court (the residences in London of the legal societies); and they also played in the private houses of great lords and civic officials. Sometimes acting companies went on tour from London into the provinces, often (but not only) when outbreaks of bubonic plague in the capital forced the closing of theaters to reduce the possibility of contagion in crowded audiences. In the provinces the actors usually staged their plays in churches (until around 1600) or in guildhalls. Though surviving records show only a handful of occasions when actors played at inns while on tour, London inns were important playing places up until the 1590s.

The building of theaters in London had begun only shortly before Shakespeare wrote his first plays in the 1590s. These theaters were of two kinds: outdoor or public playhouses that could accommodate large numbers of playgoers, and indoor or private theaters for much smaller audiences. What is usually regarded as the first London outdoor public playhouse was called simply the Theatre. James Burbage—the father of Richard Burbage, who was perhaps the most famous actor in Shakespeare's company—built it in 1576 in an area north of the city of London called Shoreditch. Among the more famous of the other public playhouses that capitalized on the new fashion were the Curtain and the Fortune (both also built north of the city), and the Rose, the Swan, the Globe, and the

Hope (all located on the Bankside, a region just across the Thames south of the city of London). All these playhouses had to be built outside the jurisdiction of the city of London because many civic officials were hostile to the performance of drama and repeatedly petitioned the royal council to abolish it.

The theaters erected on the Bankside (a region under the authority of the Church of England, whose head was the monarch) shared the neighborhood with houses of prostitution and with the Paris Garden, where the blood sports of bearbaiting and bullbaiting were carried on. There may have been no clear distinction between playhouses and buildings for such sports, because the Hope was used for plays and baiting, and Philip Henslowe, owner of the Rose and, later, partner in the ownership of the Fortune, was also a partner in a monopoly on baiting. All these forms of entertainment were easily accessible to Londoners by boat across the Thames or over London Bridge.

Evidently Shakespeare's company prospered on the Bankside. They moved there in 1599. Threatened by difficulties in renewing the lease on the land where their first playhouse (the Theatre) had been built, Shakespeare's company took advantage of the Christmas holiday in 1598 to dismantle the Theatre and transport its timbers across the Thames to the Bankside, where, in 1599, these timbers were used in the building of the Globe. The weather in late December 1598 is recorded as having been especially harsh. It was so cold that the Thames was "nigh [nearly] frozen," and there was heavy snow. Perhaps the weather aided Shakespeare's company in eluding their landlord, the snow hiding their activity and the freezing of the Thames allowing them to slide the timbers across to the Bankside without paying tolls for repeated trips over London Bridge. Attractive as this narrative is, it remains just as likely that the heavy snow hampered transport of the timbers in wagons through the London streets to the river. It also must be remembered that the Thames was, according to report, only "nigh frozen" and therefore as impassable as it ever was. Whatever the precise circumstances of this fascinating event in English theater history, Shakespeare's company was able to begin playing at their new Globe theater on the Bankside in 1599. After the first Globe burned down in 1613 during the staging of Shakespeare's *Henry VIII* (its thatch roof was set alight by cannon fire called for by the play), Shakespeare's company immediately rebuilt on the same location. The second Globe seems to have been a grander structure than its predecessor. It remained in use until the beginning of the English Civil War in 1642, when Parliament officially closed the theaters. Soon thereafter it was pulled down.

The public theaters of Shakespeare's time were very different buildings from our theaters today. First of all, they were open-air playhouses. As recent excavations of the Rose and the Globe confirm, some were polygonal or roughly circular in shape; the Fortune, however, was square. The most recent estimates of their size put the diameter of these buildings at 72 feet (the Rose) to 100 feet (the Globe), but they were said to hold vast audiences of two or three thousand, who must have been squeezed together quite tightly. Some of these spectators paid extra to sit or stand in the two or three levels of roofed galleries that extended, on the upper levels, all the way around the theater and surrounded an open space. In this space were the stage and, perhaps, the tiring house (what we would call dressing rooms), as well as the so-called yard. In the yard stood the spectators who chose to pay less, the ones whom Hamlet contemptuously called "groundlings."

For a roof they had only the sky, and so they were exposed to all kinds of weather. They stood on a floor that was sometimes made of mortar and sometimes of ash mixed with the shells of hazelnuts, which, it has recently been discovered, were standard flooring material in the period.

Unlike the yard, the stage itself was covered by a roof. Its ceiling, called "the heavens," is thought to have been elaborately painted to depict the sun, moon, stars, and planets. Just how big the stage was remains hard to determine. We have a single sketch of part of the interior of the Swan. A Dutchman named Johannes de Witt visited this theater around 1596 and sent a sketch of it back to his friend, Arend van Buchel. Because van Buchel found de Witt's letter and sketch of interest, he copied both into a book. It is van Buchel's copy, adapted, it seems, to the shape and size of the page in his book, that survives. In this sketch, the stage appears to be a large rectangular platform that thrusts far out into the yard, perhaps even as far as the center of the circle formed by the surrounding galleries. This drawing, combined with the specifications for the size of the stage in the building contract for the Fortune, has led scholars to conjecture that the stage on which Shakespeare's plays were performed must have measured approximately 43 feet in width and 27 feet in depth, a vast acting area. But the digging up of a large part of the Rose by archaeologists has provided evidence of a quite different stage design. The Rose stage was a platform tapered at the corners and much shallower than what seems to be depicted in the van Buchel sketch. Indeed, its measurements seem to be about 37.5 feet across at its widest point and only 15.5 feet deep. Because the surviving indications of stage size and design differ from each other so much, it is possible that the stages in other playhouses, like the

Theatre, the Curtain, and the Globe (the outdoor play-houses where Shakespeare's plays were performed), were different from those at both the Swan and the Rose.

After about 1608 Shakespeare's plays were staged not only at the Globe but also at an indoor or private playhouse in Blackfriars. This theater had been constructed in 1596 by James Burbage in an upper hall of a former Dominican priory or monastic house. Although Henry VIII had dissolved all English monasteries in the 1530s (shortly after he had founded the Church of England), the area remained under church, rather than hostile civic, control. The hall that Burbage had purchased and renovated was a large one in which Parliament had once met. In the private theater that he constructed, the stage, lit by candles, was built across the narrow end of the hall, with boxes flanking it. The rest of the hall offered seating room only. Because there was no provision for standing room, the largest audience it could hold was less than a thousand, or about a quarter of what the Globe could accommodate. Admission to Blackfriars was correspondingly more expensive. Instead of a penny to stand in the yard at the Globe, it cost a minimum of sixpence to get into Blackfriars. The best seats at the Globe (in the Lords' Room in the gallery above and behind the stage) cost sixpence; but the boxes flanking the stage at Black-friars were half a crown, or five times sixpence. Some spectators who were particularly interested in displaying themselves paid even more to sit on stools on the Blackfriars stage.

Whether in the outdoor or indoor playhouses, the stages of Shakespeare's time were different from ours. They were not separated from the audience by the dropping of a curtain between acts and scenes. Therefore the playwrights of the time had to find other ways of signaling to the audience that one scene (to be imagined as occurring in one location at a given time) had ended and the next (to be imagined at perhaps a different location at a later time) had begun. The customary way used by Shakespeare and many of his contemporaries was to have everyone onstage exit at the end of one scene and have one or more different characters enter to begin the next. In a few cases, where characters remain onstage from one scene to another, the dialogue or stage action makes the change of location clear, and the characters are generally to be imagined as having moved from one place to another. For example, in *Romeo and Juliet*, Romeo and his friends remain onstage in Act 1 from scene 4 to scene 5, but they are represented as having moved between scenes from the street that leads to Capulet's house into the house itself. The new location is signaled in part by the appearance onstage of Capulet's servingmen carrying napkins, something they would not take into the streets. Playwrights had to be quite resourceful in the use of hand properties, like the napkin, or in the use of dialogue to specify where the action was taking place in their plays because, in contrast to most of today's theaters, the playhouses of Shakespeare's time did not use stage sets to make the location precise. As another consequence of this difference, however, the playwrights of Shakespeare's time did not have to specify exactly where the action of their plays was set when they did not choose to do so, and much of the action of their plays is tied to no specific place.

Usually Shakespeare's stage is referred to as a "bare stage," to distinguish it from the stages of the past two or three centuries with their elaborate sets. But the stage in Shakespeare's time was not completely bare: Philip Henslowe, owner of the Rose, lists in his inventory of stage properties a rock, three tombs, and two mossy banks. Stage directions in plays of the time also call for such things as thrones (or "states"), banquets (presumably tables with plaster replicas of food on them), and beds and tombs to be pushed onto the stage. Thus the stage often held more than the actors.

The actors did not limit their performing to the stage alone. Occasionally they went beneath the stage, as the Ghost appears to do in the first act of *Hamlet*. From there they could emerge onto the stage through a trapdoor. They could retire behind the hangings across the back of the stage, as, for example, the actor playing Polonius does when he hides behind the arras. Sometimes the hangings could be drawn back during a performance to "discover" one or more actors behind them. When performance required that an actor appear "above," as when Juliet is imagined to stand at the window of her chamber in the famous and misnamed "balcony scene," then the actor probably climbed the stairs to the gallery over the back of the stage and temporarily shared it with some of the spectators. The stage was also provided with ropes and winches so that actors could descend from, and re-ascend to, the "heavens."

Perhaps the greatest difference between dramatic performances in Shakespeare's time and ours was that in Shakespeare's England the roles of women were played by boys. (Some of these boys grew up to take male roles in their maturity.) There were no women in the acting companies, only in the audience. It had not always been so in the history of the English stage. There are records of women on English stages in the thirteenth and fourteenth centuries, two hundred years before Shakespeare's plays were performed. After the accession of James I in 1603, the queen of England and her ladies took part in entertainments at court called masques, and with the reopening of the theaters in

1660 at the restoration of Charles II, women again took their place on the public stage.

The chief competitors for the companies of adult actors, such as the one to which Shakespeare belonged and for which he wrote, were companies of exclusively boy actors. The competition was most intense in the early 1600s. There were then two principal children's companies: the Children of Paul's (the choirboys from St. Paul's Cathedral, whose private playhouse was near the cathedral); and the Children of the Chapel Royal (the choirboys from the monarch's private chapel, who performed at the Blackfriars theater built by Burbage in 1596, which Shakespeare's company had been stopped from using by local residents who objected to crowds). In *Hamlet* Shakespeare writes of "an aerie [nest] of children, little eyases [hawks], that cry out on the top of question and are most tyrannically clapped for 't. These are now the fashion and . . . berattle the common stages [attack the public theaters]." In the long run, the adult actors prevailed. The Children of Paul's dissolved around 1606. By about 1608 the Children of the Chapel Royal had been forced to stop playing at the Blackfriars theater, which was then taken over by the king's company of players, Shakespeare's own troupe.

Acting companies and theaters of Shakespeare's time seem to have been organized in various ways. With the building of the Globe, Shakespeare's company apparently managed itself, with the principal actors, Shakespeare among them, having the status of "sharers" and the right to a share in the takings, as well as the responsibility for a part of the expenses. Five of the sharers, including Shakespeare, owned the Globe. As actor, as sharer in an acting company and in ownership of theaters, and as playwright, Shakespeare was about as involved in the theatrical industry as one could imagine. Although Shakespeare and his fellows prospered, their status under the law was conditional upon the protection of powerful patrons. "Common players"—those who did not have patrons or masters—were classed in the language of the law with "vagabonds and sturdy beggars." So the actors had to secure for themselves the official rank of servants of patrons. Among the patrons under whose protection Shakespeare's company worked were the lord chamberlain and, after the accession of King James in 1603, the king himself.

In the early 1990s we seemed on the verge of learning a great deal more about the theaters in which Shakespeare and his contemporaries performed—or, at least, opening up new questions about them. At that time about 70 percent of the Rose had been excavated, as had about 10 percent of the second Globe, the one built in 1614. It was then hoped that more would become available for study. However, excavation was halted at that point, and while it is not known if or when it will resume at these sites, archaeological discoveries in Shoreditch in 2008 in the vicinity of the Theatre may yield new information about the playhouses of Shakespeare's London.

THE
TWO
NOBLE
KINSMEN:

Presented at the Blackfriers
by the Kings Maiesties servants,
with great applause:

Written by the memorable Worthies
of their time;
{ M^r. *John Fletcher*, and } Gent.
{ M^r. *William Shakspeare*. }

Printed at *London* by *Tho. Cotes*, for *John Waterson*:
and are to be sold at the signe of the *Crowne*
in *Pauls* Church-yard. 1 6 3 4.

Title page of *The Two Noble Kinsmen* 1634 Quarto,
copy STC11075.
(From the Folger Shakespeare Library Collection.)

The Publication of
Shakespeare's Plays

Eighteen of Shakespeare's plays found their way into print during the playwright's lifetime, but there is nothing to suggest that he took any interest in their publication. These eighteen appeared separately in editions in quarto or, in the case of *Henry VI, Part 3*, octavo format. The quarto pages are not much larger than the ones you are now reading, and the octavo pages are even smaller; these little books were sold unbound for a few pence. The earliest of the quartos that still survive were printed in 1594, the year that both *Titus Andronicus* and a version of the play now called *Henry VI, Part 2* became available. While almost every one of these early quartos displays on its title page the name of the acting company that performed the play, only about half provide the name of the playwright, Shakespeare. The first quarto edition to bear the name Shakespeare on its title page is *Love's Labor's Lost* of 1598. A few of the quartos were popular with the book-buying public of Shakespeare's lifetime; for example, quarto *Richard II* went through five editions between 1597 and 1615. But most of the quartos were far from best sellers; *Love's Labor's Lost* (1598), for instance, was not reprinted in quarto until 1631. After Shakespeare's death, two more of his plays appeared in quarto format: *Othello* in 1622 and *The Two Noble Kinsmen*, coauthored with John Fletcher, in 1634.

In 1623, seven years after Shakespeare's death, *Mr. William Shakespeares Comedies, Histories, & Tragedies* was published. This printing offered readers in a single book thirty-six of the thirty-eight plays now thought to have been written by Shakespeare, including eighteen that had never been printed before. And it offered them in a style that was then reserved for serious literature and scholarship. The plays were arranged in double columns on pages nearly a foot high. This large page size is called "folio," as opposed to the smaller "quarto," and the 1623 volume is usually called the Shakespeare First Folio. It is reputed to have sold for the lordly price of a pound. (One copy at the Folger Shakespeare Library is marked fifteen shillings—that is, three-quarters of a pound.)

In a preface to the First Folio entitled "To the great Variety of Readers," two of Shakespeare's former fellow actors in the King's Men, John Heminge and Henry Condell, wrote that they themselves had collected their dead companion's plays. They suggested that they had seen his own papers: "we have scarce received from him a blot in his papers." The title page of the Folio declared that the plays within it had been printed "according to the True Original Copies." Comparing the Folio to the quartos, Heminge and Condell disparaged the quartos, advising their readers that "before you were abused with divers stolen and surreptitious copies, maimed, and deformed by the frauds and stealths of injurious impostors." Many Shakespeareans of the eighteenth and nineteenth centuries believed Heminge and Condell and regarded the Folio plays as superior to anything in the quartos.

Once we begin to examine the Folio plays in detail, it becomes less easy to take at face value the word of Heminge and Condell about the superiority of the Folio texts. For example, of the first nine plays in the Folio (one-quarter of the entire collection), four were essentially reprinted from earlier quarto printings that Heminge and Condell had disparaged, and four have now been identified as printed from copies written in the hand of a professional scribe of the 1620s named

Ralph Crane; the ninth, *The Comedy of Errors*, was apparently also printed from a manuscript, but one whose origin cannot be readily identified. Evidently, then, eight of the first nine plays in the First Folio were not printed, in spite of what the Folio title page announces, "according to the True Original Copies," or Shakespeare's own papers, and the source of the ninth is unknown. Because today's editors have been forced to treat Heminge and Condell's pronouncements with skepticism, they must choose whether to base their own editions upon quartos or the Folio on grounds other than Heminge and Condell's story of where the quarto and Folio versions originated.

Editors have often fashioned their own narratives to explain what lies behind the quartos and Folio. They have said that Heminge and Condell meant to criticize only a few of the early quartos, the ones that offer much shorter and sometimes quite different, often garbled, versions of plays. Among the examples of these are the 1600 quarto of *Henry V* (the Folio offers a much fuller version) or the 1603 *Hamlet* quarto. (In 1604 a different, much longer form of the play got into print as a quarto.) Early-twentieth-century editors speculated that these questionable texts were produced when someone in the audience took notes from the plays' dialogue during performances and then employed "hack poets" to fill out the notes. The poor results were then sold to a publisher and presented in print as Shakespeare's plays. More recently this story has given way to another in which the shorter versions are said to be re-creations from memory of Shakespeare's plays by actors who wanted to stage them in the provinces but lacked manuscript copies. Most of the quartos offer much better texts than these so-called bad quartos. Indeed, in most of the quartos we find texts that are at least equal to or better than what is printed in the Folio. Many Shakespeare enthusiasts persuaded themselves that most of the quartos were set into type directly from Shakespeare's own papers, although there is nothing on which to base this conclusion except the desire for it to be true. Thus speculation continues about how the Shakespeare plays got to be printed. All that we have are the printed texts.

The book collector who was most successful in bringing together copies of the quartos and the First Folio was Henry Clay Folger, founder of the Folger Shakespeare Library in Washington, D.C. While it is estimated that there survive around the world only about 300 copies of the First Folio, Mr. Folger was able to acquire more than seventy-five copies, as well as a large number of fragments, for the library that bears his name. He also amassed a substantial number of quartos. For example, only fourteen copies of the First Quarto of *Love's Labor's Lost* are known to exist, and three are at the Folger Shakespeare Library. As a consequence of Mr. Folger's labors, scholars visiting the Folger have been able to learn a great deal about sixteenth- and seventeenth-century printing and, in particular, about the printing of Shakespeare's plays. And Mr. Folger did not stop at the First Folio, but collected many copies of later editions of Shakespeare, beginning with the Second Folio (1632), the Third (1663–64), and the Fourth (1685). Each of these later folios was based on its immediate predecessor and was edited anonymously. The first editor of Shakespeare whose name we know was Nicholas Rowe, whose first edition came out in 1709. Mr. Folger, and the library named for him, collected this edition and many, many more by Rowe's successors, and the collecting continues.

An Introduction to This Text

This play was first printed in 1634 in a quarto titled *The Two Noble Kinsmen: Presented at the Blackfriers by the Kings Maiesties servants, with great applause: Written by the memorable Worthies of their time; M*ʳ*. John Fletcher and M*ʳ*. William Shakspeare. Gent.* [i.e., Gentlemen]. (See picture, page lii.) The play subsequently appeared in the 1679 collection titled *Fifty comedies and tragedies written by Francis Beaumont and John Fletcher, Gentlemen;* it thereby entered the Beaumont and Fletcher canon, rather than the Shakespeare canon, and remained there until late in the twentieth century, in spite of occasional scholarly claims that it had an equal right to a place in both canons. Now it generally appears in so-called complete works of Shakespeare.

The present edition is based directly on the 1634 printing.* For the convenience of the reader, we have modernized the punctuation and the spelling of the Quarto. Sometimes we go so far as to modernize certain old forms of words; for example, usually when *a* means *he,* we change it to *he;* we change *mo* to *more,* and *ye* to *you.* It is not our practice in editing any of the plays to modernize words that sound distinctly different from modern forms. For example, when the early printed texts read *sith* or *apricocks* or *porpentine,* we have not modernized to *since, apricots, porcupine.* When the forms *an, and,* or *and if* appear instead of the modern form *if,* we have reduced *and* to *an* but have

---

*We have also consulted the computerized text of the Quarto provided by the Text Archive of the Oxford University Computing Centre, to which we are grateful.

lvii

not changed any of these forms to their modern equivalent, *if*. We also modernize and, where necessary, correct passages in foreign languages, unless an error in the early printed text can be reasonably explained as a joke.

Whenever we change the wording of the Quarto or add anything to its stage directions, we mark the change by enclosing it in superior half-brackets (⌐ ¬). We want our readers to be immediately aware when we have intervened. (Only when we correct an obvious typographical error in the Quarto does the change not get marked.) Whenever we change either the Quarto's wording or its punctuation so that meaning changes, we list the change in the textual notes at the back of the book, even if all we have done is fix an obvious error.

We regularize spellings of a number of the proper names in the dialogue and stage directions, as is the usual practice in editions of the play. For example, the Quarto uses the forms "Pyrithous," "Pirothous," and "Perithous," as well as "Pirithous," the only form used in our edition.

This edition differs from many earlier ones in its efforts to aid the reader in imagining the play as a performance. Thus stage directions are written with reference to the stage. For example, the 1634 Quarto's opening stage direction to Act 1, scene 4, reads in part *"Then Enter Theseus (victor) the three Queenes meete him, and fall on their faces before him."* In the fiction of the play Theseus is leaving the battlefield, from which the queens have kept their distance, watching the outcome and now seeking him. In production, this separation of the queens from Theseus would be indicated by their coming onstage from different directions or through different doors. In emending the Quarto's stage direction, we indicate this feature of the staging: *"Then enter, ⌐through one door,¬ Theseus, victor, ⌐accompanied*

by Lords and Soldiers. Entering through another door,
the three Queens meet him, and fall on their faces before
him." This emended stage direction is designed to aid
our readers in imagining not just the fictive action but
also the way that action would be realized in a production on stage. Through such directions, we hope to help
our readers stage the play in their own imaginations in
a way that more closely approximates an experience in
the theater.

Whenever it is reasonably certain, in our view, that
a speech is accompanied by a particular action, we
provide a stage direction describing the action, setting
the added direction in brackets to signal that it is not
found in the Quarto. (Occasional exceptions to this
rule occur when the action is so obvious that to add a
stage direction would insult the reader). Stage directions for the entrance of a character in mid-scene are,
with rare exceptions, placed so that they immediately
precede the character's participation in the scene, even
though these entrances may appear somewhat earlier
in the early printed texts. Whenever we move a stage
direction, we record this change in the textual notes.
Latin stage directions (e.g., *Exeunt*) are translated into
English (e.g., *They exit*).

We expand the often severely abbreviated forms of
names used as speech headings in early printed texts
into the full names of the characters. We also regularize the speakers' names in speech headings, using only
a single designation for each character, even though the
early printed texts sometimes use a variety of designa-
tions. For example, the Jailer is sometimes *"Iailer."* or
"Iailor." or *"Iai."* and sometimes *"Keeper."* or *"Keep."* in
the Quarto's speech prefixes. However, in this edition,
he has a single speech prefix, "JAILER." Variations in the
speech headings of the early printed texts are recorded
in the textual notes.

In the present edition, as well, we mark with a dash any change of address within a speech, unless a stage direction intervenes. When the *-ed* ending of a word is to be pronounced, we mark it with an accent. Like editors for the past two centuries, we print metrically linked lines in the following way:

PALAMON
  How do you, noble cousin?
ARCITE   How do you, sir?
                                      (2.2.1–2)

However, when there are a number of short verse-lines that can be linked in more than one way, we do not, with rare exceptions, indent any of them.

The Explanatory Notes

The notes that appear on the pages facing the text are designed to provide readers with the help that they may need to enjoy the play. Whenever the meaning of a word in the text is not readily accessible in a good contemporary dictionary, we offer the meaning in a note. Sometimes we provide a note even when the relevant meaning is to be found in the dictionary but when the word has acquired other potentially confusing meanings since the early seventeenth century. In our notes, we try to offer modern synonyms for meanings the words had when written. We also try to indicate to the reader the connection between the word in the play and the modern synonym. For example, seventeenth-century writers sometimes use the word *head* to mean *source*, but, for modern readers, there may be no connection evident between these two words. We provide the connection by explaining the play's usage as follows: "**head:** fountainhead, source." On some occasions, a whole phrase or clause needs explanation. Then, as space allows, we rephrase in our own words the difficult passage, and add at the end synonyms for individual words in the passage. When scholars have been unable to determine the meaning of a word or phrase, we acknowledge the uncertainty. Biblical quotations are from the Geneva Bible (1560), modernized.

When we find the work of a particular editor especially helpful to the reader, we occasionally refer to that editor's notes. The following are editions that provide especially useful commentary:

Evans, G. B., ed. *The Riverside Shakespeare*, 2nd ed. (Boston, 1997)

Potter, Lois, ed. *The Two Noble Kinsmen*, The Third Arden Shakespeare (Walton-on-Thames, 1997)

Waith, Eugene, ed. *The Two Noble Kinsmen*, The Oxford Shakespeare (Oxford, 1989).

First page of "The Knight's Tale," the primary source for
The Two Noble Kinsmen.
From the Thomas Speght edition of Chaucer's *Works* (1602).

Characters in the Play

PROLOGUE

ARCITE ⎱ the two noble kinsmen, cousins,
PALAMON ⎰ nephews of Creon, King of Thebes

THESEUS, Duke of Athens

HIPPOLYTA, Queen of the Amazons, later Duchess of Athens

EMILIA, her sister

PIRITHOUS, friend to Theseus

Three QUEENS, widows of the kings killed in laying siege
to Thebes

The JAILER of Theseus's prison

The Jailer's DAUGHTER

The Jailer's BROTHER

The WOOER of the Jailer's daughter

Two FRIENDS of the Jailer

A DOCTOR

ARTESIUS, an Athenian soldier

VALERIUS, a Theban

WOMAN, attending on Emilia

An Athenian GENTLEMAN

Six KNIGHTS, three accompanying Arcite, three Palamon

Six COUNTRYMEN, one dressed as a BAVIAN or baboon

A SCHOOLMASTER

NELL, a countrywoman

A TABORER

A singing BOY, a HERALD, MESSENGERS, a SERVANT

EPILOGUE

Hymen (god of weddings), lords, soldiers, four countrywomen (Fritz, Maudlin, Luce, and Barbary), nymphs,
attendants, maids, executioner, guard

3

Prologue The audience is welcomed to the play's opening performance. The speaker apologizes for its inferiority to Chaucer, whose tale provides the plot.

---

0 SD. **Flourish:** a horn fanfare announcing an entrance

2. **followed:** i.e., sought after

3. **stand:** are; remain; **sound:** healthy, robust

4. **his marriage day:** i.e., its first performance

5. **shake:** i.e., fear; **his:** its

6. **holy tie:** marriage ceremony; **stir:** i.e., sexual activity (but with an allusion to the excitement of a play's opening [**first**] performance)

7. **is modesty:** i.e., **is** the image of **modesty**

8. **maid:** young unmarried woman, virgin; **to sight:** i.e., in appearance; **pains:** efforts

10. **breeder:** father; source; **a pure:** i.e., one of unblemished character

12. **Po and silver Trent:** i.e., the **Po** River in Italy **and** the silvery **Trent** River in England (Italy was famous for its great poets, many of whom influenced **Chaucer** [line 13].)

13. **Chaucer . . . gives: The story** dramatized in the play had appeared as "The Knight's Tale" in Chaucer's *Canterbury Tales.* (See picture, page 275.)

14. **constant:** unchanging, fixed

16. **child:** i.e., play, offspring of **Chaucer; hiss:** noise of audience disapproval

18–19. **fan . . . chaff:** The image is of removing the **chaff** (husks, worthless matter) from the grain with a winnowing fan.

(continued)

4

Flourish. ⌈*Enter Prologue.*⌉

PROLOGUE
New plays and maidenheads are near akin:
Much followed both, for both much money giv'n,
If they stand sound and well. And a good play,
Whose modest scenes blush on his marriage day
And shake to lose his honor, is like her   5
That after holy tie and first night's stir
Yet still is modesty, and still retains
More of the maid, to sight, than husband's pains.
We pray our play may be so, for I am sure
It has a noble breeder and a pure,   10
A learnèd, and a poet never went
More famous yet 'twixt Po and silver Trent.
Chaucer, of all admired, the story gives;
There, constant to eternity, it lives.
If we let fall the nobleness of this,   15
And the first sound this child hear be a hiss,
How will it shake the bones of that good man
And make him cry from underground "O, fan
From me the witless chaff of such a writer
That blasts my bays and my famed works makes   20
    lighter
Than Robin Hood!" This is the fear we bring;
For, to say truth, it were an endless thing
And too ambitious, to aspire to him,
Weak as we are, and, almost breathless, swim   25
In this deep water. Do but you hold out
Your helping hands, and we shall ⌈tack⌉ about
And something do to save us. You shall hear
Scenes, though below his art, may yet appear
Worth two hours' travel. To his bones sweet sleep; 30

5

20. **blasts:** shrivels, blights; **bays:** i.e., poetic reputation (literally, bay-laurel leaves woven into a garland to reward conquerors and great poets) See picture, page 134.

21. **lighter:** more trivial, of less value

22. **Robin Hood:** i.e., a **Robin Hood** ballad or play (Proverbial: "Tales of **Robin Hood** are good for fools.")

23. **endless:** never-ending

26–27. **hold out . . . hands:** i.e., applaud

27. **tack about:** i.e., turn our ship in the wind of audience applause and shouts

28. **us:** ourselves

29. **his:** Chaucer's; **may:** which **may**

30. **two hours' travel:** perhaps alluding to the performance time of the play, which, in lines 26–27, is imaged as **travel** (with probable wordplay on *travail* or labor; the two spellings were used interchangeably.) **To . . . sleep:** i.e., we wish **to his bones sweet sleep** (See line 17, above.)

31. **Content to you:** i.e., we wish **you content**

Content to you. If this play do not keep
A little dull time from us, we perceive
Our losses fall so thick we must needs leave.

Flourish. ⌜*He exits.*⌝

1.1 The wedding procession of Duke Theseus and his Amazonian bride Hippolyta is interrupted by three weeping queens whose dead kings lie unburied on the battlefield in Thebes. With the support of Hippolyta, Emilia, and Pirithous, the queens persuade Theseus to leave immediately for Thebes in order to protect their husbands' rights against Creon.

---

0 SD. **Hymen:** in classical mythology, the god of marriage, represented as a young man carrying **a torch** (See picture, page 250.) **before:** i.e., walking in front of **Hymen; singing:** See lines 1–24, below. **Nymph:** semi-divine being, represented as a beautiful maiden; **encompassed in her tresses:** i.e., with her hair hanging loose (a symbol of virginity); **wheaten:** i.e., made of stalks of wheat; **chaplets:** garlands; **another:** i.e., someone else; **likewise hanging:** i.e., **hanging** loose, like the Nymph's; **her train:** i.e., the **train** of Hippolyta's gown

1. **Roses:** Since **the Boy** is described as **strewing flowers** (0 SD), he presumably scatters the flowers he names in his song. **spines:** thorns

3. **But: but** also

4. **Maiden pinks:** a variety of sweet-smelling garden flowers

5. **quaint:** pretty

7. **Ver:** spring

9. **her bells:** i.e., its flowers (Because the **primrose** blossom does not resemble a bell, editors often change "**her bells**" to "harebells.")

(continued)

ACT 1

⌜Scene 1⌝

Music. Enter Hymen with a torch burning, a Boy in
a white robe before, singing and strewing flowers.
After Hymen, a Nymph encompassed in her tresses,
bearing a wheaten garland; then Theseus between
two other Nymphs with wheaten chaplets on their
heads. Then Hippolyta, the bride, led by ⌜Pirithous,⌝
and another holding a garland over her head, her
tresses likewise hanging. After her, Emilia, holding
up her train. ⌜Then Artesius and Attendants.⌝

 The Song, ⌜sung by the Boy.⌝
 Roses, their sharp spines being gone,
 Not royal in their smells alone,
  But in their hue;
 Maiden pinks, of odor faint,
 Daisies smell-less, yet most quaint,   5
  And sweet thyme true;
 Primrose, firstborn child of Ver,
 Merry springtime's harbinger,
  With her bells dim;
 Oxlips in their cradles growing,   10
 Marigolds on deathbeds blowing,
  Lark's-heels trim;
 All dear Nature's children ⌜sweet
 Lie⌝ 'fore bride and bridegroom's feet,
        Strew flowers.

10. **Oxlips . . . growing:** The leaves of the oxlip (a variety of **primrose**) surround the bud as it grows, making a kind of cradle.

11. **blowing:** blossoming, blooming

12. **Lark's-heels:** perhaps, larkspur; perhaps, nasturtiums

14 SD. **Strew flowers:** instructions for the actor playing **the Boy**

15. **sense:** i.e., senses

17. **fair:** beautiful

19. **sland'rous:** The call of **the cuckoo** was said to mock husbands by pronouncing them cuckolds, men with unfaithful wives. (See picture, page 72.)

20. **boding:** ominous; **chough hoar:** i.e., gray-headed jackdaw

21. **pie:** magpie

22. **bridehouse:** i.e., wedding site

24 SD. **stained:** perhaps, dyed (black, for mourning); or, perhaps, discolored (with travel or tears); **imperial crowns: crowns** worn by monarchs of independent or sovereign kingdoms

26. **respect:** heed, pay attention to

31. **Jove:** Roman king of the gods (See picture, page 150.) **marked:** destined

33. **clear:** unsullied

35–36. **raze . . . there:** i.e., remove **all** the sins **set down** against **you** in heaven's record **book raze:** literally, obliterate by scraping

40. **What:** whatever

    Blessing their sense.   15
Not an angel of the air,
Bird melodious or bird fair,
    Is absent hence.
The crow, the sland'rous cuckoo, nor
The boding raven, nor ⌜*chough hoar,*⌝   20
    Nor chatt'ring pie,
May on our bridehouse perch or sing,
Or with them any discord bring,
    But from it fly.

Enter three Queens in black, with veils stained, with
imperial crowns. The first Queen falls down at the foot
of Theseus; the second falls down at the foot of
Hippolyta; the third before Emilia.

FIRST QUEEN, ⌜*to Theseus*⌝
For pity's sake and true gentility's,   25
Hear and respect me.
SECOND QUEEN, ⌜*to Hippolyta*⌝ For your mother's sake,
And as you wish your womb may thrive with fair
    ones,
Hear and respect me.   30
THIRD QUEEN, ⌜*to Emilia*⌝
Now for the love of him whom Jove hath marked
The honor of your bed, and for the sake
Of clear virginity, be advocate
For us and our distresses. This good deed
Shall raze you out o' th' book of trespasses   35
All you are set down there.
THESEUS, ⌜*to First Queen*⌝
Sad lady, rise.
HIPPOLYTA, ⌜*to Second Queen*⌝ Stand up.
EMILIA, ⌜*to Third Queen*⌝   No knees to me.
What woman I may stead that is distressed   40
Does bind me to her.

42. **Deliver you:** speak

44. **Creon:** king of **Thebes** (line 46) See longer note, page 251. **who:** i.e., the **three sovereigns** (line 43)

45. **kites:** birds of prey (See picture, page 74.)

46. **crows:** See picture, page 48. **fields:** battle-fields

47. **suffer:** allow

48. **urn:** put in an urn; **offense:** offensiveness

49-50. **blest . . . Phoebus:** i.e., the sun (**Phoebus** was the Roman god of the sun.) See picture, page xvi.

52. **purger:** one who gets rid of whatever is impure (See longer note, page 251.)

54. **chapel them:** i.e., bury them in a chapel

66. **should:** was to; **season:** occasion

68. **Mars's altar:** i.e., the **altar** of the god of war; **that time fair:** i.e., then beautiful (See longer note, page 251, and picture, page 198.)

69. **Juno's mantle:** i.e., cloak of the Roman queen of the gods (See picture, page 68.)

70. **Nor . . . spread her:** i.e., **nor** encompassed **her more** abundantly

70-71. **wheaten wreath:** bridal garland

72. **nor threshed:** i.e., neither beaten (as if to separate the grain from the chaff); **blasted:** blighted

72-73. **Fortune . . . smiles:** To have the goddess Fortuna smile on one was to experience great good luck. (See picture, page 54.)

73. **Hercules:** in mythology, a hero of extraordinary strength; **our:** i.e., my (the royal plural)

75. **weaker than:** i.e., conquered by; **club:** weapon (See picture, page xvii.)

THESEUS, ⌜*to First Queen*⌝
  What's your request? Deliver you for all.
FIRST QUEEN
  We are three queens whose sovereigns fell before
  The wrath of cruel Creon; who endured
  The beaks of ravens, talons of the kites,   45
  And pecks of crows in the foul fields of Thebes.
  He will not suffer us to burn their bones,
  To urn their ashes, nor to take th' offense
  Of mortal loathsomeness from the blest eye
  Of holy Phoebus, but infects the winds   50
  With stench of our slain lords. O, pity, duke!
  Thou purger of the earth, draw thy feared sword
  That does good turns to th' world; give us the bones
  Of our dead kings, that we may chapel them;
  And of thy boundless goodness take some note   55
  That for our crownèd heads we have no roof
  Save this, which is the lion's and the bear's,
  And vault to everything.
THESEUS   Pray you, kneel not.
  I was transported with your speech and suffered   60
  Your knees to wrong themselves. I have heard the
      fortunes
  Of your dead lords, which gives me such lamenting
  As wakes my vengeance and revenge for 'em.
  King Capaneus was your lord. The day   65
  That he should marry you, at such a season
  As now it is with me, I met your groom
  By Mars's altar. You were that time fair—
  Not Juno's mantle fairer than your tresses,
  Nor in more bounty spread her. Your wheaten   70
      wreath
  Was then nor threshed nor blasted. Fortune at you
  Dimpled her cheek with smiles. Hercules, our
      kinsman,
  Then weaker than your eyes, laid by his club;   75

76. **Nemean hide:** i.e., the **hide** worn by **Hercules** after skinning the slain **Nemean** lion

77. **thawed:** i.e., melted

77–78. **grief ... devour:** Proverbial: "**Time** devours **all** things."

78. **Fearful:** dreadful, terrible

81. **Whereto:** to which (i.e., to **your manhood**); **press you forth:** i.e., **press you** into service as (also, perhaps, urge you to be; or, stamp you as)

82. **undertaker:** supporter, helper

84. **Bellona:** Roman goddess of war (See picture, page 248.)

88. **dreaded:** dread, awe-inspiring; **Amazonian:** Hippolyta was queen of the warrior women known as Amazons. (See picture, page 148.)

90–91. **wast near ... captive:** i.e., had almost conquered (Theseus's) **male** army

92. **uphold creation:** i.e., preserve intact that which God (or **nature**) has created (The assumption here is that both God and **nature** create the male as superior to the female.)

92–93. **in that honor ... it in:** i.e., **in that** sense of what is right and proper according to **nature** **styled:** ordered

94. **The bound ... o'erflowing:** the limits you were exceeding

94–95. **subduing ... affection:** wordplay on **subduing** as (1) overpowering (her) **force** (i.e., army); (2) prevailing over (her **affection**)

96. **equally:** justly

97. **power on:** i.e., **power** over

98. **ow'st:** own, possess

(continued)

He tumbled down upon his ⌈Nemean⌉ hide
And swore his sinews thawed. O grief and time,
Fearful consumers, you will all devour!

FIRST QUEEN   O, I hope some god,
Some god hath put his mercy in your manhood,   80
Whereto he'll infuse power, and press you forth
Our undertaker.

THESEUS   O, no knees, none, widow!
Unto the helmeted Bellona use them
And pray for me, your soldier. ⌈*The First Queen rises.*⌉   85
Troubled I am.   *Turns away.*

SECOND QUEEN   Honored Hippolyta,
Most dreaded Amazonian, that hast slain
The scythe-tusked boar; that with thy arm, as strong
As it is white, wast near to make the male   90
To thy sex captive, but that this thy lord,
Born to uphold creation in that honor
First nature styled it in, shrunk thee into
The bound thou wast o'erflowing, at once subduing
Thy force and thy affection; soldieress   95
That equally canst poise sternness with pity,
Whom now I know hast much more power on him
Than ever he had on thee, who ow'st his strength
And his love too, who is a servant for
The tenor of ⌈thy⌉ speech, dear glass of ladies,   100
Bid him that we, whom flaming war doth scorch,
Under the shadow of his sword may cool us;
Require him he advance it o'er our heads;
Speak 't in a woman's key, like such a woman
As any of us three; weep ere you fail.   105
Lend us a knee;
But touch the ground for us no longer time
Than a dove's motion when the head's plucked off.
Tell him if he i' th' blood-sized field lay swoll'n,
Showing the sun his teeth, grinning at the moon,   110
What you would do.

99–100. **who is . . . speech:** i.e., **who** obeys (even) the implications of your **speech** (The reference of **who** is **he** [line 98].)

100. **glass:** mirror (hence, model, standard)

103. **Require him he:** ask or request that he; **advance:** raise, lift

105. **ere you fail:** i.e., rather than give up

106. **Lend us a knee:** i.e., kneel with (or for) us

109. **blood-sized field:** i.e., blood-covered battle-field **blood-sized:** covered with blood as if with "size," a glaze or filler

110. **Showing . . . moon:** i.e., his head a **grinning** skull

113. **lief:** gladly, willingly; **trace:** pursue

115. **Went I . . . way:** i.e., did I follow a path so willingly; **taken:** affected, seized

117. **anon:** soon

118–20. **my petition . . . drops:** i.e., the rhetorically crafted form of **my petition** (written, as it were, **in ice**) is now melted by **hot grief** into tears **Set down:** written **uncandied:** dissolved

120–21. **so sorrow . . . matter:** i.e., in the same way, **sorrow,** lacking formal expression, **is pressed** out in tears (But see longer note, page 252.)

126. **There through my tears:** i.e., in my eyes

127. **wrinkled:** i.e., distorted

130. **the center:** i.e., earth's **center**

131. **least:** most insignificant; **lead his line:** i.e., weight **his line** with lead (to make it sink deeper)

133. **Extremity:** the condition of extreme suffering

138. **The groundpiece of:** perhaps, a portrait by

(continued)

HIPPOLYTA   Poor lady, say no more.
  I had as lief trace this good action with you
  As that whereto I am going, and never yet
  Went I so willing way. My lord is taken   115
  Heart-deep with your distress; let him consider.
  I'll speak anon.   ⌜*Second Queen rises.*⌝
THIRD QUEEN   O, my petition was
  Set down in ice, which by hot grief uncandied
  Melts into drops; so sorrow, wanting form,   120
  Is pressed with deeper matter.
EMILIA   Pray stand up.
  Your grief is written in your cheek.
THIRD QUEEN   O, woe!
  You cannot read it there.   ⌜*She rises.*⌝ 125
                  There through my tears,
  Like wrinkled pebbles in a ⌜glassy⌝ stream,
  You may behold 'em. Lady, lady, alack!
  He that will all the treasure know o' th' earth
  Must know the center too; he that will fish   130
  For my least minnow, let him lead his line
  To catch one at my heart. O, pardon me!
  Extremity, that sharpens sundry wits,
  Makes me a fool.
EMILIA   Pray you say nothing, pray you.   135
  Who cannot feel nor see the rain, being in 't,
  Knows neither wet nor dry. If that you were
  The groundpiece of some painter, I would buy you
  T' instruct me 'gainst a capital grief—indeed,
  Such heart-pierced demonstration. But, alas,   140
  Being a natural sister of our sex,
  Your sorrow beats so ardently upon me
  That it shall make a counter-reflect 'gainst
  My brother's heart and warm it to some pity,
  Though it were made of stone. Pray have good   145
    comfort.

139. **'gainst:** in anticipation of; **capital:** deadly

140. **Such heart-pierced demonstration:** i.e., **such** heartbreak as you show

141. **Being . . . sex:** i.e., your **being a** real woman (and not a painting)

142. **ardently:** with such fiery heat

143. **make a counter-reflect:** i.e., reflect off me (as off a mirror)

144. **brother's:** i.e., brother-in-law's

152. **Knolls:** sounds, tolls

154. **meditance:** serious and sustained thought

156. **ospreys:** birds of prey, thought to have power over **fish** that made them turn over and wait to be caught

162–64. **Those that . . . agents:** i.e., even in the case of suicides   **drams:** small amounts of liquid (here, poisons)   **precipitance:** headlong falls

164. **grace:** favor; mercy, clemency

165. **Affords:** grants; **dust and shadow:** i.e., burial

167. **visitating:** visiting

168. **And:** i.e., **and** yet, even though they

170. **To give:** i.e., by giving

172. **presents . . . doing:** i.e., must be done now

173. **Now . . . tomorrow:** i.e., if we act **now,** the (hot) metal we are shaping will **take form;** if we wait until **tomorrow,** it will have cooled off

175. **secure:** overconfident, free from alarm

176. **your puissance: your** powerful self

178. **make petition clear:** i.e., (1) purify our supplication; (2) clarify our entreaty

THESEUS, ⌜*coming forward*⌝
  Forward to th' temple. Leave not out a jot
  O' th' sacred ceremony.
FIRST QUEEN   O, this celebration
  Will ⌜longer⌝ last and be more costly than   150
  Your suppliants' war. Remember that your fame
  Knolls in the ear o' th' world; what you do quickly
  Is not done rashly; your first thought is more
  Than others' labored meditance, your premeditating
  More than their actions. But, O Jove, your actions,   155
  Soon as they ⌜move,⌝ as ospreys do the fish,
  Subdue before they touch. Think, dear duke, think
  What beds our slain kings have!
SECOND QUEEN   What griefs our beds,
  That our dear lords have none!   160
THIRD QUEEN   None fit for th' dead.
  Those that with cords, knives, drams, precipitance,
  Weary of this world's light, have to themselves
  Been death's most horrid agents, human grace
  Affords them dust and shadow.   165
FIRST QUEEN   But our lords
  Lie blist'ring 'fore the visitating sun,
  And were good kings when living.
THESEUS
  It is true, and I will give you comfort
  To give your dead lords graves;   170
  The which to do must make some work with Creon.
FIRST QUEEN
  And that work presents itself to th' doing.
  Now 'twill take form; the heats are gone tomorrow.
  Then, bootless toil must recompense itself
  With its own sweat. Now he's secure,   175
  Not dreams we stand before your puissance,
  Rinsing our holy begging in our eyes
  To make petition clear.

184. **draw out:** detach (troops) from the main body of soldiers; **fit:** proper, appropriate

185. **prim'st:** most prime or excellent

186. **carry:** conduct, manage; **forth:** go or set **forth; levy:** enlist, muster

187. **instruments:** i.e., soldiers (literally, agents)

190. **Dowagers:** i.e., **widows** (line 191); **take hands:** i.e., shake **hands** in farewell

192. **Commends us to:** i.e., delivers **us** over **to**

194. **unseasonably:** at an unfitting time

195. **Cull forth:** choose, pick out; **unpanged:** *To pang* is to afflict with mental or physical anguish.

198. **service:** wordplay on (1) duty of a soldier; (2) ceremony (here, of marriage)

199. **any was:** i.e., **any service** that has ever been (often changed to "**any** war"); **more imports:** i.e., has **more** importance for

200. **actions:** wordplay on (1) military engagements; (2) acts, deeds; **foregone:** perhaps, undertaken in the past (literally, that have gone before)

201. **futurely:** in future; **cope:** encounter

204. **lock:** exclude, prevent (as if by locking up); **synod:** assembly (here, of the gods)

205. **warranting:** approving; **corselet:** encircle

206. **twinning cherries:** i.e., lips (*To twin* can mean both "to join, combine" and "to part, divide.") **fall:** i.e., let **fall,** drop

207. **tasteful:** able to taste; or, flavorful

208. **blubbered:** i.e., weeping

211. **Mars . . . drum:** The **drum,** which in Shakespeare's day often symbolized military action or zeal, is here portrayed as the instrument of the god of war.

SECOND QUEEN   Now you may take him,
  Drunk with his victory.   180
THIRD QUEEN   And his army full
  Of bread and sloth.
THESEUS   Artesius, that best knowest
  How to draw out, fit to this enterprise,
  The prim'st for this proceeding, and the number   185
  To carry such a business: forth and levy
  Our worthiest instruments, whilst we dispatch
  This grand act of our life, this daring deed
  Of fate in wedlock.
FIRST QUEEN, ⌜*to Second and Third Queens*⌝
               Dowagers, take hands.   190
  Let us be widows to our woes. Delay
  Commends us to a famishing hope.
ALL ⌜the QUEENS⌝   Farewell.
SECOND QUEEN
  We come unseasonably; but when could grief
  Cull forth, as unpanged judgment can, fitt'st time   195
  For best solicitation?
THESEUS   Why, good ladies,
  This is a service whereto I am going
  Greater than any was; it more imports me
  Than all the actions that I have foregone,   200
  Or futurely can cope.
FIRST QUEEN   The more proclaiming
  Our suit shall be neglected when her arms,
  Able to lock Jove from a synod, shall
  By warranting moonlight corselet thee. O, when   205
  Her twinning cherries shall their sweetness fall
  Upon thy tasteful lips, what wilt thou think
  Of rotten kings or blubbered queens? What care
  For what thou feel'st not, what thou feel'st being
    able   210
  To make Mars spurn his drum? O, if thou couch
  But one night with her, every hour in 't will

213. **Take . . . hundred:** i.e., make you want to spend **a hundred** more

216. **much unlike:** i.e., (it is) highly unlikely

217. **so transported:** i.e., out of control or enraptured as feared (See lines 254–66.) **as much:** i.e., (and I am) equally

218. **be such a suitor:** i.e., entreat you with **such a** request

219. **th' abstaining of:** i.e., restraining myself from

220. **surfeit:** fever, fit of illness

221. **a present:** an immediate, a speedily acting

226. **sentencing . . . dumb:** "concluding that they will always be as ineffectual as if they had not been uttered" (Waith)

230. **fee:** possession; reward

243. **get you:** i.e., **get you** to the temple

244. **success and return:** i.e., my good fortune and my **return** (from the war)

245. **pretended:** intended

246. **your soldier:** i.e., Theseus himself; **As before:** i.e., **as** I instructed you earlier (See lines 183–89.)

Take hostage of thee for a hundred, and
Thou shalt remember nothing more than what
That banquet bids thee to.   215
HIPPOLYTA, ⌜*to Theseus*⌝   Though much unlike
You should be so transported, as much sorry
I should be such a suitor, yet I think
Did I not, by th' abstaining of my joy—
Which breeds a deeper longing—cure their surfeit   220
That craves a present med'cine, I should pluck
All ladies' scandal on me.   ⌜*She kneels.*⌝
                              Therefore, sir,
As I shall here make trial of my prayers,
Either presuming them to have some force,   225
Or sentencing for aye their vigor dumb,
Prorogue this business we are going about, and
    hang
Your shield afore your heart—about that neck
Which is my fee, and which I freely lend   230
To do these poor queens service.
ALL QUEENS, ⌜*to Emilia*⌝   O, help now!
Our cause cries for your knee.
EMILIA, ⌜*to Theseus, kneeling*⌝   If you grant not
My sister her petition in that force,   235
With that celerity and nature which
She makes it in, from henceforth I'll not dare
To ask you anything, nor be so hardy
Ever to take a husband.
THESEUS   Pray stand up.   240
                ⌜*Hippolyta and Emilia rise.*⌝
I am entreating of myself to do
That which you kneel to have me.—Pirithous,
Lead on the bride; get you and pray the gods
For success and return; omit not anything
In the pretended celebration.—Queens,   245
Follow your soldier. ⌜*To Artesius.*⌝ As before, hence
    you,

248. banks of Aulis: i.e., shores of the ancient Greek port **of Aulis**

250. moiety of a number: i.e., part of a force

250–51. a business . . . looked: i.e., an enterprise larger than that against Thebes

253. currant: i.e., red, like the fruit, with wordplay on "current" (i.e., sterling, genuine, having the quality of current coin), a secondary meaning emphasized by the words **stamp** and **token** (line 254)

256. sister: i.e., sister-in-law

257. full: fully; **bate:** omit; **on 't:** i.e., of it

259. at heels: close behind, **at** your **heels; feast's solemnity:** i.e., celebratory feast

260. Shall want: i.e., will not happen (literally, will be lacking, will not exist)

261. Cousin: a courteous form of address among nobles

264. Make no abatement: i.e., omit nothing

265. still make good: continue to confirm

265–66. the tongue o' th' world: i.e., your fame

267. earn'st a deity: i.e., earn the rank of a god

269. mortal: human; **affections:** passions; **bend:** submit, yield

270. they: i.e., the gods

271. Groan under such a mast'ry: i.e., suffer under the power of their passions

273. sensually subdued: i.e., overpowered by our sensual appetites

274. human title: i.e., claim to be **human; Good cheer:** i.e., be of **good cheer,** have courage

275. comforts: i.e., relief of your sufferings

275 SD. Flourish: a horn fanfare, here accompanying the exit of a king

And at the banks of ⌜Aulis⌝ meet us with
The forces you can raise, where we shall find
The moiety of a number for a business   250
More bigger looked.   ⌜*Artesius exits.*⌝
⌜*To Hippolyta.*⌝   Since that our theme is haste,
I stamp this kiss upon thy currant lip;
Sweet, keep it as my token.—Set you forward,
For I will see you gone.   255
                    ⌜*The wedding procession begins to*⌝ *exit*
                                    towards the temple.
Farewell, my beauteous sister.—Pirithous,
Keep the feast full; bate not an hour on 't.

PIRITHOUS   Sir,
I'll follow you at heels. The feast's solemnity
Shall want till your return.   260

THESEUS   Cousin, I charge you,
Budge not from Athens. We shall be returning
Ere you can end this feast, of which I pray you
Make no abatement.—Once more, farewell all.
                    ⌜*All but Theseus and the Queens exit.*⌝

FIRST QUEEN
Thus dost thou still make good the tongue o' th'   265
  world.

SECOND QUEEN
And earn'st a deity equal with Mars.

THIRD QUEEN   If not above him, for
Thou, being but mortal, makest affections bend
To godlike honors; they themselves, some say,   270
Groan under such a mast'ry.

THESEUS   As we are men,
Thus should we do; being sensually subdued,
We lose our human title. Good cheer, ladies.
Now turn we towards your comforts.   275
                              Flourish. They exit.

1.2 Two noble cousins, Palamon and Arcite, discuss leaving Thebes, where the reign of their despised uncle Creon has corrupted the state. News comes of Theseus's advance on Thebes and, despite their hatred of Creon, they go to the city's defense.

—————

1. **blood:** i.e., kinship

2. **prime:** most valued

3. **crimes:** sins (The Ghost in *Hamlet* [1.5.17] refers to his sins as "the foul **crimes** done in my days **of nature**.")

6. **here:** i.e., **here in Thebes** (line 16); **to keep . . . shame:** i.e., we are as ashamed to continue **in abstinence**

7. **As in incontinence:** i.e., as to commit unchaste acts

8. **I' th' aid o':** i.e., when supported by

11. **should turn:** i.e., would whirl around; **if labor through:** i.e., **if** we get out of the whirlpool

14. **cried up with:** i.e., supported by

16. **bare weeds:** threadbare clothes

17. **gain:** winnings; **martialist:** warrior; **did propound:** proposed as a reward

19. **he had not:** i.e., he did not receive; **flirted:** scoffed at, scorned

20–21. **offer / To:** make an offering at

21. **Mars's . . . altar:** See note to line 1.1.68, above. **I do bleed:** i.e., I feel great sorrow

23. **her ancient fit of jealousy:** For Juno's **jealousy,** see longer note, page 252.

(continued)

Scene 2

Enter Palamon and Arcite.

ARCITE

   Dear Palamon, dearer in love than blood
   And our prime cousin, yet unhardened in
   The crimes of nature, let us leave the city
   Thebes, and the temptings in 't, before we further
   Sully our gloss of youth,   5
   And here to keep in abstinence we shame
   As in incontinence; for not to swim
   I' th' aid o' th' current were almost to sink,
   At least to frustrate striving; and to follow
   The common stream, 'twould bring us to an eddy   10
   Where we should turn or drown; if labor through,
   Our gain but life and weakness.

PALAMON   Your advice
   Is cried up with example. What strange ruins,
   Since first we went to school, may we perceive   15
   Walking in Thebes! Scars and bare weeds
   The gain o' th' martialist, who did propound
   To his bold ends honor and golden ingots,
   Which though he won, he had not, and now flirted
   By peace for whom he fought. Who then shall offer   20
   To Mars's so-scorned altar? I do bleed
   When such I meet, and wish great Juno would
   Resume her ancient fit of jealousy
   To get the soldier work, that peace might purge
   For her repletion, and retain anew   25
   Her charitable heart, now hard and harsher
   Than strife or war could be.

ARCITE   Are you not out?
   Meet you no ruin but the soldier in
   The cranks and turns of Thebes? You did begin   30
   As if you met decays of many kinds.

24–25. **purge . . . repletion:** relieve the body through evacuation to make up for eating and drinking to excess (See longer note, page 253.)

25. **retain:** i.e., engage in her service

28. **Are . . . out:** i.e., have you not forgotten your lines (an image from acting)

30. **cranks:** winding paths; **turns:** curves, bends

31. **decays:** i.e., **ruins** (line 14), debris

33. **unconsidered:** i.e., unrewarded; forgotten

36. **toil:** severe labor; net, trap, snare

39. **This is:** i.e., proper consideration of soldiers **is**

43. **color:** outward appearance

44. **e'en jump:** just exactly, precisely

48. **apes:** i.e., those who ape others

49. **manners:** conduct, behavior; morals

50. **Affect:** assume, ostentatiously make use of

51. **fond upon:** infatuated with

53. **conceived:** understood

55. **generous bond:** obligation of magnanimity; **follow:** imitate, copy

56. **Follows:** i.e., who accepts the authority of; **haply:** perhaps; **so long until:** up to the point when

59. **scissored:** trimmed; **just:** precisely

60. **To such a favorite's glass:** i.e., as if the mirror of some preferred or chosen one

63. **Before . . . foul:** i.e., even though **the street** is not muddy or filthy

64. **forehorse:** foremost horse; **none:** i.e., **none** of the horses

65. **draw:** pull (i.e., a cart or plow); **i' th' sequent trace:** i.e., in the train of horses that follow

Perceive you none that do arouse your pity
But th' unconsidered soldier?

PALAMON   Yes, I pity
Decays where'er I find them, but such most   35
That, sweating in an honorable toil,
Are paid with ice to cool 'em.

ARCITE   'Tis not this
I did begin to speak of. This is virtue
Of no respect in Thebes. I spake of Thebes—   40
How dangerous, if we will keep our honors,
It is for our residing, where every evil
Hath a good color; where every seeming good's
A certain evil; where not to be e'en jump
As they are here were to be strangers, and,   45
Such things to be, mere monsters.

PALAMON   'Tis in our power—
Unless we fear that apes can tutor 's—to
Be masters of our manners. What need I
Affect another's gait, which is not catching   50
Where there is faith? Or to be fond upon
Another's way of speech, when by mine own
I may be reasonably conceived—saved too,
Speaking it truly? Why am I bound
By any generous bond to follow him   55
Follows his tailor, haply so long until
The followed make pursuit? Or let me know
Why mine own barber is unblessed, with him
My poor chin too, for 'tis not scissored just
To such a favorite's glass? What canon is there   60
That does command my rapier from my hip
To dangle 't in my hand, or to go tiptoe
Before the street be foul? Either I am
The forehorse in the team, or I am none
That draw i' th' sequent trace. These poor slight   65
    sores

67. **plantain:** a weed whose leaves were used to stanch bleeding (See line 21 above.)

68. **heart's:** i.e., heart is

72. **Makes ... unfeared:** i.e., make people unafraid of **heaven; assured:** i.e., confident that

73–74. **puts ... fever:** i.e., makes **faith** ill

74. **alone:** only

75. **Voluble:** inconstant; **chance:** fortune

75–77. **only attributes ... nerves and act:** i.e., **attributes to** himself alone the capacities of those who serve him **nerves:** sinews

78. **in 't:** in serving him; **boot:** booty

79. **good, dares not:** dares not do good

80. **sib:** kin, related

81. **them break:** i.e., the **leeches** burst

82. **corruption:** putrid matter (i.e., the **blood** related to **Creon** [line 69])

85. **loud:** with wordplay on "manifest, flagrant"; **infamy:** shameful vileness

86. **relish of:** i.e., carry the taste of

88. **blood:** kinship; **quality:** character, nature

95. **be leaden-footed:** i.e., do not hurry (Lead is proverbially heavy.)

96–98. **Phoebus ... sun:** an allusion to the behavior of the sun god when his son Phaëthon was killed (See longer note to 5.1.99–100, page 263, and pictures, pages xvi and 166.) **whipstock:** handle of his whip **exclaimed against:** railed at

98. **but whispered to:** i.e., merely **whispered** in comparison to

99. **his fury:** i.e., Creon's fury

Need not a plantain. That which rips my bosom
Almost to th' heart's—

ARCITE   Our Uncle Creon.

PALAMON   He.   70
A most unbounded tyrant, whose successes
Makes heaven unfeared and villainy assured
Beyond its power there's nothing; almost puts
Faith in a fever, and deifies alone
Voluble chance; who only attributes   75
The faculties of other instruments
To his own nerves and act; commands men service,
And what they win in 't, boot and glory; one
That fears not to do harm; good, dares not. Let
The blood of mine that's sib to him be sucked   80
From me with leeches; let them break and fall
Off me with that corruption.

ARCITE   Clear-spirited cousin,
Let's leave his court, that we may nothing share
Of his loud infamy; for our milk   85
Will relish of the pasture, and we must
Be vile or disobedient, not his kinsmen
In blood unless in quality.

PALAMON   Nothing truer.
I think the echoes of his shames have deafed   90
    The ears of heav'nly justice. Widows' cries
    Descend again into their throats and have not
    Due audience of the gods.

Enter Valerius.

Valerius.

VALERIUS
The King calls for you; yet be leaden-footed   95
Till his great rage be off him. Phoebus, when
He broke his whipstock and exclaimed against
The horses of the sun, but whispered to
The loudness of his fury.

100. **shake:** agitate

102. **where:** i.e., wherever; **threats:** threatens

104–5. **seal...wrath:** i.e., confirm (through action) what **his wrath** promises

107. **But that:** i.e., except for the fact that

109. **Thirds:** i.e., reduces to one-third; **the case... ours:** i.e., as **is the case** with us

110. **dregged with mind assured:** i.e., hindered by his awareness **dregged:** made cloudy with dregs or sediment

112. **Leave that unreasoned:** i.e., do not think about **that**

113. **stand now for: now** take the part of

116. **With him stand...fate:** i.e., **stand with him** at the mercy of fate

117. **Who:** i.e., which; **bounded:** set the limits of

121. **On...condition:** i.e., if we fail in **some** provision or stipulation

123. **intelligence of state:** i.e., news (of the war)

123–24. **came...With:** i.e., arrived at the same moment as

128. **as for our health:** i.e., **as** if we were bled by our physicians (a common medical treatment); **which...spent:** i.e., our **blood** would not be wasted

129. **laid out for purchase:** i.e., expended **for** the **purchase** (of **honor** [line 126])

132. **th' event:** the outcome

PALAMON   Small winds shake him.   100
  But what's the matter?
VALERIUS
  Theseus, who where he threats appalls, hath sent
  Deadly defiance to him and pronounces
  Ruin to Thebes, who is at hand to seal
  The promise of his wrath.   105
ARCITE   Let him approach.
  But that we fear the gods in him, he brings not
  A jot of terror to us. Yet what man
  Thirds his own worth—the case is each of ours—
  When that his action's dregged with mind assured   110
  'Tis bad he goes about?
PALAMON   Leave that unreasoned.
  Our services stand now for Thebes, not Creon.
  Yet to be neutral to him were dishonor,
  Rebellious to oppose. Therefore we must   115
  With him stand to the mercy of our fate,
  Who hath bounded our last minute.
ARCITE   So we must.
  ⌜*To Valerius.*⌝ Is 't said this war's afoot? Or, it shall
    be,   120
  On fail of some condition?
VALERIUS   'Tis in motion;
  The intelligence of state came in the instant
  With the defier.
PALAMON   Let's to the King, who, were he   125
  A quarter carrier of that honor which
  His enemy come in, the blood we venture
  Should be as for our health, which were not spent,
  Rather laid out for purchase. But alas,
  Our hands advanced before our hearts, what will   130
  The fall o' th' stroke do damage?
ARCITE   Let th' event,
  That never-erring arbitrator, tell us

135. **becking:** beckoning; **chance:** fortune

1.3 Pirithous leaves Athens to join Theseus in Thebes. Hippolyta and Emilia praise the strength of the bond between the two men, comparing it with other close bonds, especially that of Emilia as a girl with her friend Flavina.

---

1. **No further:** i.e., come **no further** with me (toward Thebes)

3–4. **of whose . . . question:** i.e., about **whose success I** have no doubt or fear (To **make question** is to entertain doubt about.)

5. **an 't might be:** if it **be** possible

6. **dure:** endure, bear; **ill-dealing:** i.e., (1) badly behaving; (2) dispensing **ill** or evil; **Speed to:** (1) success **to;** or, perhaps, (2) hurry **to**

7. **Store:** abundance; **governors:** managers

11. **affections:** qualities, properties

12. **In:** i.e., into; **best-tempered:** i.e., highest quality (*To temper,* here, is to bring something to a proper condition by mingling it with something else.)

15. **speed:** success

16. **Bellona:** See note to 1.1.84.

17. **terrene:** earthly

21. **In 's:** i.e., (also) in his

22. **We . . . soldiers:** See note to **Amazonian,** 1.1.88.

24. **broached:** transfixed, impaled

25. **sod:** seethed, boiled

When we know all ourselves, and let us follow
The becking of our chance.   135

>   *They exit.*

Scene 3

Enter Pirithous, Hippolyta, Emilia.

PIRITHOUS
  No further.

HIPPOLYTA   Sir, farewell. Repeat my wishes
  To our great lord, of whose success I dare not
  Make any timorous question; yet I wish him
  Excess and overflow of power, an 't might be,   5
  To dure ill-dealing fortune. Speed to him.
  Store never hurts good governors.

PIRITHOUS   Though I know
  His ocean needs not my poor drops, yet they
  Must yield their tribute there.—My precious maid,   10
  Those best affections that the heavens infuse
  In their best-tempered pieces keep enthroned
  In your dear heart!

EMILIA   Thanks, sir. Remember me
  To our all-royal brother, for whose speed   15
  The great Bellona I'll solicit; and
  Since in our terrene state petitions are not
  Without gifts understood, I'll offer to her
  What I shall be advised she likes. Our hearts
  Are in his army, in his tent.   20

HIPPOLYTA   In 's bosom.
  We have been soldiers, and we cannot weep
  When our friends don their helms or put to sea,
  Or tell of babes broached on the lance, or women
  That have sod their infants in—and after ate them— 25
  The brine they wept at killing 'em. Then if

27. **stay:** wait; **spinsters:** i.e., women who spin yarn (rather than fight in wars [See line 22.])

30–31. **which . . . requiring:** i.e., **which (peace)** will no longer need to be asked for **requiring:** requesting, entreating

33. **his depart:** i.e., Theseus's departure; **his sports:** i.e., Pirithous's participation in games

34–35. **passed . . . execution:** i.e., were carried out with little care or attention

35. **nor:** neither

36. **or:** nor

37. **another:** i.e., **another business**

38–39. **nurse equal / To:** The image is of **twins** (i.e., Pirithous's participation in the games and his desire to follow Theseus) being cared for by a **nurse** (the **mind**) whose attention is divided between them.

42. **cabined:** taken shelter

44. **want:** starvation

44–45. **skiffed / Torrents:** crossed rushing waters in a small light boat or skiff

46. **I' . . . these:** i.e., even when **least** dangerous

47. **Fought . . . lodged:** an allusion to their journey to **Death's** lodging, the underworld, from which they were rescued by Hercules

48. **brought them off:** rescued them

48–51. **knot . . . undone:** i.e., the **knot** that ties them together, though it can be **outworn,** can **never be** untied (The phrase "**with so true, so long**" may refer to the **knot of love** or to the **finger.**) **finger . . . cunning:** i.e., greatly or subtly dexterous instrument of work **outworn:** obliterated by time

(continued)

You stay to see of us such spinsters, we
Should hold you here forever.

PIRITHOUS　　　　　　　　　　　Peace be to you
As I pursue this war, which shall be then　　　　　　30
Beyond further requiring.　　　　　　*Pirithous exits.*

EMILIA　　　　　　　　　　　How his longing
Follows his friend! Since his depart, his sports,
Though craving seriousness and skill, passed slightly
His careless execution, where nor gain　　　　　　35
Made him regard, or loss consider, but
Playing ⌜one⌝ business in his hand, another
Directing in his head, his mind nurse equal
To these so diff'ring twins. Have you observed him
Since our great lord departed?　　　　　　　　40

HIPPOLYTA　　　　　　　　　　With much labor,
And I did love him for 't. They two have cabined
In many as dangerous as poor a corner,
Peril and want contending; they have skiffed
Torrents whose roaring tyranny and power　　　　45
I' th' least of these was dreadful, and they have
Fought out together where Death's self was lodged.
Yet fate hath brought them off. Their knot of love,
Tied, weaved, entangled, with so true, so long,
And with a finger of so deep a cunning,　　　　　50
May be outworn, never undone. I think
Theseus cannot be umpire to himself,
Cleaving his conscience into twain and doing
Each side like justice, which he loves best.

EMILIA　　　　　　　　　　　　Doubtless　55
There is a best, and reason has no manners
To say it is not you. I was acquainted
Once with a time when I enjoyed a playfellow;
You were at wars when she the grave enriched,
Who made too proud the bed; took leave o' th' moon,　60
Which then looked pale at parting, when our count
Was each eleven.

53. **conscience:** inmost thought, heart

54. **like:** equal; **which:** i.e., himself or Pirithous

56. **a best:** i.e., one he loves best; **manners:** procedures

57. **you:** i.e., instead of Pirithous or Theseus himself

61. **count:** number (of years)

66. **ground:** foundation

67. **buckled:** fastened

70. **sigh:** i.e., sigh for

71. **for:** because; **elements:** atmospheric agencies or powers

72–73. **effect . . . operance:** i.e., bring about wonderful outcomes through their operations

76. **arraignment:** i.e., trial or examination

78. **long:** be impatient for

80. **the like:** the same kind of

80–81. **Phoenix-like . . . perfume:** The mythical Phoenix immolates itself on a fire of sweet-smelling wood and is then reborn from the ashes. (See picture, page 96.)

81. **toy:** trifling ornament

82. **her affections:** i.e., those things that she liked

83. **haply:** perhaps (See longer note, page 253.)

84. **my most serious decking:** i.e., clothing myself for important occasions

85. **air:** tune; **at adventure:** by chance

86. **coinage:** improvisation; **note:** melody

87. **sojourn:** make a temporary stay

87–88. **dwell on:** linger over (with the added sense of **dwell** as "remain as in a permanent residence")

89. **rehearsal:** account

(continued)

40

HIPPOLYTA   'Twas ⌜Flavina.⌝
EMILIA   Yes.
　You talk of Pirithous' and Theseus' love.   65
　Theirs has more ground, is more maturely seasoned,
　More buckled with strong judgment, and their needs
　The one of th' other may be said to water
　Their intertangled roots of love. But I,
　And she I sigh and spoke of, were things innocent,   70
　Loved for we did, and like the elements
　That know not what nor why, yet do effect
　Rare issues by their operance, our souls
　Did so to one another. What she liked
　Was then of me approved, what not, condemned,   75
　No more arraignment. The flower that I would pluck
　And put between my breasts—O, then but beginning
　To swell about the blossom—she would long
　Till she had such another, and commit it
　To the like innocent cradle, where, Phoenix-like,   80
　They died in perfume. On my head no toy
　But was her pattern; her affections—pretty,
　Though haply ⌜hers⌝ careless were—I followed
　For my most serious decking. Had mine ear
　Stol'n some new air, or at adventure hummed one   85
　From musical coinage, why, it was a note
　Whereon her spirits would sojourn—rather, dwell
　　on—
　And sing it in her slumbers. This rehearsal—
　Which fury-innocent wots well comes in   90
　Like old importment's bastard—has this end,
　That the true love 'tween maid and maid may be
　More than in sex individual.
HIPPOLYTA   You're out of breath,
　And this high-speeded pace is but to say   95
　That you shall never—like the maid Flavina—
　Love any that's called man.
EMILIA   I am sure I shall not.

90. **fury-innocent:** perhaps, innocent passion (The phrase is often emended.) **wots:** knows; **comes in:** enters, arrives at its destination

91. **old importment's bastard:** i.e., the illegitimate offspring of something significant; **end:** (1) purpose; (2) conclusion

92. **maid:** girl, maiden

93. **in sex individual:** i.e., **in** (the love between) a man and a woman joined indissolubly (in marriage); or, **in** (the fact that) the maidens share a single **sex** or are indivisible in more ways than in sharing this **sex individual:** (1) inseparable; (2) single (See longer note, page 254.)

99. **weak:** i.e., easily deceived, credulous

104. **ripe for your persuasion:** i.e., prepared to be persuaded by you

107. **now in: now** go **in**

108. **That we:** i.e., **that** I (the royal plural)

1.4 A victorious Theseus bids farewell to the three queens just as Palamon and Arcite are brought in wounded on stretchers. Theseus insists that doctors tend to them quickly so that he may imprison them.

---

0 SD. **Cornets:** wind instruments made of horn (See longer note, page 255, and picture, page 70.) **struck within:** i.e., fought offstage; **retreat:** i.e., the signal for a withdrawal from the battlefield; **Flourish:** trumpet signal for a noble's entrance

(continued)

HIPPOLYTA   Now, alack, weak sister,
  I must no more believe thee in this point—   100
  Though in 't I know thou dost believe thyself—
  Than I will trust a sickly appetite,
  That loathes even as it longs. But sure, my sister,
  If I were ripe for your persuasion, you
  Have said enough to shake me from the arm   105
  Of the all-noble Theseus, for whose fortunes
  I will now in and kneel, with great assurance
  That we, more than his Pirithous, possess
  The high throne in his heart.
EMILIA   I am not   110
  Against your faith, yet I continue mine.

                             They exit.

Scene 4

Cornets. A battle struck within; then a retreat.
Flourish. Then enter, ⌜through one door,⌝ Theseus,
victor, ⌜accompanied by Lords and Soldiers.
Entering through another door,⌝ the three Queens
meet him, and fall on their faces before him.

FIRST QUEEN
  To thee no star be dark!
SECOND QUEEN   Both heaven and earth
  Friend thee forever.
THIRD QUEEN   All the good that may
  Be wished upon thy head, I cry "Amen" to 't!   5
THESEUS
  Th' impartial gods, who from the mounted heavens
  View us their mortal herd, behold who err
  And, in their time, chastise. Go and find out
  The bones of your dead lords and honor them
  With treble ceremony; rather than a gap   10
  Should be in their dear rites, we would supply 't;

1. **no star be dark:** i.e., may **no star** or planet **be** malignant (a reference to the supposed astrological power of celestial bodies)

6. **mounted:** high, elevated

11. **dear:** noble, honorable; **rites:** a spelling used interchangeably with *rights;* **we would supply 't:** i.e., I would like to make it whole or complete

12. **those . . . which:** i.e., **I will depute those** who; **invest:** clothe

13. **and:** i.e., **and shall** (line 12); **even:** make **even,** i.e., complete

15. **good:** i.e., favorable

16. **What:** i.e., who

17. **great quality:** i.e., high rank or position

18. **appointment:** equipment, trappings

20. **By . . . Mars:** an oath, "by Mars's helmet"

22. **Make . . . aghast:** cut their way through horrified **troops; note:** attention

23. **mark:** i.e., object of attention

24. **view:** beholding

26. **Wi' leave:** i.e., with your permission to speak

30. **taken:** captured

32. **recovered:** restored to life or consciousness

35. **lees of such:** i.e., dregs **of such** men; **millions of rates:** "by a multiple of **millions**" (G. B. Evans)

37. **Convent:** summon (accent on first syllable); **in their behoof:** i.e., to help them; **balms:** healing ointments

38. **niggard:** use sparingly; **waste:** squander

But those we will depute which shall invest
You in your dignities and even each thing
Our haste does leave imperfect. So, adieu,
And heaven's good eyes look on you.   *Queens exit.*   15

⌜*Enter a Herald and Soldiers bearing Palamon
and Arcite on biers.*⌝

                                                     What are those?
HERALD
Men of great quality, as may be judged
By their appointment. Some of Thebes have told 's
They are sisters' children, nephews to the King.
THESEUS
By th' helm of Mars, I saw them in the war,   20
Like to a pair of lions, smeared with prey,
Make lanes in troops aghast. I fixed my note
Constantly on them, for they were a mark
Worth a god's view. What prisoner was't that told me
When I enquired their names?   25
HERALD   ⌜Wi'⌝ leave, they're called
Arcite and Palamon.
THESEUS   'Tis right; those, those.
They are not dead?
HERALD
Nor in a state of life. Had they been taken   30
When their last hurts were given, 'twas possible
They might have been recovered. Yet they breathe
And have the name of men.
THESEUS   Then like men use 'em.
The very lees of such, millions of rates,   35
Exceed the wine of others. All our surgeons
Convent in their behoof; our richest balms,
Rather than niggard, waste. Their lives concern us
Much more than Thebes is worth. Rather than have
  'em   40

42. **would 'em:** wish them

45. **unkind:** i.e., unhealthy (because fresh **air** was thought harmful to wounds)

45–46. **minister . . . do:** i.e., do what is humanly possible

47–51. **Since . . . imposition:** This difficult passage argues that urgent pressures enable accomplishments beyond what **nature** can **reach to. mark:** goal, target **imposition:** i.e., the imposing of external stimuli (such as those listed in lines 47–49)

51–52. **sickness . . . reason:** i.e., the inflamed or deeply affected **will** overpowering **reason**

53. **Apollo's mercy:** Phoebus Apollo, the Greek god of the sun, was also the god of healing. **our best:** i.e., **our best surgeons** (line 36)

54. **tender:** i.e., apply (literally, "offer, present")

55. **post:** travel with speed

1.5 The three queens take farewell of each other as the bodies of their dead husbands are carried off for separate burials.

————————

0 SD. **knights:** i.e., kings, husbands; **&c.:** i.e., other mourners or with funeral accoutrements; **dirge:** to be sung or recited, perhaps by the queens

1. **Urns . . . away:** i.e., **bring** burial **urns** and incense

2. **Vapors:** smoky matter from flames

3. **dole:** mourning

(continued)

Freed of this plight, and in their morning state,
Sound and at liberty, I would 'em dead.
But forty-thousandfold we had rather have 'em
Prisoners to us than Death. Bear 'em speedily
From our kind air, to them unkind, and minister   45
What man to man may do—for our sake, more,
Since I have known frights, fury, friends' behests,
Love's provocations, zeal, a mistress' task,
Desire of liberty, a fever, madness,
Hath set a mark which nature could not reach to   50
Without some imposition, sickness in will
⌜O'er-wrestling⌝ strength in reason. For our love
And great Apollo's mercy, all our best
Their best skill tender.—Lead into the city,
Where, having bound things scattered, we will post   55
To Athens ⌜'fore⌝ our army.

                             Flourish. They exit.

Scene 5

*Music. Enter the Queens with the hearses of their
knights, in a funeral solemnity, &c.*

          ⌜*The dirge.*⌝
   Urns and odors bring away;
   Vapors, sighs, darken the day;
Our dole more deadly looks than dying;
    Balms and gums and heavy cheers,
    Sacred vials filled with tears,   5
And clamors through the wild air flying.
    Come, all sad and solemn shows
    That are quick-eyed Pleasure's foes;
    We convent naught else but woes.
    We convent naught else but woes.   10

4. **Balms:** aromatic material for embalming the dead; **gums:** resinous substances burned as incense; **heavy cheers:** sad faces

8. **quick-eyed:** capable of keen perception

9. **convent:** call together

11. **brings:** leads; **household's grave:** i.e., family mausoleum or burial ground

13. **this:** i.e., **this path** (line 11)

14–16. **Heavens . . . end:** Proverbial: "Death has **a thousand** doors to let out life." **lend:** provide **ways:** paths

17–18. **This . . . meets:** Proverbial: "Many **ways** (line 16) meet in one town." **straying:** wandering

18 SD. **severally:** i.e., through (three) separate doors

Pecking crows. (1.1.46)
From Guillaume de La Perrière,
Le théâtre des bons engins . . . [1539?].

THIRD QUEEN, ⌜*to Second Queen*⌝
  This funeral path brings to your household's grave.
  Joy seize on you again; peace sleep with him.
SECOND QUEEN, ⌜*to First Queen*⌝
  And this to yours.
FIRST QUEEN, ⌜*to Third Queen*⌝ Yours this way. Heavens
    lend   15
  A thousand differing ways to one sure end.
THIRD QUEEN
  This world's a city full of straying streets,
  And death's the market-place where each one meets.
                                        They exit severally.

THE TWO NOBLE KINSMEN

ACT 2

2.1 The keeper of a jail in Athens discusses the terms of his daughter's dowry with her wooer. The daughter enters bringing straw for the cells of the jail's new prisoners, Palamon and Arcite. She praises their attitude and behavior.

---

1. **depart with:** give away, bestow
2. **cast to:** i.e., confer or bestow upon; **keep:** guard, have charge of
3. **great ones:** i.e., persons of high rank (Prisoners paid the jailer.)
5. **given out:** reputed; **better lined:** i.e., richer
6. **report:** rumor, repute; **would:** wish
7. **that:** i.e., **that** which; **delivered:** reported, declared; **Marry:** a mild oath
8. **assure upon:** i.e., transfer legally to, hand down to
11. **estate . . . in:** provide . . . with
13–14. **solemnity:** celebration, ceremonial occasion
14. **a full promise of her:** i.e., her unequivocal **promise**
15. **that . . . seen:** i.e., I know **that** to have happened; **tender:** offer
17–18. **chanced to name:** i.e., happened to speak of
18. **upon:** about
19. **hurry:** commotion
20. **have an end of it:** i.e., bring it to completion

ACT 2

Scene 1

Enter Jailer and Wooer.

JAILER I may depart with little while I live; something I
may cast to you, not much. Alas, the prison I keep,
though it be for great ones, yet they seldom come;
before one salmon you shall take a number of min-
nows. I am given out to be better lined than it can   5
appear to me report is a true speaker. I would I
were really that I am delivered to be. Marry, what
I have, be it what it will, I will assure upon my
daughter at the day of my death.

WOOER Sir, I demand no more than your own offer,   10
and I will estate your daughter in what I have
promised.

JAILER Well, we will talk more of this when the solemnity is past. But have you a full promise of her?
When that shall be seen, I tender my consent.   15

Enter ⌜the Jailer's⌝ Daughter, ⌜carrying rushes.⌝

WOOER I have sir. Here she comes.

JAILER, ⌜to Daughter⌝ Your friend and I have chanced
to name you here, upon the old business. But no
more of that now; so soon as the court hurry is
over, we will have an end of it. I' th' meantime,   20

21. **look tenderly to:** i.e., take good care of
23. **strewings:** i.e., fresh rushes for the floor
28. **famed:** rumored, reported
29. **By my troth:** a mild oath
30. **grise:** step, rung
32. **only:** sole
37. **toy:** trifle
41. **merrily:** i.e., cheerful, agreeable
42. **restraint:** captivity
43. **divided:** broken off, cut off
45. **presently:** immediately
49. **privately:** secretly
50 SD. **above:** in a window or gallery over the stage

Fortune spinning her wheel. (1.1.72; 2.2.42; 3.1.16)
From Charles de Bouelles,
Que hoc volumine continentur . . . [1510].

look tenderly to the two prisoners. I can tell you
they are princes.

DAUGHTER   These strewings are for their chamber. 'Tis
pity they are in prison, and 'twere pity they should
be out. I do think they have patience to make any   25
adversity ashamed. The prison itself is proud of
'em, and they have all the world in their chamber.

JAILER   They are famed to be a pair of absolute men.

DAUGHTER   By my troth, I think fame but stammers
'em. They stand a grise above the reach of report.   30

JAILER   I heard them reported in the battle to be the
only doers.

DAUGHTER   Nay, most likely, for they are noble suff'rers.
I marvel how they would have looked had they
been victors, that with such a constant nobility en-   35
force a freedom out of bondage, making misery
their mirth and affliction a toy to jest at.

JAILER   Do they so?

DAUGHTER   It seems to me they have no more sense
of their captivity than I of ruling Athens. They eat   40
well, look merrily, discourse of many things, but
nothing of their own restraint and disasters. Yet
sometimes a divided sigh, martyred as 'twere i' th'
deliverance, will break from one of them—when
the other presently gives it so sweet a rebuke that   45
I could wish myself a sigh to be so chid, or at least
a sigher to be comforted.

WOOER   I never saw 'em.

JAILER   The Duke himself came privately in the night,
and so did they.   50

Enter Palamon and Arcite, ⌜in shackles,⌝ above.

What the reason of it is, I know not. Look, yonder
they are; that's Arcite looks out.

DAUGHTER   No, sir, no, that's Palamon. Arcite is the

54. **lower:** a reference either to his height or to his position at the window

56. **Go to:** an expression of remonstrance; **leave your:** i.e., stop

2.2 Palamon and Arcite, after lamenting their prospect of lifelong imprisonment, rejoice that they are imprisoned together where nothing can ever come between them. Through the prison window Palamon sees Emilia below in a garden, immediately falls in love with her, and announces his love to Arcite. When the same fate befalls Arcite, the two cousins become bitter rivals. Arcite is then freed and banished from the kingdom while Palamon is moved to a cell without a view of the garden.

----

4. **chance:** i.e., unpredictable course

8. **Laid up:** put away; **hour to come:** i.e., future

12. **Must we:** i.e., will we be allowed to

14. **Hung:** decorated; **painted:** brightly colored; **favors:** scarves or other love tokens

15. **start:** rush, go quickly

16. **as:** i.e., like; **east wind:** proverbially unpleasant and injurious to health

18. **Even . . . leg:** i.e., quickly; or, perhaps, effortlessly **wanton:** playful

19. **won the garlands:** i.e., gained the victory (See picture, page 134.)

21–22. **exercise . . . arms:** i.e., do battle **like** heroic **twins**

lower of the twain; you may perceive a part of   55
him.

JAILER   Go to, leave your pointing; they would not
make us their object. Out of their sight.

DAUGHTER   It is a holiday to look on them. Lord, the
diff'rence of men!

⌜*Jailer, Daughter, and Wooer*⌝ *exit.*

Scene 2

Palamon and Arcite ⌜*remain, above.*⌝

PALAMON
How do you, noble cousin?

ARCITE   How do you, sir?

PALAMON
Why, strong enough to laugh at misery
And bear the chance of war; yet we are prisoners
I fear forever, cousin.   5

ARCITE   I believe it,
And to that destiny have patiently
Laid up my hour to come.

PALAMON   O, cousin Arcite,
Where is Thebes now? Where is our noble country?   10
Where are our friends and kindreds? Never more
Must we behold those comforts, never see
The hardy youths strive for the games of honor,
Hung with the painted favors of their ladies,
Like tall ships under sail; then start amongst 'em   15
And as an east wind leave 'em all behind us,
Like lazy clouds, whilst Palamon and Arcite,
Even in the wagging of a wanton leg,
Outstripped the people's praises, won the garlands
Ere they have time to wish 'em ours. O, never   20
Shall we two exercise, like twins of honor,
Our arms again, and feel our fiery horses

24. **Better . . . wore:** i.e., Mars never **wore better swords** (line 23) than ours (See picture, page 198.)

25. **Ravished:** torn from

26. **deck:** adorn; **gods that hate us:** As Thebans, they would have been hated by Athena and Juno. (See longer note to 1.2.23, page 252, and pictures, pages 154 and 68.)

28. **blast:** i.e., destroy (blight, wither)

32. **Like . . . spring:** i.e., **like** blossoms that appear too early in the **spring**

33. **heaviest:** saddest

35. **Loaden:** laden, weighed down; **armed:** furnished (with wordplay on *arms* as upper limbs); **Cupids:** Cupid, in Roman mythology, is the god of love. (See picture, page 66.)

36. **issue:** offspring

37. **figures:** images, likenesses

38. **glad our age:** i.e., cause us in old **age** to rejoice

38–39. **like young . . . arms:** i.e., as eaglets are taught **to gaze** into the sun, so the offspring of warriors should be taught **to gaze** unblinking at **bright** military armor

41. **fair-eyed maids:** girls with beautiful eyes

42. **ever-blinded Fortune:** The goddess Fortuna, called "blind **Fortune**," was often pictured as blindfolded. (See pictures, pages 54 and 222.)

46. **tells:** counts (with wordplay on "narrates")

49. **inhabit:** dwell; **still:** always, continually

51. **echoes:** i.e., echoing yelps and cries

52. **must we halloo:** i.e., are we allowed to urge on with shouts

(continued)

Like proud seas under us. Our good swords now—
Better the red-eyed god of war ne'er ⌜wore⌝—
Ravished our sides, like age must run to rust   25
And deck the temples of those gods that hate us;
These hands shall never draw 'em out like lightning
To blast whole armies more.

ARCITE   No, Palamon,
Those hopes are prisoners with us. Here we are   30
And here the graces of our youths must wither
Like a too-timely spring. Here age must find us
And—which is heaviest, Palamon—unmarried.
The sweet embraces of a loving wife,
Loaden with kisses, armed with thousand Cupids,   35
Shall never clasp our necks; no issue know us—
No figures of ourselves shall we e'er see,
To glad our age, and like young eagles teach 'em
Boldly to gaze against bright arms and say
"Remember what your fathers were, and conquer!"   40
The fair-eyed maids shall weep our banishments
And in their songs curse ever-blinded Fortune
Till she for shame see what a wrong she has done
To youth and nature. This is all our world.
We shall know nothing here but one another,   45
Hear nothing but the clock that tells our woes.
The vine shall grow, but we shall never see it;
Summer shall come, and with her all delights,
But dead-cold winter must inhabit here still.

PALAMON
'Tis too true, Arcite. To our Theban hounds   50
That shook the agèd forest with their echoes
No more now must we halloo; no more shake
Our pointed javelins whilst the angry swine
Flies like a Parthian quiver from our rages,
Struck with our well-steeled darts. All valiant uses, 55
The food and nourishment of noble minds,
In us two here shall perish; we shall die,

53. **swine:** wild boar (hunted with **javelins**)

54. **Flies:** flees; **Parthian quiver:** i.e., quiverful of arrows carried by horsemen from the ancient kingdom of Parthia (See longer note, page 255.)

55. **well-steeled darts:** i.e., **darts** overlaid, pointed, or edged with steel; **uses:** practices

58. **lastly:** i.e., at last, finally

59. **Children . . . ignorance:** perhaps, sad and ignored

63. **mere:** pure, unmixed

64. **hold:** maintain; **brave:** "an indeterminate word, used to express the superabundance of any valuable quality in men or things" (Samuel Johnson)

65. **enjoying:** experiencing; **griefs:** suffering; wrongs, injuries

69. **main goodness:** great benefit or advantage

71. **let 'em suffer:** even if they **suffer**

72. **gall of hazard:** bitterness of fortune; **so:** if

74. **A willing man:** i.e., **a man** who accepts his fate; **sleeping:** i.e., peacefully (Proverbial: "To go to one's grave like a bed.")

77. **gentle:** a complimentary epithet

80. **yet:** still; **ways:** paths

81. **common conversation:** i.e., frequent dealing with others

84. **Can be:** i.e., **can** exist

86. **endless mine:** infinite source of riches

Which is the curse of honor, lastly,
Children of grief and ignorance.

ARCITE   Yet, cousin,   60
Even from the bottom of these miseries,
From all that fortune can inflict upon us,
I see two comforts rising, two mere blessings,
If the gods please: to hold here a brave patience,
And the enjoying of our griefs together.   65
Whilst Palamon is with me, let me perish
If I think this our prison!

PALAMON   Certainly
'Tis a main goodness, cousin, that our fortunes
Were twined together. 'Tis most true, two souls   70
Put in two noble bodies, let 'em suffer
The gall of hazard, so they grow together,
Will never sink; they must not, say they could.
A willing man dies sleeping and all's done.

ARCITE
Shall we make worthy uses of this place   75
That all men hate so much?

PALAMON   How, gentle cousin?

ARCITE
Let's think this prison holy sanctuary
To keep us from corruption of worse men.
We are young and yet desire the ways of honor   80
That liberty and common conversation,
The poison of pure spirits, might like women
Woo us to wander from. What worthy blessing
Can be but our imaginations
May make it ours? And here being thus together,   85
We are an endless mine to one another;
We are one another's wife, ever begetting
New births of love; we are father, friends,
    acquaintance;
We are, in one another, families;   90
I am your heir, and you are mine. This place

92. **inheritance:** estate, property

94. **surfeits:** fevers, fits

98. **Quarrels:** i.e., our involvement in others' disputes **might** (line 97)

98–99. **envy . . . acquaintance:** For editorial attempts to explain these lines, see longer note, page 256. **Crave:** require, call for, demand

102. **chances:** mishaps, unfortunate accidents

106. **wanton:** i.e., delighted (literally, unrestrained in merriment)

108. **abroad:** at large

109. **like a beast:** i.e., the way **a beast** lives; **methinks:** it seems to me

109–10. **I . . . content:** i.e., **I find** greater **content** in **the court** we have created **here** (See 2.1.27: "they have all the world in their chamber.")

110–14. **all those pleasures . . . takes with him:** These lines summarize Ecclesiastes 1–2 on the transitoriness of the **pleasures** in which humans delight. (See longer note, page 256.) **vanity:** that which is futile or worthless **sufficient:** able **gaudy:** brilliantly fine **shadow:** unreal appearance, delusive semblance

115. **What . . . old:** i.e., **what** might **we** have become had we grown **old**

119. **they:** i.e., **the great ones** (line 117); **ill:** wicked

120. **had their epitaphs:** received the **epitaphs** that **they do** (line 119)

122. **would:** want to; **still:** without interruption or cessation

Is our inheritance; no hard oppressor
Dare take this from us; here with a little patience
We shall live long and loving. No surfeits seek us;
The hand of war hurts none here, nor the seas   95
Swallow their youth. Were we at liberty,
A wife might part us lawfully, or business;
Quarrels consume us; envy of ill men
Crave our acquaintance. I might sicken, cousin,
Where you should never know it, and so perish   100
Without your noble hand to close mine eyes,
Or prayers to the gods. A thousand chances,
Were we from hence, would sever us.

PALAMON   You have made
    me—   105
I thank you, cousin Arcite—almost wanton
With my captivity. What a misery
It is to live abroad and everywhere!
'Tis like a beast, methinks. I find the court here,
I am sure, a more content; and all those pleasures   110
That woo the wills of men to vanity
I see through now, and am sufficient
To tell the world 'tis but a gaudy shadow
That old Time as he passes by takes with him.
What had we been, old in the court of Creon,   115
Where sin is justice, lust and ignorance
The virtues of the great ones? Cousin Arcite,
Had not the loving gods found this place for us,
We had died as they do, ill old men, unwept,
And had their epitaphs, the people's curses.   120
Shall I say more?

ARCITE   I would hear you still.

PALAMON   You shall.
Is there record of any two that loved
Better than we do, Arcite?   125

ARCITE   Sure there cannot.

129 SD. **Woman:** i.e., personal attendant (perhaps a "waiting gentlewoman")

131. **To those:** i.e., **to** the abode of **those**

136–37. **That . . . himself:** In mythology, the **boy** Narcissus fell in love with **himself** on seeing his reflection in water. On the spot where he died of lovesickness, the **narcissus** flower grew. (See Ovid, *Metamorphoses* 3.413–510, and picture, below.)

137. **maids:** young women

138. **Pray, forward:** i.e., please go on with what you were saying

141. **fair:** beautiful, handsome

144. **wench:** girl

149. **go forward:** i.e., continue

151. **work:** embroider

Narcissus. (2.2.135; 4.2.35)
From Geoffrey Whitney, *A choice of emblemes . . .* (1586).

64

PALAMON
  I do not think it possible our friendship
  Should ever leave us.

ARCITE   Till our deaths it cannot.

  Enter Emilia and her Woman, ⌜below.⌝

  And after death our spirits shall be led   130
  To those that love eternally.   ⌜*Palamon catches sight
                                         of Emilia.*⌝
                            Speak on, sir.
⌜EMILIA, *to her Woman*⌝
  This garden has a world of pleasures in 't.
  What flower is this?
WOMAN   'Tis called narcissus, madam.   135
EMILIA
  That was a fair boy certain, but a fool
  To love himself. Were there not maids enough?
ARCITE, ⌜*to Palamon, who is stunned by the sight of Emilia*⌝
  Pray, forward.
PALAMON   Yes.
EMILIA, ⌜*to Woman*⌝ Or were they all hard-hearted?   140
WOMAN
  They could not be to one so fair.
EMILIA   Thou wouldst not.
WOMAN
  I think I should not, madam.
EMILIA   That's a good wench.
  But take heed to your kindness, though.   145
WOMAN   Why,
  madam?
EMILIA   Men are mad things.
ARCITE, ⌜*to Palamon*⌝   Will you go forward,
  cousin?   150
EMILIA, ⌜*to Woman*⌝
  Canst not thou work such flowers in silk, wench?
WOMAN   Yes.

155. **Rarely:** remarkably well

163. **Do reverence:** bow or kneel in veneration

167. **gentle:** See note to line 77, above.

168. **maid:** chaste young woman, virgin

169. **her:** the **rose** (line 166)

170. **blows:** blossoms; **paints the sun:** colors the sunlight

171. **north: north** wind

173. **Rude:** rough

175. **leaves . . . briers:** i.e., allows **him to** blow (only) on wild rose bushes (considered **base** or inferior to the garden **rose** [line 166]) See longer note, page 257.

178. **falls:** wordplay on (1) **falls** off the stem; (2) surrenders her chastity; **for 't:** i.e., because of it

180. **take example by her:** i.e., follow the **example** of the **rose** (line 166)

181. **wanton:** i.e., naughty, unseemly

Cupid, the god of love. (2.2.35; 2.6.8–9)
From Francesco Petrarca, *Opera* . . . [1508].

EMILIA
  I'll have a gown full of 'em, and of these.
  This is pretty color. Will 't not do
  Rarely upon a skirt, wench?   155
WOMAN   Dainty, madam.
ARCITE, ⌜*to Palamon*⌝
  Cousin, cousin! How do you, sir? Why, Palamon!
PALAMON
  Never till now I was in prison, Arcite.
ARCITE
  Why, what's the matter, man?
PALAMON   Behold, and wonder!   160
  By heaven, she is a goddess.
ARCITE, ⌜*seeing Emilia*⌝   Ha!
PALAMON   Do reverence.
  She is a goddess, Arcite.
EMILIA, ⌜*to Woman*⌝   Of all flowers   165
  Methinks a rose is best.
WOMAN   Why, gentle madam?
EMILIA
  It is the very emblem of a maid.
  For when the west wind courts her gently,
  How modestly she blows and paints the sun   170
  With her chaste blushes! When the north comes
      near her,
  Rude and impatient, then, like chastity,
  She locks her beauties in her bud again,
  And leaves him to base briers.   175
WOMAN   Yet, good madam,
  Sometimes her modesty will blow so far
  She falls for 't. A maid,
  If she have any honor, would be loath
  To take example by her.   180
EMILIA   Thou art wanton!
ARCITE, ⌜*to Palamon*⌝
  She is wondrous fair.

186. **how near art:** i.e., **how** closely embroidery; **come near:** approximate

188. **lie down:** Proverbial (with sexual connotations): "**Laugh** (line 187) and **lie down.**"

189. **take one:** i.e., **take** someone

190–91. **That's . . . then:** For two possible ways of reading these lines, see longer note, page 257.

197. **I have:** i.e., **I have** lost myself **and love her**

198. **Beshrew:** curse (a mild oath)

202. **Before:** more than, in preference to

The goddess Juno. (1.1.69; 1.2.22; 4.2.22)
From Johann Theodore de Bry,
Proscenium vitae humanae . . . (1627).

PALAMON   She is all the beauty extant.
EMILIA, ⌈*to Woman*⌉
  The sun grows high. Let's walk in. Keep these
    flowers.   185
  We'll see how near art can come near their colors.
  I am wondrous merry-hearted. I could laugh now.
WOMAN
  I could lie down, I am sure.
EMILIA   And take one with you?
WOMAN
  That's as we bargain, madam.   190
EMILIA   Well, agree then.
                  Emilia and Woman exit.
PALAMON
  What think you of this beauty?
ARCITE   'Tis a rare one.
PALAMON
  Is 't but a rare one?
ARCITE   Yes, a matchless beauty.   195
PALAMON
  Might not a man well lose himself and love her?
ARCITE
  I cannot tell what you have done; I have,
  Beshrew mine eyes for 't! Now I feel my shackles.
PALAMON
  You love her, then?
ARCITE   Who would not?   200
PALAMON   And desire her?
ARCITE
  Before my liberty.
PALAMON   I saw her first.
ARCITE
  That's nothing.
PALAMON   But it shall be.   205
ARCITE   I saw her, too.
PALAMON   Yes, but you must not love her.

208. **will not:** i.e., **will not love her**

208–10. **to worship . . . enjoy her:** In Chaucer's "Knight's Tale," Arcite makes the same distinction: "Thine is affection of holiness, / And mine is love, as to a creature" (1158–59, spelling modernized).

217. **entertain'st:** i.e., harbor, cherish

218. **fellow:** worthless person (term of contempt)

219. **blood:** kinship

223. **name:** family, people; **lay:** depended, hung

227. **free:** noble, honorable

229. **any living:** i.e., anyone alive

232. **moved:** angered, disturbed

234. **coldly:** dispassionately

Early modern cornets, here carried by satyrs. (1.4.0; 2.5.0; 3.1.0, 108; 5.1.8; 5.3.66, 75, 84, 93, 107, 112, 126 SDD)
From Stephen Harrison, *The arches of triumph* (1694).

ARCITE
  I will not, as you do, to worship her
  As she is heavenly and a blessèd goddess.
  I love her as a woman, to enjoy her.   210
  So both may love.
PALAMON   You shall not love at all.
ARCITE   Not love at all! Who shall deny me?
PALAMON
  I, that first saw her; I that took possession
  First with mine eye of all those beauties   215
  In her revealed to mankind. If thou lov'st her,
  Or entertain'st a hope to blast my wishes,
  Thou art a traitor, Arcite, and a fellow
  False as thy title to her. Friendship, blood,
  And all the ties between us I disclaim   220
  If thou once think upon her.
ARCITE   Yes, I love her,
  And, if the lives of all my name lay on it,
  I must do so. I love her with my soul.
  If that will lose you, farewell, Palamon.   225
  I say again, I love, and in loving her maintain
  I am as worthy and as free a lover
  And have as just a title to her beauty
  As any Palamon or any living
  That is a man's son.   230
PALAMON   Have I called thee friend?
ARCITE
  Yes, and have found me so. Why are you moved
    thus?
  Let me deal coldly with you: am not I
  Part of ⌜your⌝ blood, part of your soul? You have   235
    told me
  That I was Palamon and you were Arcite.
PALAMON
  Yes.

239. **liable to:** subject to the operations of; **affections:** feelings

241. **suffer:** undergo, experience

244. **So strangely:** i.e., in **so** unfriendly a way

251. **charge:** attack

252. **he be but one:** i.e., **the enemy** (line 250) is alone (The code of chivalry would forbid two charging against **one.**)

256. **use thy freedom:** i.e., act without restraint

257–58. **Be . . . villain:** i.e., take upon you the infamy of being a traitor (who may be **branded** with a hot iron, or who may carry a less tangible stigma)

262. **hazard thee:** i.e., put your life at risk, endanger you

269. **thy friend:** i.e., I; **fortune:** good luck

"The sland'rous cuckoo." (1.1.19)
From Konrad Gesner, . . . *Historiae animalium* . . . (1585–1604).

ARCITE   Am not I liable to those affections,
   Those joys, griefs, angers, fears, my friend shall   240
     suffer?

PALAMON
   You may be.

ARCITE   Why then would you deal so cunningly,
   So strangely, so unlike a noble kinsman,
   To love alone? Speak truly, do you think me   245
   Unworthy of her sight?

PALAMON   No, but unjust
   If thou pursue that sight.

ARCITE   Because another
   First sees the enemy, shall I stand still   250
   And let mine honor down, and never charge?

PALAMON
   Yes, if he be but one.

ARCITE   But say that one
   Had rather combat me?

PALAMON   Let that one say so,   255
   And use thy freedom. Else, if thou pursuest her,
   Be as that cursèd man that hates his country,
   A branded villain.

ARCITE   You are mad.

PALAMON   I must be.   260
   Till thou art worthy, Arcite, it concerns me.
   And in this madness if I hazard thee
   And take thy life, I deal but truly.

ARCITE   Fie, sir!
   You play the child extremely. I will love her;   265
   I must, I ought to do so, and I dare,
   And all this justly.

PALAMON   O, that now, that now,
   Thy false self and thy friend had but this fortune
   To be one hour at liberty, and grasp   270
   Our good swords in our hands, I would quickly
     teach thee

274. **cutpurse:** i.e., pickpocket
276. **nail thy life to 't:** i.e., **nail** you **to this window** (thus ending your **life**)
280. **pitch:** perhaps, (1) hurl myself; or perhaps, (2) take up my abode
284. **By your leave:** a polite request for permission
285. **honest:** a rather patronizing epithet of praise
286. **presently:** i.e., go immediately
289. **bereave:** deprive
293. **goodly:** well-favored, handsome
294. **like enough:** it is probable
295. **blood:** high birth

A kite. (1.1.45)
From Konrad Gesner, . . . *Historiae animalium* . . . (1585–1604).

What 'twere to filch affection from another.
Thou art baser in it than a cutpurse.
Put but thy head out of this window more   275
And, as I have a soul, I'll nail thy life to 't.

ARCITE
Thou dar'st not, fool; thou canst not; thou art feeble.
Put my head out? I'll throw my body out
And leap the garden when I see her next,
And pitch between her arms to anger thee.   280

Enter ⌐Jailer, above.⌐

PALAMON
No more; the keeper's coming. I shall live
To knock thy brains out with my shackles.

ARCITE   Do!

JAILER
By your leave, gentlemen.

PALAMON   Now, honest keeper?   285

JAILER
Lord Arcite, you must presently to th' Duke;
The cause I know not yet.

ARCITE   I am ready, keeper.

JAILER
Prince Palamon, I must awhile bereave you
Of your fair cousin's company.   290

Arcite and Jailer exit.

PALAMON   And me too,
Even when you please, of life.—Why is he sent for?
It may be he shall marry her; he's goodly,
And like enough the Duke hath taken notice
Both of his blood and body. But his falsehood!   295
Why should a friend be treacherous? If that
Get him a wife so noble and so fair,
Let honest men ne'er love again. Once more
I would but see this fair one. Blessèd garden

302. **would:** I wish

303. **For . . . hereafter:** i.e., in exchange **for all my** future good luck

304. **apricock:** i.e., apricot tree

305. **wanton arms:** i.e., amorous branches

308. **Still as:** whenever

309. **not heavenly:** i.e., mortal

314. **Prince Pirithous:** Pirithous's action here may have its origin in the fact that, in Chaucer's "Knight's Tale," Arcite and **Pirithous** are boyhood friends.

318. **He's a blessèd man:** This speech (lines 318–30) should perhaps be marked as an "aside," since the information it reveals would ordinarily be considered private. However, it is possible that in the world of this play, a nobleman would not be concerned if a lower-class person overheard personal revelations.

319. **call to arms:** summon to prepare for battle

321. **Fall on:** attack; **fortune:** chance

322. **worthy lover:** i.e., a man **worthy** of wooing (Emilia)

323. **strike:** fight

328. **virtuous:** valiant

332. **charge:** mandate, order

333. **discharge:** get rid of (with wordplay on **charge,** line 332)

And fruit and flowers more blessèd that still   300
   blossom
As her bright eyes shine on you, would I were,
For all the fortune of my life hereafter,
Yon little tree, yon blooming apricock!
How I would spread and fling my wanton arms   305
In at her window; I would bring her fruit
Fit for the gods to feed on; youth and pleasure
Still as she tasted should be doubled on her;
And, if she be not heavenly, I would make her
So near the gods in nature, they should fear her.   310

Enter ⌜*Jailer, above.*⌝

And then I am sure she would love me.—How now,
   keeper,
Where's Arcite?
JAILER   Banished. Prince Pirithous
  Obtained his liberty, but never more   315
  Upon his oath and life must he set foot
  Upon this kingdom.
PALAMON   He's a blessèd man.
  He shall see Thebes again, and call to arms
  The bold young men that, when he bids 'em charge,   320
  Fall on like fire. Arcite shall have a fortune,
  If he dare make himself a worthy lover,
  Yet in the field to strike a battle for her,
  And, if he lose her then, he's a cold coward.
  How bravely may he bear himself to win her   325
  If he be noble Arcite—thousand ways!
  Were I at liberty, I would do things
  Of such a virtuous greatness that this lady,
  This blushing virgin, should take manhood to her
  And seek to ravish me.   330
JAILER   My lord, for you
  I have this charge to—
PALAMON   To discharge my life?

335. **open:** unprotected, accessible, unobstructed

337. **envious:** malicious, spiteful; **Prithee:** i.e., I pray you

339. **By this good light:** an oath on the sun

342. **pelting, scurvy:** contemptible

345. **May I:** i.e., shall I be able to

348. **for:** because

350. **irons:** shackles (See picture, below.)

353. **morris: morris** dance (with rattling shackles in place of bells)

356. **rude:** rough

A man in gyves, or shackles. (2.2.350; 2.6.8; 3.1.81)
From Cesare Vecellio, *Degli habiti antichi et moderni . . .* (1590).

JAILER
  No, but from this place to remove your Lordship;
  The windows are too open.   335
PALAMON   Devils take 'em
  That are so envious to me! Prithee, kill me.
JAILER
  And hang for 't afterward!
PALAMON   By this good light,
  Had I a sword I would kill thee.   340
JAILER   Why, my lord?
PALAMON
  Thou bringst such pelting, scurvy news continually,
  Thou art not worthy life. I will not go.
JAILER
  Indeed ⌜you⌝ must, my lord.
PALAMON   May I see the garden?   345
JAILER
  No.
PALAMON   Then I am resolved, I will not go.
JAILER
  I must constrain you then; and, for you are
     dangerous,
  I'll clap more irons on you.   350
PALAMON   Do, good keeper.
  I'll shake 'em so, you shall not sleep;
  I'll make you a new morris. Must I go?
JAILER
  There is no remedy.
PALAMON   Farewell, kind window.   355
  May rude wind never hurt thee. O, my lady,
  If ever thou hast felt what sorrow was,
  Dream how I suffer.—Come; now bury me.
                          Palamon and Jailer exit.

2.3 Arcite decides he will not leave Athens and Emilia. Countrymen enter talking about their plans to dance at a May Day celebration and about competitive games to take place before Duke Theseus. Arcite decides to assume a disguise and become a competitor in the games.

---

4. **studied:** intentional, premeditated
7. **pluck:** bring, draw
8. **start:** advantage
9–10. **Her . . . window:** The image is of the dawn breaking, with **her bright eyes** as the **morning** sun.
15. **come:** be brought in the course of events
16. **gentle:** generous, courteous; **fair:** beautiful
18. **wanton:** playful; amorous
19. **Come what can come:** Proverbial. (See longer note, page 257.)
21. **mine own:** i.e., Thebes
23. **shape:** assumed appearance, disguise
25. **or no more:** i.e., **or** be **no more**
25 SD. **before:** i.e. leading
26. **masters:** a polite term of address

Scene 3

Enter Arcite.

ARCITE
  Banished the kingdom? 'Tis a benefit,
  A mercy I must thank 'em for; but banished
  The free enjoying of that face I die for,
  O, 'twas a studied punishment, a death
  Beyond imagination—such a vengeance   5
  That, were I old and wicked, all my sins
  Could never pluck upon me. Palamon,
  Thou hast the start now; thou shalt stay and see
  Her bright eyes break each morning 'gainst thy
      window   10
  And let in life into thee; thou shalt feed
  Upon the sweetness of a noble beauty
  That nature ne'er exceeded nor ne'er shall.
  Good gods, what happiness has Palamon!
  Twenty to one he'll come to speak to her,   15
  And if she be as gentle as she's fair,
  I know she's his. He has a tongue will tame
  Tempests and make the wild rocks wanton.
  Come what can come,
  The worst is death. I will not leave the kingdom.   20
  I know mine own is but a heap of ruins,
  And no redress there. If I go, he has her.
  I am resolved another shape shall make me
  Or end my fortunes. Either way I am happy.
  I'll see her and be near her, or no more.   25

      *Enter four Country people, and one with
          a garland before them.*

                              ⌐*Arcite steps aside.*⌐

FIRST COUNTRYMAN   My masters, I'll be there, that's cer-
    tain.
SECOND COUNTRYMAN   And I'll be there.

30. **have with you:** i.e., count me in

31. **'Tis but a chiding:** i.e., it will cost no more than a scolding

32. **tickle:** beat; **jades':** A *jade* is a broken-down horse.

36–37. **Clap . . . stow her:** i.e., have sex with her (The image is of boarding a ship and filling its hold with cargo.)

38. **put . . . fist:** again, have sex with her, here using the image of the schoolroom **fescue:** a small pin used to point out letters to children learning to read

40. **hold:** i.e., keep our promise; **against:** with regard to; **Maying:** celebration of May Day

46. **dainty:** fine; **domine:** a Latinate form for **schoolmaster; keep touch:** i.e., **keep** his promise

48. **hornbook:** small board on which was mounted a printed leaf of paper covered with translucent horn (See picture, page 214.) **fail:** is absent

49. **Go to:** an expression of impatience; **too far driven: too** close to being decided (with possible sexual connotations)

50. **the tanner's daughter:** presumably one of the **wenches** expected for the **Maying** (lines 45, 40); **let slip:** allow her to escape; or, miss an opportunity (a phrase from hunting)

50–51. **must see:** i.e., insists on seeing

52. **lusty:** merry, lively

53–54. **All . . . breech on 's:** i.e., may **all the boys in Athens** pant and puff behind us

54. **here . . . I'll be:** He presumably dances around during these lines.

(continued)

THIRD COUNTRYMAN   And I.

FOURTH COUNTRYMAN   Why, then, have with you, boys.   30
'Tis but a chiding. Let the plough play today; I'll
tickle 't out of the jades' tails tomorrow.

FIRST COUNTRYMAN   I am sure to have my wife as jealous as a turkey, but that's all one. I'll go through;
let her mumble.   35

SECOND COUNTRYMAN   Clap her aboard tomorrow night
and stow her, and all's made up again.

THIRD COUNTRYMAN   Ay, do but put a fescue in her fist
and you shall see her take a new lesson out and be
a good wench. Do we all hold against the Maying?   40

FOURTH COUNTRYMAN   Hold? What should ail us?

THIRD COUNTRYMAN   Arcas will be there.

SECOND COUNTRYMAN   And Sennois and Rycas; and
three better lads ne'er danced under green tree.
And ⌜you⌝ know what wenches, ha! But will the   45
dainty domine, the Schoolmaster, keep touch, do
you think? For he does all, you know.

THIRD COUNTRYMAN   He'll eat a hornbook ere he fail.
Go to, the matter's too far driven between him and
the tanner's daughter to let slip now; and she must   50
see the Duke, and she must dance too.

FOURTH COUNTRYMAN   Shall we be lusty?

SECOND COUNTRYMAN   All the boys in Athens blow wind
i' th' breech on 's. And here I'll be and there I'll be,
for our town, and here again, and there again. Ha,   55
boys, hey for the weavers!

FIRST COUNTRYMAN   This must be done i' th' woods.

FOURTH COUNTRYMAN   O pardon me.

SECOND COUNTRYMAN   By any means; our thing of learning ⌜says⌝ so—where he himself will edify the Duke   60
most parlously in our behalfs. He's excellent i' th'
woods; bring him to th' plains, his learning makes
no cry.

55. **for our town: for** the honor of **our town**

57. **i' th' woods:** where the May Day hunting takes place

58. **pardon me:** an expression of doubt or disbelief

59. **By any means:** by all **means,** certainly

59–60. **thing of learning:** schoolmaster (perhaps sarcastic)

61. **parlously:** cleverly, cunningly

62. **plains:** i.e., court (literally, flat meadowland)

62–63. **makes no cry:** goes unheard (like silenced hunting dogs)

64. **the sports:** i.e., **the games** (line 76)

65. **tackle:** equipment (for the morris dance)

66. **any means:** all **means**

69. **hold:** i.e., keep your word

70. **By your leaves:** a polite apology for intruding; **honest:** See note to 2.2.285.

77. **bred:** brought up

84. **pretty:** fine, admirable; agreeable

89–91. **My mind . . . hip:** i.e., I fear **this fellow** is an excellent wrestler **vengeance:** i.e., astounding **trick o' th' hip:** a reference to the wrestler's hip movement that enables him to throw his opponent (Proverbial: "To have one on the **hip.**") See picture, page 112.

91. **Mark:** notice

94. **plum porridge:** here, a term of contempt (literally, a thick sweet broth); **roast eggs:** Proverbial: "Set a fool to **roast eggs** and a wise man to eat them."

THIRD COUNTRYMAN We'll see the sports, then every
    man to 's tackle. And, sweet companions, let's re- 65
    hearse, by any means, before the ladies see us, and
    do sweetly, and God knows what may come on 't.
FOURTH COUNTRYMAN Content. The sports once ended,
    we'll perform. Away, boys, and hold.

                              ⌜*Arcite comes forward.*⌝

ARCITE By your leaves, honest friends: pray you, 70
    whither go you?
FOURTH COUNTRYMAN Whither?
    Why, what a question's that?
ARCITE   Yes, 'tis a question
    To me that know not. 75
THIRD COUNTRYMAN   To the games, my friend.
SECOND COUNTRYMAN
    Where were you bred, you know it not?
ARCITE   Not far, sir.
    Are there such games today?
FIRST COUNTRYMAN   Yes, marry, are there, 80
    And such as you never saw. The Duke himself
    Will be in person there.
ARCITE   What pastimes are they?
SECOND COUNTRYMAN
    Wrestling and running.—'Tis a pretty fellow.
THIRD COUNTRYMAN
    Thou wilt not go along? 85
ARCITE   Not yet, sir.
FOURTH COUNTRYMAN   Well, sir,
    Take your own time.—Come, boys.
FIRST COUNTRYMAN, ⌜*aside to the others*⌝ My mind mis-
    gives me. This fellow has a vengeance trick o' th' 90
    hip. Mark how his body's made for 't.
SECOND COUNTRYMAN, ⌜*aside to the others*⌝ I'll be
    hanged, though, if he dare venture. Hang him,
    plum porridge! He wrestle? He roast eggs! Come,
    let's be gone, lads.   *The four exit.* 95

97. **durst not wish:** i.e., dared not have wished; **Well . . . wrestled:** i.e., I once knew how to wrestle well

98–100. **run . . . flew:** i.e., could **run swifter than wind** ever **flew** through a **field of** grain, twisting **the** abundant **ears corn:** grain **wealthy:** abundant **never:** i.e., ever

101. **poor disguise:** i.e., **disguise** as one of lower rank

102. **girt with garlands:** i.e., adorned **with garlands** of victory (See picture, page 134.)

103. **happiness:** good luck, success; **prefer me to a place:** i.e., promote **me to** an office at court

2.4 The jailer's daughter, having fallen in love with Palamon, decides to find a way to free him from prison in the hope that he will love her in return.

----

1. **'Tis odds:** i.e., it is probable that

2. **affect:** care for, love; **base:** lower-class

3. **mean:** lowly

5. **witless:** foolish, irrational; **Out upon 't:** an expression of abhorrence or reproach

6. **pushes:** extremes

12. **o' my conscience:** a mild oath

13. **vowed her maidenhead:** promised her virginity

18. **what . . . keeps:** i.e., **what a** disturbance **he** creates

ARCITE
    This is an offered opportunity
    I durst not wish for. Well I could have wrestled—
    The best men called it excellent—and run
    Swifter than wind upon a field of corn,
    Curling the wealthy ears, never flew. I'll venture,   100
    And in some poor disguise be there. Who knows
    Whether my brows may not be girt with garlands,
    And happiness prefer me to a place
    Where I may ever dwell in sight of her?
                                        Arcite exits.

                        Scene 4
              Enter Jailer's Daughter, alone.

DAUGHTER
    Why should I love this gentleman? 'Tis odds
    He never will affect me. I am base,
    My father the mean keeper of his prison,
    And he a prince. To marry him is hopeless;
    To be his whore is witless. Out upon 't!   5
    What pushes are we wenches driven to
    When fifteen once has found us! First, I saw him;
    I, seeing, thought he was a goodly man;
    He has as much to please a woman in him,
    If he please to bestow it so, as ever   10
    These eyes yet looked on. Next, I pitied him,
    And so would any young wench, o' my conscience,
    That ever dreamed, or vowed her maidenhead
    To a young handsome man. Then I loved him,
    Extremely loved him, infinitely loved him!   15
    And yet he had a cousin, fair as he too.
    But in my heart was Palamon, and there,
    Lord, what a coil he keeps! To hear him
    Sing in an evening, what a heaven it is!

24. **maid:** i.e., maiden; **good morrow: good** morning

25. **happy:** fortunate

27. **Would:** i.e., I wish

28. **me as much:** i.e., it **grieves me as much** as it does him

30. **fain:** gladly, happily

32. **Thus much:** presumably accompanied by a contemptuous or dismissive gesture

2.5 Arcite, having won the competition disguised as a poor gentleman, is made an attendant upon Emilia. He and the other courtiers are told to be ready to celebrate May Day on the following morning.

———————

0 SD. **cornets:** See longer note to 1.4.0 SD, page 255. **garland:** as a sign of victory

4. **allow:** i.e., boast of

10. **to . . . life:** i.e., bred me to gentlemanly pursuits

And yet his songs are sad ones. Fairer spoken   20
Was never gentleman. When I come in
To bring him water in a morning, first
He bows his noble body, then salutes me thus:
"Fair, gentle maid, good morrow. May thy goodness
Get thee a happy husband." Once he kissed me;   25
I loved my lips the better ten days after.
Would he would do so ev'ry day! He grieves much—
And me as much to see his misery.
What should I do to make him know I love him?
For I would fain enjoy him. Say I ventured   30
To set him free? What says the law then?
Thus much for law or kindred! I will do it,
And this night, or tomorrow, he shall love me.

                                   She exits.

Scene ⌈5⌉

This short flourish of cornets and shouts within.
Enter Theseus, Hippolyta, Pirithous, Emilia, Arcite
⌈*in disguise,*⌉ *with a garland,* ⌈*Attendants, and others.*⌉

THESEUS, ⌈*to Arcite*⌉
  You have done worthily. I have not seen,
  Since Hercules, a man of tougher sinews.
  Whate'er you are, you run the best and wrestle
  That these times can allow.
ARCITE   I am proud to please you.   5
THESEUS
  What country bred you?
ARCITE   This; but far off, prince.
THESEUS
  Are you a gentleman?
ARCITE   My father said so,
  And to those gentle uses gave me life.   10

14. **Sure:** i.e., certainly; **happy:** fortunate; **proves you:** i.e., shows you (to be thus bred)

15. **noble qualities:** i.e., skills associated with nobility

16–17. **I . . . dogs:** Both hawking and hunting with hounds were aristocratic pursuits. **could have kept:** knew how to keep   **hallowed:** i.e., urged on by shouting   **cry of dogs:** yelping of hounds in the chase (See picture, below.)

20. **would be thought:** i.e., am considered

21. **perfect:** fully accomplished

22. **proper:** worthy, admirable

25. **admire:** marvel at

27. **sort:** social rank

28. **Believe:** i.e., **believe** me

35. **got:** begotten, fathered

38. **purchase name:** acquire fame

39. **well-found:** well-approved, commendable

Hunting with hounds. (2.5.16–17; 3.5.173–77)
From [George Turberville,]
The noble arte of venerie or hunting . . . (1611).

THESEUS
  Are you his heir?
ARCITE   His youngest, sir.
THESEUS   Your father,
  Sure, is a happy sire, then. What proves you?
ARCITE
  A little of all noble qualities.   15
  I could have kept a hawk and well have hallowed
  To a deep cry of dogs. I dare not praise
  My feat in horsemanship, yet they that knew me
  Would say it was my best piece. Last, and greatest,
  I would be thought a soldier.   20
THESEUS   You are perfect.
PIRITHOUS
  Upon my soul, a proper man.
EMILIA   He is so.
PIRITHOUS, ⌜to Hippolyta⌝
  How do you like him, lady?
HIPPOLYTA   I admire him.   25
  I have not seen so young a man so noble,
  If he say true, of his sort.
EMILIA   Believe,
  His mother was a wondrous handsome woman;
  His face, methinks, goes that way.   30
HIPPOLYTA   But his body
  And fiery mind illustrate a brave father.
PIRITHOUS
  Mark how his virtue, like a hidden sun,
  Breaks through his baser garments.
HIPPOLYTA   He's well got, sure.   35
THESEUS, ⌜to Arcite⌝
  What made you seek this place, sir?
ARCITE   Noble Theseus,
  To purchase name and do my ablest service
  To such a well-found wonder as thy worth;

43. **travel:** perhaps, journey from **far off** (line 7); or, perhaps, *travail*, the strenuous work of the competition (The two spellings were used interchangeably.)

45. **Dispose of:** i.e., find a suitable situation or employment for

50. **observe her goodness:** i.e., treat **her goodness** with ceremonious respect

53. **due:** payment, fee; **hers:** i.e., in her service

57. **but offends:** merely vexes or annoys

61. **mine:** i.e., my **servant** (line 56)

62. **use:** treat

63. **furnished:** equipped, properly clothed

65. **rough one:** i.e., horse that is temperamental, hard **to ride**

Theseus.
From Plutarch,
The Lives of the Noble Grecians and Romanes . . . (1579).

92

For only in thy court, of all the world,   40
Dwells fair-eyed Honor.

PIRITHOUS   All his words are worthy.

THESEUS
Sir, we are much indebted to your travel,
Nor shall you lose your wish.—Pirithous,
Dispose of this fair gentleman.   45

PIRITHOUS   Thanks, Theseus.—
Whate'er you are, you're mine, and I shall give you
To a most noble service: to this lady,
This bright young virgin.

⌜*He brings Arcite to Emilia.*⌝
                        Pray observe her goodness;   50
You have honored her fair birthday with your
    virtues,
And, as your due, you're hers. Kiss her fair hand, sir.

ARCITE
Sir, you're a noble giver.—Dearest beauty,
Thus let me seal my vowed faith.   55

⌜*He kisses her hand.*⌝
                    When your servant,
Your most unworthy creature, but offends you,
Command him die, he shall.

EMILIA   That were too cruel.
If you deserve well, sir, I shall soon see 't.   60
You're mine, and somewhat better than your rank
I'll use you.

PIRITHOUS, ⌜*to Arcite*⌝
I'll see you furnished, and because you say
You are a horseman, I must needs entreat you
This afternoon to ride—but 'tis a rough one.   65

ARCITE
I like him better, prince; I shall not then
Freeze in my saddle.

THESEUS, ⌜*to Hippolyta*⌝ Sweet, you must be ready,—
And you, Emilia,—and you, friend,—and all,

70. **by the sun:** i.e., by sunrise

70–71. **do observance . . . May:** celebrate May Day (with a hunt, a morris dance, games, etc.)

71. **Dian's wood:** i.e., the forest dedicated to Diana, goddess of the hunt, the moon, and chastity (See picture, page xviii.)

71–72. **Wait . . . mistress:** i.e., serve **your mistress well** (See longer note, page 257.)

76. **want:** lack

79. **do not:** i.e., **do not serve faithfully** (line 77)

80. **find that:** i.e., experience **that** which

82. **won it:** i.e., **won** this distinction

83. **dues:** i.e., rewards

85. **Sister:** i.e., sister-in-law; **beshrew my heart:** a mild oath

2.6 The jailer's daughter, having set Palamon free and sent him off to await her in the woods, plans to bring him food, along with files to free him from his shackles, and clothes for herself so that they may escape the country together.

---

2. **ventured:** risked myself

5. **plane:** plane tree (a lofty spreading tree)

6. **Fast:** near; **keep close:** stay hidden

8. **bracelets:** fetters, shackles (See picture, page 78.) **Love:** i.e., Cupid, often imaged as a **child** (line 9) See picture, page 66.

10. **Durst . . . done it:** i.e., would have **endured** (1) prison fetters, or (2) being stabbed rather **than** do what I have just **done**

Tomorrow by the sun, to do observance   70
To flowery May in Dian's wood.—Wait well, sir,
Upon your mistress.—Emily, I hope
He shall not go afoot.

EMILIA   That were a shame, sir,
While I have horses.—Take your choice, and what   75
You want at any time, let me but know it.
If you serve faithfully, I dare assure you
You'll find a loving mistress.

ARCITE   If I do not,
Let me find that my father ever hated,   80
Disgrace and blows.

THESEUS   Go lead the way; you have won it.
It shall be so; you shall receive all dues
Fit for the honor you have won. 'Twere wrong else.—
Sister, beshrew my heart, you have a servant   85
That, if I were a woman, would be master;
But you are wise.

EMILIA   I hope too wise for that, sir.

Flourish. They all exit.

Scene 6

Enter Jailer's Daughter alone.

DAUGHTER
Let all the dukes and all the devils roar!
He is at liberty. I have ventured for him,
And out I have brought him; to a little wood
A mile hence I have sent him, where a cedar
Higher than all the rest spreads like a plane   5
Fast by a brook, and there he shall keep close
Till I provide him files and food, for yet
His iron bracelets are not off. O Love,
What a stout-hearted child thou art! My father
Durst better have endured cold iron than done it.   10

11. **him:** i.e., Palamon
12. **wit:** intelligence; **made ... it:** i.e., told him
17. **way:** path, course
18. **purpose:** resolve
19. **unmanly:** dishonorable
20. **maids:** maidens
25. **made such scruples of:** i.e., felt **such** reluctance because **of**
29. **so:** provided that
31. **presently:** immediately, at once
33. **where:** anywhere
36. **I am then:** i.e., I will be at that moment
38. **Get:** (1) acquire (**prisoners**); (2) beget (**daughters**)
39. **keep:** i.e., guard only; **him:** Palamon

Phoenix. (1.3.80)
From Conrad Lycosthenes, *Prodigiorum* ... [1557].

I love him beyond love and beyond reason
Or wit or safety. I have made him know it;
I care not, I am desperate. If the law
Find me and then condemn me for 't, some wenches,
Some honest-hearted maids, will sing my dirge   15
And tell to memory my death was noble,
Dying almost a martyr. That way he takes
I purpose is my way too. Sure he cannot
Be so unmanly as to leave me here.
If he do, maids will not so easily   20
Trust men again. And yet he has not thanked me
For what I have done; no, not so much as kissed me,
And that, methinks, is not so well; nor scarcely
Could I persuade him to become a free man,
He made such scruples of the wrong he did   25
To me and to my father. Yet I hope,
When he considers more, this love of mine
Will take more root within him. Let him do
What he will with me, so he use me kindly;
For use me so he shall, or I'll proclaim him,   30
And to his face, no man. I'll presently
Provide him necessaries and pack my clothes up,
And where there is a path of ground I'll venture,
So he be with me. By him like a shadow
I'll ever dwell. Within this hour the hubbub   35
Will be all o'er the prison. I am then
Kissing the man they look for. Farewell, father!
Get many more such prisoners and such daughters,
And shortly you may keep yourself. Now to him.
⌜*She exits.*⌝

THE TWO NOBLE KINSMEN

ACT 3

3.1 Arcite, now Emilia's attendant, is confronted by a still-shackled Palamon in the woods where the court is celebrating May Day. They challenge each other to a trial by combat to determine who has the right to Emilia. Arcite promises to bring food for Palamon and files to remove his shackles.

———————————

0 SD. **Cornets:** See longer note to 1.4.0 SD, page 255. **in sundry places:** from various **places** offstage; **hallowing:** shouting; **as:** i.e., **as** if made by; **a-Maying:** celebrating May Day

1. **took:** chose, selected; entered

2. **several:** different; **laund:** glade

3. **pay it:** discharge this obligation

4. **To . . . ceremony:** i.e., most ceremoniously; **Queen:** perhaps, **Queen** of the **May** (line 5)

6. **buttons:** buds

7. **enameled knacks:** i.e., many-colored trifles; **mead:** meadow

8. **challenge too:** i.e., claim (that she is also more lovely **than** [line 6]); **bank . . . nymph:** i.e., **bank** of **flowers** (line 9) inhabited by **any** semi-divine maiden or **nymph**

10. **likewise:** i.e., like the **nymph** (line 8); **pace:** narrow passage

11. **sole:** mere

11–12. **In thy . . . between:** i.e., if only **I, poor man, might** occasionally **come** into your thoughts

13. **chop on:** perhaps, break in upon; or, perhaps, seize upon (a hunting term); **cold:** chaste

15. **drop on:** happen upon

(continued)

ACT 3

Scene 1

*Cornets in sundry places. Noise and hallowing
as people a-Maying. Enter Arcite alone.*

ARCITE
    The Duke has lost Hippolyta; each took
    A several laund. This is a solemn rite
    They owe bloomed May, and the Athenians pay it
    To th' heart of ceremony. O Queen Emilia,
    Fresher than May, sweeter   5
    Than her gold buttons on the boughs, or all
    Th' enameled knacks o' th' mead or garden—yea,
    We challenge too the bank of any nymph
    That makes the stream seem flowers; thou, O jewel
    O' th' wood, o' th' world, hast likewise blessed a pace   10
    With thy sole presence. In thy rumination
    That I, poor man, might eftsoons come between
    And chop on some cold thought! Thrice blessèd
      chance
    To drop on such a mistress, expectation   15
    Most guiltless on 't. Tell me, O Lady Fortune,
    Next after Emily my sovereign, how far
    I may be proud. She takes strong note of me,
    Hath made me near her; and this beauteous morn,
    The prim'st of all the year, presents me with   20
    A brace of horses; two such steeds might well

16. **guiltless on 't:** i.e., innocent of any such hope; **Lady Fortune:** the goddess Fortuna (See picture, page 54.)

17–18. **how . . . proud:** i.e., **how** gratified or pleased dare **I be**

18. **takes . . . of:** i.e., pays a lot of attention to

19. **made me near her:** a reference to the positioning of attendants around a master or mistress

20. **prim'st:** most excellent, most important

22. **backed:** mounted; **field:** battle

23. **their . . . tried:** i.e., determined **their** rights to **their** crowns

26. **happier:** more fortunate

27. **deem'st:** imagine

30. **eared:** gave ear to

31. **passion:** impassioned anger

31 SD. **as:** i.e., **as** if; **bends:** raises

36–37. **I . . . traitor:** i.e., **I would** prove you **a traitor** in a formal trial by combat (See longer note, page 258.)

38. **gently looked:** i.e., bore the marks of a nobleman; **void'st:** most destitute or devoid

39. **bore gentle token:** i.e., **gently looked** (line 38)

42. **Void of appointment:** without equipment

43. **chaffy lord:** i.e., a **lord** worthless as chaff

45. **house clogs:** i.e., shackles

47. **Cozener:** deceiver (with wordplay on **cousin** [line 46])

48. **feat:** deeds, overt action

50. **circuit:** limits; **gross stuff:** common or inferior material

51. **form . . . blazon:** i.e., fashion myself as you describe me

(continued)

102

Be by a pair of kings backed, in a field
That their crowns' titles tried. Alas, alas,
Poor cousin Palamon, poor prisoner, thou
So little dream'st upon my fortune that   25
Thou think'st thyself the happier thing, to be
So near Emilia; me thou deem'st at Thebes,
And therein wretched, although free. But if
Thou knew'st my mistress breathed on me, and that
I eared her language, lived in her eye—O coz,   30
What passion would enclose thee!

Enter Palamon as out of a bush, with his shackles;
⌜*he*⌝ *bends his fist at Arcite.*

PALAMON   Traitor kinsman,
Thou shouldst perceive my passion if these signs
Of prisonment were off me, and this hand
But owner of a sword. By all oaths in one,   35
I and the justice of my love would make thee
A confessed traitor, O thou most perfidious
That ever gently looked, the ⌜void'st⌝ of honor
That e'er bore gentle token, falsest cousin
That ever blood made kin! Call'st thou her thine?   40
I'll prove it in my shackles, with these hands,
Void of appointment, that thou liest, and art
A very thief in love, a chaffy lord,
Nor worth the name of villain. Had I a sword,
And these house clogs away—   45
ARCITE   Dear cousin Palamon—
PALAMON
Cozener Arcite, give me language such
As thou hast showed me feat.
ARCITE   Not finding in
The circuit of my breast any gross stuff   50
To form me like your blazon holds me to
This gentleness of answer: 'tis your passion
That thus mistakes, the which, to you being enemy,

51–52. **holds . . . answer:** i.e., makes me continue to use courteous **language** (line 47)

53. **the which:** i.e., **your passion** (line 52)

56. **skip:** fail to see

57. **maintain:** defend, uphold; **proceedings:** actions; **Pray be pleased:** a polite form of request

58. **show:** declare; **generous terms:** i.e., language appropriate to one of noble birth; **griefs:** grievances

59. **question's:** quarrel or dispute is

60. **To clear . . . way:** i.e., **to prove his** course of action blameless

62. **That thou durst:** i.e., if only you dared

63. **advertised:** informed, warned (accent on second syllable)

65. **of another:** i.e., from the mouth of someone else

66–67. **your . . . sanctuary:** i.e., you would speak up loudly (in my defense) even if in a church

69. **such a place:** i.e., a tournament or battlefield

70. **justify your manhood:** affirm **your** valor

73. **temper:** disposition, constitution

75. **compelled bears:** i.e., **bears tied** (line 76) to a stake and forced to **fight** the attacking dogs; **would fly:** i.e., which **would** flee

78. **glass:** looking **glass,** mirror

81. **Quit:** free; **gyves:** shackles

83. **lend:** grant, give

87. **carry 't:** i.e., kill me (literally, win the battle); **brave:** See note to 2.2.64. **shades:** i.e., the world of the dead, Hades

Cannot to me be kind. Honor and honesty
I cherish and depend on, howsoe'er 55
You skip them in me, and with them, fair coz,
I'll maintain my proceedings. Pray be pleased
To show in generous terms your griefs, since that
Your question's with your equal, who professes
To clear his own way with the mind and sword 60
Of a true gentleman.

PALAMON   That thou durst, Arcite!

ARCITE
My coz, my coz, you have been well advertised
How much I dare; you've seen me use my sword
Against th' advice of fear. Sure, of another 65
You would not hear me doubted, but your silence
Should break out, though i' th' sanctuary.

PALAMON   Sir,
I have seen you move in such a place which well
Might justify your manhood; you were called 70
A good knight and a bold. But the whole week's not
      fair
If any day it rain; their valiant temper
Men lose when they incline to treachery,
And then they fight like compelled bears—would fly 75
Were they not tied.

ARCITE   Kinsman, you might as well
Speak this and act it in your glass as to
His ear which now disdains you.

PALAMON   Come up to me; 80
Quit me of these cold gyves, give me a sword
Though it be rusty, and the charity
Of one meal lend me. Come before me then,
A good sword in thy hand, and do but say
That Emily is thine, I will forgive 85
The trespass thou hast done me—yea, my life,
If then thou carry 't; and brave souls in shades
That have died manly, which will seek of me

92. **betake you:** go; **your hawthorn house:** i.e., **your** hiding place, the **bush** (line 31 SD)

93. **With . . . night:** i.e., in secrecy (literally, confiding only in **the night**)

97. **stretch yourself:** stand up straight

98. **in plight:** i.e., ready (literally, **in** health, **in** good condition)

101. **bear . . . business:** i.e., be attached to a blameworthy matter

108 SD. **Wind:** sound; **off:** offstage

110. **muset:** i.e., hiding place (literally, hare's lair)

111. **crossed:** prevented; **met:** i.e., begun (literally, come together in the shock of conflict)

114. **Pray hold:** please keep

115. **bent brow:** knit **brow,** frown

116. **rough:** harsh, uncivil, angry

117. **By this air:** a mild oath

118. **cuff:** blow with the fist; **stomach:** anger, vexation

121. **pardon me hard language:** i.e., do not ask that I speak harshly **pardon me:** excuse me from (speaking)

Some news from earth, they shall get none but this:
That thou art brave and noble.   90
ARCITE   Be content.
Again betake you to your hawthorn house.
With counsel of the night I will be here
With wholesome viands. These impediments
Will I file off. You shall have garments and   95
Perfumes to kill the smell o' th' prison. After,
When you shall stretch yourself and say but "Arcite,
I am in plight," there shall be at your choice
Both sword and armor.
PALAMON   O you heavens, dares any   100
So noble bear a guilty business? None
But only Arcite. Therefore none but Arcite
In this kind is so bold.
ARCITE   Sweet Palamon.
PALAMON
I do embrace you and your offer; for   105
Your offer do 't I only. Sir, your person
Without hypocrisy I may not wish
More than my sword's edge on 't.
                              Wind horns off; ⌜*sound*⌝ *cornets.*
ARCITE   You hear the horns.
Enter your ⌜muset,⌝ lest this match between 's   110
Be crossed ere met. Give me your hand; farewell.
I'll bring you every needful thing. I pray you,
Take comfort and be strong.
PALAMON   Pray hold your promise,
And do the deed with a bent brow. Most certain   115
You love me not; be rough with me, and pour
This oil out of your language. By this air,
I could for each word give a cuff, my stomach
Not reconciled by reason.
ARCITE   Plainly spoken,   120
Yet pardon me hard language. When I spur
My horse, I chide him not; content and anger

126. **office there:** duty or function at **the banquet** (line 125)

128. **office:** position; function

130. **good title:** i.e., earned right

131. **persuaded:** convinced; **question:** quarrel

132. **bleeding:** wordplay on (1) bloodletting as a medical treatment, and (2) flowing of blood from wounds; **I . . . suitor:** i.e., I beg

133. **bequeath this plea:** commit **this** quarrel (The words **plea, question** [line 131], and **suitor** [line 132] echo legal language, as if the dispute were a legal suit being assigned to trial by combat.)

137. **note you:** pay close attention

140. **breed me strength:** engender **strength** in **me**

143. **a vantage:** an advantage

3.2 The jailer's daughter, unable to find Palamon, fearing that he has been eaten by wild animals and that her father will be hanged for Palamon's escape, falls into despair.

---

1. **mistook:** mistaken; **brake:** thicket

2. **After his fancy:** i.e., following **his** own **fancy**

3. **would:** I wish

5. **but for:** except for

7. **reck:** care; **jaw me:** seize me with their jaws; **so:** i.e., **so** long as

In me have but one face.   *Wind horns.*
                          Hark, sir, they call
The scattered to the banquet; you must guess   125
I have an office there.

PALAMON   Sir, your attendance
Cannot please heaven, and I know your office
Unjustly is achieved.

ARCITE   ⌜'Tis⌝ a good title.   130
I am persuaded this question, sick between 's,
By bleeding must be cured. I am a suitor
That to your sword you will bequeath this plea,
And talk of it no more.

PALAMON   But this one word: 135
You are going now to gaze upon my mistress,
For note you, mine she is—

ARCITE   Nay then,—

PALAMON   Nay, pray you,
You talk of feeding me to breed me strength.   140
You are going now to look upon a sun
That strengthens what it looks on; there
You have a vantage o'er me, but enjoy 't till
I may enforce my remedy. Farewell.

                                    They exit.

                    Scene 2

            Enter Jailer's Daughter, alone.

DAUGHTER
He has mistook the ⌜brake⌝ I meant, is gone
After his fancy. 'Tis now well-nigh morning.
No matter; would it were perpetual night,
And darkness lord o' th' world. Hark, 'tis a wolf!
In me hath grief slain fear, and but for one thing,   5
I care for nothing, and that's Palamon.
I reck not if the wolves would jaw me, so

8. **hallowed:** shouted loudly

9. **whooped:** i.e., made a whooping sound

11. **that service:** perhaps, the benefit (1) of attracting the **wolf** to Palamon; or, perhaps, (2) of getting eaten

15. **fell:** savage

17. **set it down:** put it on record

20. **Be bold:** i.e., feel free; **the bell:** i.e., **the** passing **bell,** tolled to announce a death; **How stand I:** what is my situation

21. **chared:** done

22. **for his:** i.e., for Palamon's

23–24. **Myself . . . act:** i.e., **if I** saved **my** own **life** by lying about what I have done, I would have **to beg** for food after **my father's** death (line 22)

25. **try . . . dozens:** i.e., experience **death** in **dozens** of ways; **moped:** bewildered, stupefied

28. **brine:** i.e., tears

29. **sense:** i.e., reason, wits

31. **state of nature:** perhaps, (my) physical and mental being; **together:** all at once

32. **props:** supports

33. **next:** shortest, most direct

34. **errant step beside:** i.e., **step** that strays away from **the next way to a grave** (line 33) **beside:** away from

37. **offices:** tasks

He had this file. What if I hallowed for him?
I cannot hallow. If I whooped, what then?
If he not answered, I should call a wolf,   10
And do him but that service. I have heard
Strange howls this livelong night; why may 't not be
They have made prey of him? He has no weapons;
He cannot run; the jingling of his gyves
Might call fell things to listen, who have in them   15
A sense to know a man unarmed and can
Smell where resistance is. I'll set it down
He's torn to pieces; they howled many together,
And then they ⌜fed⌝ on him; so much for that.
Be bold to ring the bell. How stand I then?   20
All's chared when he is gone. No, no, I lie.
My father's to be hanged for his escape;
Myself to beg, if I prized life so much
As to deny my act, but that I would not,
Should I try death by dozens. I am moped;   25
Food took I none these two days;
Sipped some water. I have not closed mine eyes
Save when my lids scoured off their brine. Alas,
Dissolve, my life! Let not my sense unsettle,
Lest I should drown, or stab, or hang myself.   30
O state of nature, fail together in me,
Since thy best props are warped! So, which way now?
The best way is the next way to a grave;
Each errant step beside is torment. Lo,
The moon is down, the crickets chirp, the screech   35
    owl
Calls in the dawn. All offices are done
Save what I fail in. But the point is this—
An end, and that is all.

                                         She exits.

3.3 Arcite brings Palamon food, wine, and files. He promises to return in two hours bringing swords and armor for their combat.

---

2 SD. **within:** offstage

5. **honest:** honorable

7. **hereafter:** later

8. **beastly:** like a beast

12. **must:** would have to; **good now:** an interjection of entreaty

13. **vain:** idle; futile

14. **ancient:** long-established; also, perhaps, former

15. **Make talk:** i.e., provide gossip

16. **Do:** perhaps, **do** drink (But see longer note, page 258.)

21. **pledge:** drink a toast to

A wrestler "o' th' hip." (2.3.90–91)
From Romein de Hoogue,
L'academie de l'admirable art de la lutte . . . [1712].

Scene 3

Enter Arcite with meat, wine, and files.

ARCITE
  I should be near the place.—Ho! Cousin Palamon!
PALAMON, ⌜*within*⌝
  Arcite?
ARCITE   The same. I have brought you food and files.
  Come forth and fear not; here's no Theseus.

Enter Palamon.

PALAMON
  Nor none so honest, Arcite.   5
ARCITE   That's no matter.
  We'll argue that hereafter. Come, take courage;
  You shall not die thus beastly. Here, sir, drink—
  I know you are faint—then I'll talk further with you.
PALAMON
  Arcite, thou mightst now poison me.   10
ARCITE   I might;
  But I must fear you first. Sit down and, good now,
  No more of these vain parleys. Let us not,
  Having our ancient reputation with us,
  Make talk for fools and cowards. To your health.   15
                                          ⌜*He drinks.*⌝
PALAMON   Do!
ARCITE
  Pray sit down, then, and let me entreat you,
  By all the honesty and honor in you,
  No mention of this woman; 'twill disturb us.
  We shall have time enough.   20
PALAMON   Well, sir, I'll pledge you.
                                          ⌜*He drinks.*⌝

22. **it ... blood:** Proverbial: "Good wine makes good blood."

25. **Stay:** wait

27. **Spare it not:** i.e., do **not** be frugal (in drinking **it**)

31. **stomach:** appetite

33. **so ... to 't:** i.e., such **good** food for it

34. **mad lodging:** i.e., a foolish or unwise place to lodge

37. **wild:** savage; rebellious; wayward

40. **Your ... sauce:** Proverbial: "**Hunger** is the best **sauce**."

42. **yours ... tart:** an allusion to the verb "to sauce" (to speak abusively) and to the adjective "saucy" (insolent, presumptuous)

45. **lusty:** i.e., hearty, fortifying

51. **After you:** perhaps, you speak first

A falcon with its bells. (3.5.82)
From George Turberville, *The booke of faulconrie ...* (1575).

ARCITE
  Drink a good hearty draught; it breeds good blood,
    man.
  Do not you feel it thaw you?
PALAMON   Stay, I'll tell you   25
  After a draught or two more.
ARCITE   Spare it not.
  The Duke has more, coz. Eat now.
PALAMON   Yes.   ⌜*He eats.*⌝
ARCITE   I am glad   30
  You have so good a stomach.
PALAMON   I am gladder
  I have so good meat to 't.
ARCITE   Is 't not mad lodging
  Here in the wild woods, cousin?   35
PALAMON   Yes, for ⌜them⌝
  That have wild consciences.
ARCITE   How tastes your
    victuals?
  Your hunger needs no sauce, I see.   40
PALAMON   Not much.
  But if it did, yours is too tart, sweet cousin.
  What is this?
ARCITE   Venison.
PALAMON   'Tis a lusty meat.   45
  Give me more wine. Here, Arcite, to the wenches
  We have known in our days!
              ⌜*He raises his cup in a toast.*⌝
                       The Lord Steward's
    daughter!
  Do you remember her?   50
ARCITE   After you, coz.
PALAMON
  She loved a black-haired man.
ARCITE   She did so; well, sir?

55. **faith:** a mild oath

57. **virginals:** a musical instrument resembling a small upright piano (with wordplay on virginity and its loss) See picture, below.

64. **Else:** otherwise; **tales:** falsehoods, idle stories

66. **brown:** brunette

68. **thereby . . . tale:** proverbial

69. **Heigh ho:** indicating the sound of a **sigh** (line 72)

70. **upon my life:** a mild oath

71. **strained:** artificial, forced

73. **break:** violate (our agreement that there be "**No mention of this woman**" [lines 17–19])

74. **wide:** mistaken, **wide** of the mark (language from archery)

Playing "o' th' virginals." (3.3.57)
From Henry Playford, *The banquet of musick . . .* (1688).

PALAMON
  And I have heard some call him Arcite, and—
ARCITE
  Out with 't, faith.   55
PALAMON   She met him in an arbor.
  What did she there, coz? Play o' th' virginals?
ARCITE
  Something she did, sir.
PALAMON   Made her groan a month
     for 't—   60
  Or two, or three, or ten.
ARCITE   The Marshal's sister
  Had her share, too, as I remember, cousin,
  Else there be tales abroad. You'll pledge her?
PALAMON   Yes.   65
      ⌜*He lifts his cup and then drinks.*⌝
ARCITE
  A pretty brown wench 'tis. There was a time
  When young men went a-hunting, and a wood,
  And a broad beech—and thereby hangs a tale.
  Heigh ho!
PALAMON   For Emily, upon my life! Fool,   70
  Away with this strained mirth. I say again
  That sigh was breathed for Emily. Base cousin,
  Dar'st thou break first?
ARCITE   You are wide.
PALAMON   By heaven and   75
     earth,
  There's nothing in thee honest.
ARCITE   Then I'll leave you.
  You are a beast now.
PALAMON   As thou mak'st me, traitor.   80
ARCITE
  There's all things needful: files and shirts and
     perfumes.

84. **That that:** i.e., **that** which

86. **Fear:** doubt; **foul:** offensive

87. **trinkets:** i.e., fetters; **want naught:** lack nothing

88. **Sirrah:** As a term of address to a social inferior or child, its use here is an insult.

90. **keep touch:** keeps his promise

3.4 The jailer's daughter, convinced that Palamon is dead and that her father will be hanged, begins to hallucinate.

---

1. **out:** extinguished (However, the word could also mean "alight, shining.")

2. **aglets:** spangles

5. **Yonder's . . . ship:** Potter (Arden 3 edition, page 48) traces the source of this hallucination to Ariadne's lament in Ovid's *Heroides*.

8. **sound:** substantial

9. **Open her:** i.e., unfurl **her** sails, let **her** run

10. **course:** sail ("The courses are the main-sail, fore-sail, and mizzen . . ."; Falconer's *Dict. Marine* [1769].) **tack about:** run obliquely against the wind

15. **carrack:** large, three-masted sailing ship (See picture, page 164.) **cockleshell:** small saucer-shaped shell of a cockle or other shellfish

17. **rarely:** splendidly

I'll come again some two hours hence and bring
That that shall quiet all.

PALAMON   A sword and armor.   85

ARCITE
Fear me not. You are now too foul. Farewell.
Get off your trinkets; you shall want naught.

PALAMON   Sirrah—

ARCITE
I'll hear no more.

                                              He exits.

PALAMON   If he keep touch, he dies for 't.   90

                                              He exits.

Scene 4

Enter Jailer's Daughter.

DAUGHTER
I am very cold, and all the stars are out too,
The little stars and all, that look like aglets.
The sun has seen my folly.—Palamon!
Alas, no; he's in heaven. Where am I now?
Yonder's the sea, and there's a ship. How 't tumbles!   5
And there's a rock lies watching under water.
Now, now, it beats upon it; now, now, now,
There's a leak sprung, a sound one! How they cry!
⌜Open⌝ her before the wind; you'll lose all else.
Up with a course or two, and ⌜tack⌝ about, boys!   10
Good night, good night; you're gone. I am very
     hungry.
Would I could find a fine frog; he would tell me
News from all parts o' th' world; then would I make
A carrack of a cockleshell, and sail   15
By east and northeast to the king of pygmies,
For he tells fortunes rarely. Now my father,

18. **is trussed . . . trice:** will be hanged quickly

20–27. **For . . . nonny:** The ballad on which this song is based tells the story of a young woman who serves the man she loves disguised as his page.   **eye:** probably pronounced "e'e" (to rhyme with **knee** [line 20])   **He's:** i.e., he shall   **cut:** horse (perhaps, cut-tail horse, or, perhaps, gelding)

28. **prick:** thorn (The **nightingale** was said to press its **breast** [line 29] against a thorn in order to stay awake at night to sing.)

29. **sleep like a top:** proverbial for sleeping soundly

3.5 The countrymen and the schoolmaster gather for the morris dance to be performed for Duke Theseus. When the countrywomen arrive, it is discovered that one woman is missing. At that moment, the jailer's daughter, now completely mad, arrives and becomes one of the dancers. Theseus and his court appear and the morris dance is performed.

---

0 SD. **Bavian:** i.e., babion, baboon

1. **tediosity, disinsanity:** the Schoolmaster's terms for "tediousness" and "gross insanity"

2. **rudiments:** basic teachings

3. **milked:** i.e., fed like mother's milk

4. **figure:** i.e., **figure** of speech; **plum broth and marrow:** delicacies, choicest foods

6. **Wherefore:** why

7–8. **coarse-frieze capacities, jean judgments:**

(continued)

Twenty to one, is trussed up in a trice
Tomorrow morning. I'll say never a word.
(*Sing.*)
> For I'll cut my green coat a foot above my knee,   20
> And I'll clip my yellow locks an inch below mine
>   eye.
>   *Hey nonny, nonny, nonny.*
> He's buy me a white cut, forth for to ride,
> And I'll go seek him through the world that is so   25
>   wide.
>   *Hey nonny, nonny, nonny.*

O, for a prick now, like a nightingale,
To put my breast against. I shall sleep like a top else.
                                             She exits.

Scene ⌜5⌝

Enter a Schoolmaster and ⌜six⌝ Countrymen,
⌜*one dressed as a Bavian.*⌝

SCHOOLMASTER Fie, fie, what tediosity and disinsanity
is here among you! Have my rudiments been labored so long with you, milked unto you, and, by a
figure, even the very plum broth and marrow of
my understanding laid upon you, and do you still   5
cry "Where?" and "How?" and "Wherefore?" You
most coarse-frieze capacities, you ⌜jean⌝ judgments, have I said "Thus let be" and "There let be"
and "Then let be" and no man understand me? *Proh*
deum, medius fidius, you are all dunces! Forwhy,   10
here stand I; here the Duke comes; there are you,
close in the thicket; the Duke appears; I meet him
and unto him I utter learnèd things and many figures; he hears, and nods, and hums, and then cries
"Rare!" and I go forward. At length I fling my cap   15
up—mark there! Then do you as once did Melea-

Here, mental abilities are imaged as fabrics. (**Coarse-frieze** [rough wool cloth] and **jean** [twilled cotton cloth] are worn by the lower classes.) **capacities:** talents **judgments:** critical faculties

9–10. **Proh deum, medius fidius:** Latin oaths that mean, in effect, "God help me"

10. **Forwhy:** because

12. **close:** hidden

13–14. **figures:** See note to line 4, above.

14. **hums:** makes sounds of warm approval

15. **go forward:** i.e., **go** on, continue

16. **mark there:** i.e., watch this (He presumably flings up his **cap.**)

16–17. **do you ... comely out:** With this inapt allusion to **Meleager** and the Calydonian **boar,** the Schoolmaster instructs the countrymen to spring from concealment in a seemly manner. (See longer note, page 258.)

18. **like true lovers:** perhaps, in couples; or, perhaps, **like** loving subjects (of Theseus); **cast ... body:** dispose or arrange **yourselves; decently:** suitably, becomingly

19. **by a figure:** i.e., to use **a figure** of speech; **trace and turn:** i.e., dance

22. **Draw ... company:** i.e., bring **the company** into proper order

23. **taborer:** one who plays the small drum called the tabor

25. **Have at you!:** words signaling a coming action (here, perhaps, a burst of drumming)

32. **Swim:** glide smoothly

33. **carry it:** behave, act

33–34. **deliverly:** deftly, cleverly

(continued)

ger and the boar—break comely out before him;
like true lovers, cast yourselves in a body decently,
and sweetly, by a figure, trace and turn, boys.

FIRST COUNTRYMAN And sweetly we will do it, Master   20
Gerald.

SECOND COUNTRYMAN Draw up the company. Where's
the taborer?

THIRD COUNTRYMAN Why, Timothy!

⌜*Enter the*⌝ *Taborer.*

TABORER Here, my mad boys. Have at you!   25

SCHOOLMASTER But I say, where's their women?

Enter ⌜*five*⌝ *Wenches.*

FOURTH COUNTRYMAN Here's Fritz and Maudlin.

SECOND COUNTRYMAN And little Luce with the white
legs, and bouncing Barbary.

FIRST COUNTRYMAN And freckled Nell, that never failed   30
her master.

SCHOOLMASTER Where be your ribbons, maids? Swim
with your bodies, and carry it sweetly and deliverly, and now and then a favor and a frisk.

NELL Let us alone, sir.   35

SCHOOLMASTER Where's the rest o' th' music?

THIRD COUNTRYMAN Dispersed, as you commanded.

SCHOOLMASTER Couple, then, and see what's wanting.
Where's the Bavian?—My friend, carry your tail
without offense or scandal to the ladies; and be   40
sure you tumble with audacity and manhood, and
when you bark, do it with judgment.

BAVIAN Yes, sir.

SCHOOLMASTER *Quo usque tandem?* Here is a woman
wanting.   45

FOURTH COUNTRYMAN We may go whistle; all the fat's i'
th' fire.

SCHOOLMASTER We have, as learnèd authors utter,

34. **frisk:** caper, jig

35. **Let us alone:** i.e., don't worry about us

36. **music:** company of musicians

38. **Couple:** join up in pairs; **wanting:** missing

39. **Bavian:** See note to 0 SD.

42. **bark:** make animal sounds

44. **Quo usque tandem:** How long then (quoting Cicero's familiar Latin "How long then . . . will you abuse our patience?")

46–49. **We may . . . tile:** These three proverbs are versions of "**We have . . . labored vainly**" (lines 49–50).

49. **fatuus:** foolish (Latin)

51. **This:** i.e., the missing woman; **piece:** woman

52. **scurvy hilding:** worthless strumpet

53. **sempster's:** tailor's

54. **dogskin:** i.e., the cheapest leather

55. **an she:** if she

56. **break:** i.e., **break** her promise (to take part)

57–59. **An eel . . . fail:** Proverbial: "Who has a **woman** has **an eel** by the **tail**." **either:** i.e., both

59–60. **In manners . . . position:** i.e., her **manners** were as deplorable as **false** logic

61. **fire:** perhaps, pox, venereal disease; **take:** attack; **flinch:** draw back

64–65. **a nullity:** a mere nothing

67. **to be frampold:** i.e., (for her) **to be** peevish

67–68. **piss o' th' nettle:** proverbial for "to be in a bad temper"

68. **Go thy ways:** a contemptuous dismissal; **fit:** provide with a fit punishment

(continued)

washed a tile; we have been *fatuus* and labored
vainly.   50

SECOND COUNTRYMAN   This is that scornful piece, that
scurvy hilding that gave her promise faithfully she
would be here—Cicely, the sempster's daughter.
The next gloves that I give her shall be dogskin;
nay, an she fail me once—you can tell, Arcas, she   55
swore by wine and bread she would not break.

SCHOOLMASTER   An eel and woman, a learnèd poet
says, unless by th' tail and with thy teeth thou hold,
will either fail. In manners, this was false position.   60

FIRST COUNTRYMAN   A fire ill take her! Does she flinch
now?

THIRD COUNTRYMAN   What shall we determine, sir?

SCHOOLMASTER   Nothing. Our business is become a
nullity, yea, and a woeful and a piteous nullity.   65

FOURTH COUNTRYMAN   Now, when the credit of our town
lay on it, now to be frampold, now to piss o' th'
nettle! Go thy ways; I'll remember thee. I'll fit
thee!

Enter Jailer's Daughter.

DAUGHTER, ⌈*sings*⌉
    The George Alow came from the south,   70
        From the coast of Barbary-a,
    And there he met with brave gallants of war,
        By one, by two, by three-a.
    "Well hailed, well hailed, you jolly gallants,
        And whither now are you bound-a?   75
    O, let me have your company
        Till ⌈I⌉ come to the sound-a."

There was three fools, fell out about an owlet—
⌈*Sings*⌉   *The one ⌈he⌉ said it was an owl,*
                The other he said nay,   80

70. **The George Alow:** the name of a ship in an early ballad (See longer note, page 259.)

72. **gallants of war:** perhaps, galleons, warships

78. **fell out:** i.e., who argued

82. **bells:** Falconers tie decorative small **bells** to the legs of hawks and falcons. (See picture, page 114.)

83. **dainty:** splendid, fine

84. **i' th' nick:** at the critical moment; **mad . . . hare:** proverbial

85. **dance:** i.e., to **dance; we are made:** i.e., our success in life is assured

85–86. **I warrant her:** I guarantee

86. **rarest gambols:** most splendid leaps

93. **Tell ten:** count to **ten; posed:** perplexed

94. **Buzz:** an exclamation of impatience

97. **stop . . . should:** Proverbial: "A **tinker** stops one hole and makes two," here with sexual innuendo.

98. **Dii boni:** good gods (Latin)

99. **Raise me:** i.e., conjure up (See picture, page 194.)

100. **Chi passa:** Music for *Chi passa questa strada* (1557) survives in many English instrumental settings. **bones:** used for percussion for rural dances

102–3. **Et opus . . . ignis:** "And I have completed a work which neither the anger of Jove nor fire [will undo]." (Latin, quoting Ovid's *Metamorphoses* 15.871)

109. **meditation:** i.e., time to think; **mark:** i.e., listen for

110. **Pallas: Pallas** Athena, goddess of wisdom

112. **edify:** gain instruction

> *The third he said it was a hawk,*
> *And her bells were cut away.*

THIRD COUNTRYMAN   There's a dainty madwoman, master, comes i' th' nick, as mad as a March hare. If we can get her dance, we are made again. I warrant her, she'll do the rarest gambols.   85

FIRST COUNTRYMAN   A madwoman? We are made, boys.

SCHOOLMASTER, ⌈*to Jailer's Daughter*⌉ And are you mad, good woman?

DAUGHTER   I would be sorry else. Give me your hand.   90

SCHOOLMASTER   Why?

DAUGHTER   I can tell your fortune. ⌈*She looks at his hand.*⌉ You are a fool. Tell ten.—I have posed him. Buzz!—Friend, you must eat no white bread; if you do, your teeth will bleed extremely. Shall we   95
dance, ho? I know you, you're a tinker. Sirrah tinker, stop no more holes but what you should.

SCHOOLMASTER   *Dii boni!* A tinker, damsel?

DAUGHTER   Or a conjurer. Raise me a devil now, and let him play ⌈*Chi*⌉ *passa* o' th' bells and bones.   100

SCHOOLMASTER   Go, take her, and fluently persuade her to a peace. *Et opus exegi, quod nec Iovis ira, nec ignis.* Strike up, and lead her in.

SECOND COUNTRYMAN   Come, lass, let's trip it.

DAUGHTER   I'll lead.   105

THIRD COUNTRYMAN   Do, do!

SCHOOLMASTER   Persuasively, and cunningly.

Wind horns.

Away, boys! I hear the horns. Give me some meditation, and mark your cue.

All but Schoolmaster exit.

Pallas, inspire me!   110

Enter Theseus, Pirithous, Hippolyta, Emilia, and train.

THESEUS   This way the stag took.

SCHOOLMASTER   Stay, and edify!

117. **stay:** await

119. **cold:** wordplay on **hail** (line 118) as ice

120. **favor:** approve; **made is:** succeeds

122. **ruder:** perhaps, more impolite; or, perhaps, more unsophisticated; **distinguish:** classify as

124. **rout:** band

125. **figure:** i.e., **figure** of speech; **chorus:** perhaps alluding to the **chorus** of a Greek tragedy

126. **thy dignity:** perhaps, "your Honor"

128. **pedagogus:** schoolmaster (Latin)

129. **birch: birch** rod used to whip schoolboys

130. **ferula:** ferule, cane

131. **machine, frame:** structure; device (perhaps, a structure on the stage, or the dance itself)

132. **dismal:** terrible (to his enemies) But see longer note, page 259.

133. **Dis:** god of the underworld; **Daedalus:** creator of the Cretan Labyrinth

134. **well-willer:** well-wisher

136–38. **this . . . Morris:** Two costumed actors may enact "**Morr**" (perhaps "Moor") and "**is**" (perhaps "ice"), or may carry signs that spell out the syllables. **mickle:** much

139. **body of our sport:** main part of our show; **of no small study:** i.e., put together with great effort

140. **rude:** unpolished; **raw:** crude; **muddy:** vague, confused

141. **tenner:** ten-syllable line

142. **penner:** pen case

143. **Lord of May and Lady:** For the pairs of dancers presented by the Schoolmaster in lines 143–50, see longer note, page 259.

(continued)

THESEUS   What have we here?

PIRITHOUS   Some country sport, upon my life, sir.

⌜THESEUS, *to Schoolmaster*⌝ Well, sir, go forward. We   115
    will "edify."   *Chairs and stools* ⌜*brought*⌝ *out.*
    Ladies, sit down. We'll stay it.
                 ⌜*Theseus, Hippolyta, and Emilia sit.*⌝

SCHOOLMASTER
    Thou doughty duke, all hail!—All hail, sweet ladies!

THESEUS, ⌜*aside*⌝ This is a cold beginning.

SCHOOLMASTER
    If you but favor, our country pastime made is.   120
    We are a few of those collected here
    That ruder tongues distinguish "villager."
    And to say verity, and not to fable,
    We are a merry rout, or else a rabble,
    Or company, or by a figure, chorus,   125
    That 'fore thy dignity will dance a morris.
    And I that am the rectifier of all,
    By title *pedagogus*, that let fall
    The birch upon the breeches of the small ones,
    And humble with a ferula the tall ones,   130
    Do here present this machine, or this frame.
    And, dainty duke, whose doughty dismal fame
    From Dis to Daedalus, from post to pillar,
    Is blown abroad, help me, thy poor well-willer,
    And with thy twinkling eyes look right and straight   135
    Upon this mighty "Morr," of mickle weight—
    "Is" now comes in, which being glued together
    Makes "Morris," and the cause that we came hither.
    The body of our sport, of no small study,
    I first appear, though rude, and raw, and muddy,   140
    To speak before thy noble grace this tenner,
    At whose great feet I offer up my penner.
    The next, the Lord of May and Lady bright,
    The Chambermaid and Servingman by night
    That seek out silent hanging; then mine Host   145

144–45. by night...hanging: i.e., **that, by night, seek out** a **silent** place behind a wall **hanging** or tapestry

146. welcomes to their cost: i.e., gives them a costly welcome (See longer note, page 260.)

149. beest-eating Clown: i.e., ignorant or unsophisticated countryman (The **beest**, or thick milk given by animals after parturition, was considered dangerous or unpalatable.)

150. eke: also; **tool:** penis

151. Cum multis aliis: with many others (Latin)

153. any means: i.e., all **means; Domine:** See note to 2.3.46.

155. Intrate, filii: come in, boys (Latin)

155 SD. Enter: In the anti-masque from which this dance is taken, the dancers **enter** with "the men issuing out of one side of the boscage [i.e., thicket], and the women from the other." (See longer note to 3.5.143, page 259.)

157–58. derry, down: words used in ballad refrains

165. make...rout: i.e., **make** you **and all this** company of people **laugh**

169. preface: prologue

170. One: someone

And his fat Spouse, that welcomes to their cost
The gallèd traveler, and with a beck'ning
Informs the tapster to inflame the reck'ning;
Then the beest-eating Clown; and next the Fool,
The Bavian with long tail and eke long tool,   150
Cum multis aliis that make a dance;
Say "ay," and all shall presently advance.

THESEUS
Ay, ay, by any means, dear Domine.

PIRITHOUS   Produce!

SCHOOLMASTER
Intrate, filii. Come forth and foot it.   155

Music. ⌜*Enter the Countrymen, Countrywomen, and
    Jailer's Daughter; they perform a morris*⌝ *dance.*

⌜SCHOOLMASTER⌝
          Ladies, if we have been merry
          And have pleased ⌜ye⌝ with a derry,
          And a derry and a down,
          Say the Schoolmaster's no clown.—
          Duke, if we have pleased ⌜thee⌝ too   160
          And have done as good boys should do,
          Give us but a tree or twain
          For a Maypole, and again,
          Ere another year run out,
          We'll make thee laugh, and all this rout.   165

THESEUS
Take twenty, Domine.—How does my sweetheart?

HIPPOLYTA
Never so pleased, sir.

EMILIA   'Twas an excellent dance,
And, for a preface, I never heard a better.

THESEUS
Schoolmaster, I thank you.—One see 'em all   170
    rewarded.   ⌜*An Attendant gives money.*⌝

172. **withal:** with

173. **sports:** i.e., hunting

174. **stand long:** perhaps, hold out against the hunting **dogs** (and thus provide good sport)

176. **lets:** impediments, hindrances

177. **dowsets:** testicles (considered a delicacy)

178. **we ... made:** See note to line 85, above. **Dii deaeque omnes:** all you gods and goddesses (Latin)

179. **rarely:** splendidly

3.6 Arcite arrives in the forest with armor and swords. The two cousins dress each other in armor and prepare as if for a formal trial by combat. Theseus comes upon the combat, arrests them, and sentences them both to immediate death. He is persuaded to pardon them; but in order to end their violent rivalry, he sets up a competition that will include companion knights from Thebes and that will end with the victor winning Emilia and the loser and his companions being executed.

———————

1. **gave his faith:** pledged his word

3. **armors:** See note to 17 SD, below.

7. **wants:** starvation

10. **outdure:** i.e., prevail over; **it:** the combat

11–12. **comes to hearing:** becomes known

13. **fatting ... fight:** preparing for the fight **like a swine** being fattened up for slaughter

15. **that sword he refuses:** Palamon assumes that Arcite will choose the better **sword.**

PIRITHOUS
   And here's something to paint your pole withal.
                                    ⌜*He gives money.*⌝
THESEUS   Now to our sports again.
SCHOOLMASTER
         May the stag thou hunt'st stand long,
         And thy dogs be swift and strong;   175
         May they kill him without lets,
         And the ladies eat his dowsets.
              Wind horns ⌜within. Theseus, Hippolyta,
                  Emilia, Pirithous, and Train exit.⌝
   Come, we are all made. *Dii deaeque omnes,*
   You have danced rarely, wenches.
                                         They exit.

                     ⌜Scene 6⌝

              Enter Palamon from the bush.

PALAMON
   About this hour my cousin gave his faith
   To visit me again, and with him bring
   Two swords and two good armors. If he fail,
   He's neither man nor soldier. When he left me,
   I did not think a week could have restored   5
   My lost strength to me, I was grown so low
   And crestfall'n with my wants. I thank thee, Arcite,
   Thou art yet a fair foe, and I feel myself,
   With this refreshing, able once again
   To outdure danger. To delay it longer   10
   Would make the world think, when it comes to
      hearing,
   That I lay fatting like a swine to fight
   And not a soldier. Therefore, this blest morning
   Shall be the last; and that sword he refuses,   15

16. **hold:** remains unbroken; **'Tis justice:** For the larger context of this supposed trial by combat, in which single combat was used to determine legal right, see longer note to 3.1.36–37, page 258.

17 SD. **armors:** perhaps, suits of armor; or, more likely, pieces of armor—e.g., breastplates, **gauntlets** (line 89), casques (line 86)—needed for hand-to-hand combat

30. **quit:** repay, requite

31. **show:** seem, appear

37–38. **to . . . pertains:** i.e., the one who was born to possess **this beauty   birthright:** possession entitled by birth   **pertains:** belongs

43. **fitting:** i.e., fit

44. **stay:** wait

46. **discourse you:** bring you through conversation

A laurel wreath. (Pro. 20; 2.2.19; 2.3.102; 5.4.95)
From Giacomo Lauri, *Antiquae vrbis splendor . . .* (1612–15).

If it but hold, I kill him with. 'Tis justice.
So, love and fortune for me!

     Enter Arcite with armors and swords.

                        O, good morrow.

ARCITE
Good morrow, noble kinsman.
PALAMON   I have put you   20
To too much pains, sir.
ARCITE   That too much, fair cousin,
Is but a debt to honor and my duty.
PALAMON
Would you were so in all, sir; I could wish you
As kind a kinsman as you force me find   25
A beneficial foe, that my embraces
Might thank you, not my blows.
ARCITE   I shall think either,
Well done, a noble recompense.
PALAMON   Then I shall quit you.   30
ARCITE
Defy me in these fair terms, and you show
More than a mistress to me. No more anger,
As you love anything that's honorable!
We were not bred to talk, man; when we are armed
And both upon our guards, then let our fury,   35
Like meeting of two tides, fly strongly from us,
And then to whom the birthright of this beauty
Truly pertains—without upbraidings, scorns,
Despisings of our persons, and such poutings,
Fitter for girls and schoolboys—will be seen,   40
And quickly, yours or mine. Will 't please you arm,
   sir?
Or if you feel yourself not fitting yet
And furnished with your old strength, I'll stay,
   cousin,   45
And ev'ry day discourse you into health,

47. **As I am spared:** i.e., whenever **I am** free (of my duties at court)

49. **Though . . . died:** even if not saying so had killed me

50. **justifying:** i.e., having acknowledged the truth of

53. **lusty:** strong, vigorous; **arms:** armor

55. **exceed in all:** i.e., outdo (me) at every point

61. **find it:** i.e., **find it** so

63. **With . . . affection:** "with justice and love on my side" (Potter)

64. **pay:** punish, chastise

77. **close:** i.e., so that it fits tightly

A casque, or helmet. (3.6.86)
From Louis de Gaya, *Traité des armes . . .* (1678).

As I am spared. Your person I am friends with,
And I could wish I had not said I loved her,
Though I had died. But loving such a lady,
And justifying my love, I must not fly from 't. 50

PALAMON
Arcite, thou art so brave an enemy
That no man but thy cousin's fit to kill thee.
I am well and lusty. Choose your arms.

ARCITE   Choose you, sir.

PALAMON
Wilt thou exceed in all, or dost thou do it 55
To make me spare thee?

ARCITE   If you think so, cousin,
You are deceived, for as I am a soldier,
I will not spare you.

PALAMON   That's well said. 60

ARCITE   You'll find it.

PALAMON
Then, as I am an honest man and love
With all the justice of affection,
I'll pay thee soundly.   ⌈*He chooses armor.*⌉
                        This I'll take. 65

ARCITE ⌈*taking the other*⌉   That's mine, then.
I'll arm you first.

PALAMON   Do.   ⌈*Arcite begins arming him.*⌉
                        Pray thee tell me, cousin,
Where got'st thou this good armor? 70

ARCITE   'Tis the Duke's,
And to say true, I stole it. Do I pinch you?

PALAMON   No.

ARCITE
Is 't not too heavy?

PALAMON   I have worn a lighter, 75
But I shall make it serve.

ARCITE   I'll buckle 't close.

78. **By any means:** i.e., **by** all **means**

79. **care not:** have no desire; **grand guard:** piece of plate armor that fastened to the breastplate for extra protection of the chest and left shoulder (See longer note, page 260.)

80. **we'll use no horses:** See longer note to 3.6.79.

81. **fain . . . fight:** gladly take part in mounted combat (See picture, page 2.)

82. **I am indifferent:** i.e., it doesn't matter to me

85. **I warrant you:** i.e., certainly

86. **casque:** helmet (See picture, page 136.)

87. **bare-armed:** After the body armor is buckled on, the arm pieces would be put on next. Instead, Palamon has asked for his helmet.

89. **gauntlets:** leather gloves covered with plates of steel (See picture, below.) **o' th' least:** i.e., too small; or, perhaps, inferior

92. **fall'n much away:** i.e., much thinner

93. **love . . . kindly:** One sign of a true lover was extreme thinness.

94. **I'll warrant thee:** I guarantee; **home:** i.e., to your very heart

98. **Methinks:** it seems to me

100. **good one:** i.e., **good** armor

Gantelet

A gauntlet. (3.6.89)
From Louis de Gaya, *Traité des armes . . .* (1678).

138

PALAMON
  By any means.
ARCITE   You care not for a grand guard?
PALAMON
  No, no, we'll use no horses. I perceive   80
  You would fain be at that fight.
ARCITE   I am indifferent.
PALAMON
  Faith, so am I. Good cousin, thrust the buckle
  Through far enough.
ARCITE   I warrant you.   85
PALAMON   My casque now.
ARCITE
  Will you fight bare-armed?
PALAMON   We shall be the nimbler.
ARCITE
  But use your gauntlets though. Those are o' th' least.
  Prithee take mine, good cousin.   90
PALAMON   Thank you, Arcite.
  How do I look? Am I fall'n much away?
ARCITE
  Faith, very little; love has used you kindly.
PALAMON
  I'll warrant thee, I'll strike home.
ARCITE   Do, and spare not.   95
  I'll give you cause, sweet cousin.
PALAMON   Now to you, sir.
                    ⌈*He begins to arm Arcite.*⌉
  Methinks this armor's very like that, Arcite,
  Thou wor'st that day the three kings fell, but lighter.
ARCITE
  That was a very good one, and that day,   100
  I well remember, you outdid me, cousin.
  I never saw such valor. When you charged
  Upon the left wing of the enemy,

104. **come up: come** forward, i.e., catch **up** with you

107. **bright bay:** reddish-brown horse (**Bright bay** is one of several shades of **bay.**)

108–9. **all . . . in me:** i.e., **all** my efforts were in vain

110. **Nor could my wishes reach you:** i.e., not even **my** desire (to equal **you**) **could** match your **valor** (line 102)

112. **virtue:** manly excellence

115. **Methought:** it seemed to me

117. **still:** always

118. **Stay a little:** i.e., wait a minute

119. **strait:** tight

123. **perfect:** made ready, i.e., completely armed

125. **hold it better:** consider **it** the **better sword**

126. **lies:** depends

127. **hold:** remain unbroken

129. **me my love:** i.e., (may) **my love (guard) me**

129 SD. **bow several ways: bow** in different directions (as if to spectators at a formal trial by combat)

130. **Is . . . say:** perhaps, have we said everything requisite for combatants in such a trial

132. **mutual:** possessed in common, shared

I spurred hard to come up, and under me
I had a right good horse.   105

PALAMON   You had, indeed;
A bright bay, I remember.

ARCITE   Yes, but all
Was vainly labored in me; you outwent me,
Nor could my wishes reach you; yet a little   110
I did by imitation.

PALAMON   More by virtue;
You are modest, cousin.

ARCITE   When I saw you charge first,
Methought I heard a dreadful clap of thunder   115
Break from the troop.

PALAMON   But still before that flew
The lightning of your valor. Stay a little;
Is not this piece too strait?

ARCITE   No, no, 'tis well.   120

PALAMON
I would have nothing hurt thee but my sword.
A bruise would be dishonor.

ARCITE   Now I am perfect.

PALAMON
Stand off, then.

ARCITE   Take my sword; I hold it better.   125

PALAMON
I thank you, no; keep it; your life lies on it.
Here's one; if it but hold, I ask no more
For all my hopes. My cause and honor guard me!

ARCITE
And me my love!
          They bow several ways, then advance and stand.
                    Is there aught else to say?   130

PALAMON
This only, and no more: thou art mine aunt's son.
And that blood we desire to shed is mutual—
In me thine, and in thee mine. My sword

137. **win:** reach, attain

141. **commend thee:** perhaps, commit you to God's care

142. **fall:** i.e., **die** (line 143)

143. **just trials:** judicial **trials** by combat (which determine the truth)

146. **undone:** ruined

150. **presently:** i.e., (go) immediately

152. **Gentle:** See note to 2.2.77.

155. **contempt:** disobedience of royal command (of banishment)

156. **difference:** dispute, quarrel

157. **base . . . it:** i.e., we managed it basely

159. **nor put off:** i.e., **nor will I put off**

160. **adventure:** undertaking, venture

162. **faints:** loses heart, gives way

162–63. **Put . . . guard:** i.e., assume a position of defense immediately

Knights in combat. (3.6.145 SD, 175 SD)
From [Sir William Segar,] *The booke of honor and armes* (1590).

Is in my hand, and if thou kill'st me,
The gods and I forgive thee. If there be   135
A place prepared for those that sleep in honor,
I wish his weary soul that falls may win it.
Fight bravely, cousin. Give me thy noble hand.

ARCITE, ⌈*as they shake hands*⌉
Here, Palamon. This hand shall never more
Come near thee with such friendship.   140

PALAMON   I commend thee.

ARCITE
If I fall, curse me, and say I was a coward,
For none but such dare die in these just trials.
Once more farewell, my cousin.

PALAMON   Farewell, Arcite.   145
                                                    Fight.
                              Horns within. They stand.

ARCITE
Lo, cousin, lo, our folly has undone us!

PALAMON   Why?

ARCITE
This is the Duke, a-hunting, as I told you.
If we be found, we are wretched. O, retire,
For honor's sake, and safely, presently   150
Into your bush again. Sir, we shall find
Too many hours to die in. Gentle cousin,
If you be seen, you perish instantly
For breaking prison, and I, if you reveal me,
For my contempt. Then all the world will scorn us,   155
And say we had a noble difference,
But base disposers of it.

PALAMON   No, no, cousin,
I will no more be hidden, nor put off
This great adventure to a second trial.   160
I know your cunning, and I know your cause.
He that faints now, shame take him! Put thyself
Upon thy present guard—

167. **my fortune:** i.e., the outcome of this fight for me

169. **crosses else:** other obstacles; or, other adversities

172. **fears:** frightens

173. **The law . . . ends:** i.e., we will be executed (so that neither of us will gain **honor**)

174. **Have at thy life:** a warning of a fatal blow to come

175 SD. **Enter . . . train:** In Chaucer's "Knight's Tale," **Theseus** himself separates the combatants, and he may do so here. (See 5.4.120–21.)

177. **tenor:** substance, general meaning

178. **appointed:** fitted out, equipped

179. **leave:** permission; **officers of arms:** officials who supervise trials by combat (See longer note to 3.1.36–37, page 258.)

180. **Castor:** a figure from Greek mythology (twin brother of Pollux), famous in Roman times for his valor and horsemanship

181. **Hold:** keep

188. **begged and banished:** See lines 2.2.314–17. **contemns:** despises

192. **servant:** i.e., one who has dedicated himself to her love (and who has been thus acknowledged)

192–93. **if there . . . soul to:** i.e., **if seeing first, and first** bestowing **the soul to,** conveys **a right**

ARCITE   You are not mad?

PALAMON

    Or I will make th' advantage of this hour   165
    Mine own, and what to come shall threaten me
    I fear less than my fortune. Know, weak cousin,
    I love Emilia, and in that I'll bury
    Thee and all crosses else.

ARCITE   Then come what can come,   170
    Thou shalt know, Palamon, I dare as well
    Die as discourse or sleep. Only this fears me:
    The law will have the honor of our ends.
    Have at thy life!

PALAMON   Look to thine own well, Arcite.   175

                                 Fight again.

   Horns. Enter Theseus, Hippolyta, Emilia,
           Pirithous and train.

THESEUS

    What ignorant and mad malicious traitors
    Are you, that 'gainst the tenor of my laws
    Are making battle, thus like knights appointed,
    Without my leave and officers of arms?
    By Castor, both shall die.   180

PALAMON   Hold thy word, Theseus.
    We are certainly both traitors, both despisers
    Of thee and of thy goodness. I am Palamon,
    That cannot love thee, he that broke thy prison.
    Think well what that deserves. And this is Arcite.   185
    A bolder traitor never trod thy ground,
    A falser ne'er seemed friend. This is the man
    Was begged and banished; this is he contemns thee
    And what thou dar'st do; and in this disguise,
    Against ⌈thine⌉ own edict, follows thy sister,   190
    That fortunate bright star, the fair Emilia,
    Whose servant—if there be a right in seeing
    And first bequeathing of the soul to—justly

194. **dares:** i.e., he **dares**

195. **like:** i.e., I, behaving **like; trusty:** faithful

196. **called:** bade, i.e., challenged; **answer:** i.e., **answer** for (in combat)

197. **spoken:** described

198. **injuries:** violations of rights, unjustly inflicted sufferings

200. **Do such a justice:** inflict **such a** legal vengeance

206–7. **'Tis . . . say it:** i.e., I am **as** ready **to die as** you are **to** pronounce my death **thee:** i.e., for **thee**

208. **moved:** disturbed

210. **if in love:** i.e., **if** to **be in love**

212. **As:** because, since; **in that faith:** i.e., **in** fidelity to **that love**

213. **confirm it:** i.e., **confirm** that **I love most**

216. **let me be most:** i.e., proclaim me the worst

217. **For:** as for

218. **fair:** beautiful

221. **pity of:** i.e., **pity** on

222. **Stop:** close up, block

224–25. **thy . . . memory:** an allusion to Hercules, Theseus's cousin, famous for his **twelve** impossible **labors** (See picture, page xvii.)

226. **Let's:** i.e., let Arcite and me

I am; and, which is more, dares think her his.
This treachery, like a most trusty lover,   195
I called him now to answer. If thou be'st
As thou art spoken, great and virtuous,
The true decider of all injuries,
Say "Fight again," and thou shalt see me, Theseus,
Do such a justice thou thyself wilt envy.   200
Then take my life; I'll woo thee to 't.

PIRITHOUS   O heaven,
  What more than man is this!

THESEUS   I have sworn.

ARCITE   We seek not   205
  Thy breath of mercy, Theseus. 'Tis to me
  A thing as soon to die as thee to say it,
  And no more moved. Where this man calls me
    traitor,
  Let me say thus much: if in love be treason,   210
  In service of so excellent a beauty,
  As I love most, and in that faith will perish,
  As I have brought my life here to confirm it,
  As I have served her truest, worthiest,
  As I dare kill this cousin that denies it,   215
  So let me be most traitor, and you please me.
  For scorning thy edict, duke, ask that lady
  Why she is fair, and why her eyes command me
  Stay here to love her; and if she say "traitor,"
  I am a villain fit to lie unburied.   220

PALAMON
  Thou shalt have pity of us both, O Theseus,
  If unto neither thou show mercy. Stop,
  As thou art just, thy noble ear against us;
  As thou art valiant, for thy cousin's soul,
  Whose twelve strong labors crown his memory,   225
  Let's die together at one instant, duke;
  Only a little let him fall before me,
  That I may tell my soul he shall not have her.

236. **Will . . . else:** i.e., **will** otherwise **bear the curses**

239. **ruin:** cause of destruction

240. **kill:** i.e., kills

241. **that I will be:** i.e., to show **that I** am a

242. **but I'll:** i.e., unless I, until I

248. **faith:** pledge, promise

250. **By . . . another:** "**by** whatever **you would** invoke to arouse **pity in** someone else" (Evans)

253. **chaste . . . you:** The idea of chastity includes a celebration of married love.

254. **conjurings:** solemn appeals

255. **I'll in:** i.e., **I'll** join **in**

Amazon In archibus Jacobi Plutei Sibentini 43

An Amazon. (1.1.88)
From Giovanni Battista Cavalleriis,
Antiquarum statuarum . . . (1585–94).

THESEUS
  I grant your wish, for to say true, your cousin
  Has ten times more offended, for I gave him   230
  More mercy than you found, sir, your offenses
  Being no more than his.—None here speak for 'em,
  For ere the sun set both shall sleep forever.

HIPPOLYTA
  Alas, the pity! Now or never, sister,
  Speak not to be denied. That face of yours   235
  Will bear the curses else of after ages
  For these lost cousins.

EMILIA   In my face, dear sister,
  I find no anger to 'em, nor no ruin.
  The misadventure of their own eyes kill 'em.   240
  Yet that I will be woman and have pity,
  My knees shall grow to th' ground but I'll get mercy.
                        ⌜*She kneels.*⌝

  Help me, dear sister; in a deed so virtuous,
  The powers of all women will be with us.
                    ⌜*Hippolyta kneels.*⌝

  Most royal brother—   245
HIPPOLYTA   Sir, by our tie of marriage—
EMILIA
  By your own spotless honor—
HIPPOLYTA   By that faith,
  That fair hand, and that honest heart you gave me—
EMILIA
  By that you would have pity in another;   250
  By your own virtues infinite—
HIPPOLYTA   By valor;
  By all the chaste nights I have ever pleased you—
THESEUS
  These are strange conjurings.
PIRITHOUS   Nay, then, I'll in too.   255
                    ⌜*He kneels.*⌝

258–59. **By . . . maid:** a reference to the knight's chivalric duty to aid young women in distress

261. **went beyond:** excelled

264. **want:** lack

270. **faith:** i.e., fidelity (to my oath [lines 180, 204, 229]); **reel:** waver, become unsteady

273. **right:** true, i.e., typical

274. **want:** lack

279–80. **bring . . . question:** i.e., (1) quarrel over you **in public**; (2) **bring your honor** into **question**

281. **credit:** good name, reputation

Jove, king of the gods. (1.1.31; 4.3.37)
From Vincenzo Cartari, *Le vere e noue imagini . . .* (1615).

By all our friendship, sir, by all our dangers;
By all you love most, wars and this sweet lady—

EMILIA
By that you would have trembled to deny
A blushing maid—

HIPPOLYTA   By your own eyes; by strength,   260
In which you swore I went beyond all women,
Almost all men, and yet I yielded, Theseus—

PIRITHOUS
To crown all this: by your most noble soul,
Which cannot want due mercy, I beg first—

HIPPOLYTA
Next hear my prayers—   265

EMILIA   Last let me entreat, sir—

PIRITHOUS
For mercy.

HIPPOLYTA   Mercy.

EMILIA   Mercy on these princes.

THESEUS
You make my faith reel. (⌜*To Emilia.*⌝) Say I felt   270
Compassion to 'em both, how would you place it?
                            ⌜*They rise from their knees.*⌝

EMILIA
Upon their lives, but with their banishments.

THESEUS
You are a right woman, sister: you have pity,
But want the understanding where to use it.
If you desire their lives, invent a way   275
Safer than banishment. Can these two live,
And have the agony of love about 'em,
And not kill one another? Every day
They'd fight about you, hourly bring your honor
In public question with their swords. Be wise, then,   280
And here forget 'em; it concerns your credit
And my oath equally. I have said they die.

284. **Bow not my honor:** do not force **my honor** to bend or swerve

287. **hold:** support, maintain, uphold

288. **Stand . . . will:** i.e., are taken as final decisions **Stand:** are valid, hold good **express will:** fixed intention

291. **passion:** overpowering emotion, i.e., anger; **good heed:** i.e., careful regard

293. **home:** to the very heart, so as to touch him deeply

295. **Fit for:** fitting, appropriate for; **my modest suit:** i.e., a plea from me as a **modest** young woman; **free:** noble, honorable

299. **their lives:** i.e., your taking **their lives** (See longer note, page 261, for a different reading of these lines.)

300. **Opinion:** public **opinion**

302. **were:** would be

306. **goodly:** splendid; **groaned:** labored in childbirth

310. **woe worth:** may **woe** befall

314. **Swear 'em:** make them swear

315. **make me:** i.e., **make me** the theme of; **know me:** i.e., acknowledge our acquaintance

Better they fall by th' law than one another.
Bow not my honor.

EMILIA   O, my noble brother,   285
That oath was rashly made, and in your anger;
Your reason will not hold it. If such vows
Stand for express will, all the world must perish.
Besides, I have another oath 'gainst yours,
Of more authority, I am sure more love,   290
Not made in passion neither, but good heed.

THESEUS
What is it, sister?

PIRITHOUS   Urge it home, brave lady.

EMILIA
That you would ne'er deny me anything
Fit for my modest suit and your free granting.   295
I tie you to your word now; if you ⌜fail⌝ in 't,
Think how you maim your honor—
For now I am set a-begging, sir, I am deaf
To all but your compassion—how their lives
Might breed the ruin of my name. Opinion!   300
Shall anything that loves me perish for me?
That were a cruel wisdom. Do men prune
The straight young boughs that blush with thousand
    blossoms
Because they may be rotten? O, Duke Theseus,   305
The goodly mothers that have groaned for these,
And all the longing maids that ever loved,
If your vow stand, shall curse me and my beauty,
And in their funeral songs for these two cousins
Despise my cruelty, and cry woe worth me,   310
Till I am nothing but the scorn of women.
For heaven's sake, save their lives, and banish 'em.

THESEUS
On what conditions?

EMILIA   Swear 'em never more
To make me their contention, or to know me,   315

321. **Thy banishment:** the **banishment** you propose

322. **so:** provided that; **fairly:** properly, legally, legitimately

326. **piece:** i.e., plot of ground

328. **these:** i.e., Emilia's proposed

332. **take ... basely:** i.e., accept the gift of **my life** on such base terms

334. **affection:** i.e., serving her out of love

335. **Make ... devil:** i.e., no matter how terrifying or agonizing you **make** my **death**

337. **fall:** lapse, die out, expire

342. **goodly:** beautiful, splendid

344. **difference:** quarrel, dispute

Pallas Athena as goddess of war, of spinning, and of wisdom. (2.2.26; 3.5.110; 4.2.127)
From Vincenzo Cartari, *Le vere e noue imagini . . .* (1615).

To tread upon thy dukedom, and to be,
Wherever they shall travel, ever strangers
To one another.
PALAMON   I'll be cut a-pieces
Before I take this oath! Forget I love her?   320
O, all you gods, despise me then! Thy banishment
I not mislike, so we may fairly carry
Our swords and cause along; else never trifle,
But take our lives, duke. I must love, and will,
And for that love must and dare kill this cousin   325
On any piece the earth has.
THESEUS   Will you, Arcite,
Take these conditions?
PALAMON   He's a villain, then.
PIRITHOUS   These are men!   330
ARCITE
   No, never, duke. 'Tis worse to me than begging
   To take my life so basely; though I think
   I never shall enjoy her, yet I'll preserve
   The honor of affection, and die for her,
   Make death a devil!   335
THESEUS
   What may be done? For now I feel compassion.
PIRITHOUS
   Let it not fall again, sir.
THESEUS   Say, Emilia,
   If one of them were dead, as one must, are you
   Content to take th' other to your husband?   340
   They cannot both enjoy you. They are princes
   As goodly as your own eyes, and as noble
   As ever fame yet spoke of. Look upon 'em,
   And, if you can love, end this difference.
   I give consent.—Are you content too, princes?   345
BOTH   With all our souls.
THESEUS   He that she refuses
   Must die then.

350. from that mouth: i.e., through words pronounced by **that** speaker

356. For . . . men: i.e., not **a hair shall fall** from (either **of**) **these men** on account of **me**

359. stands: remains in force, i.e., is immutable

363. plant: put in place; **pyramid:** obelisk; **whether:** whichever one of you

367. And all his friends: i.e., as shall the **three knights** he brings with him (line 362); **grudge to fall:** complain about being executed

368. interest in: title or claim to

372. embrace you: accept your friendship

374. must: i.e., **must** be

375. miscarry: perish

The goddess Venus. (5.1.79–84; 5.4.126)
From Vincenzo Cartari, *Le vere e noue imagini* . . . (1615).

BOTH   Any death thou canst invent, duke.

PALAMON
  If I fall from that mouth, I fall with favor,   350
  And lovers yet unborn shall bless my ashes.

ARCITE
  If she refuse me, yet my grave will wed me,
  And soldiers sing my epitaph.

THESEUS, ⌜*to Emilia*⌝   Make choice, then.

EMILIA
  I cannot, sir; they are both too excellent.   355
  For me, a hair shall never fall of these men.

HIPPOLYTA
  What will become of 'em?

THESEUS   Thus I ordain it—
  And, by mine honor, once again, it stands,
  Or both shall die: you shall both to your country,   360
  And each within this month, accompanied
  With three fair knights, appear again in this place,
  In which I'll plant a pyramid; and whether,
  Before us that are here, can force his cousin
  By fair and knightly strength to touch the pillar,   365
  He shall enjoy her; the other lose his head,
  And all his friends; nor shall he grudge to fall,
  Nor think he dies with interest in this lady.
  Will this content you?

PALAMON   Yes.—Here, Cousin Arcite,   370
  I am friends again till that hour. ⌜*He offers his hand.*⌝

ARCITE   I embrace you.
                        ⌜*They shake hands.*⌝

THESEUS
  Are you content, sister?

EMILIA   Yes, I must, sir;
  Else both miscarry.   375

THESEUS, ⌜*to Palamon and Arcite*⌝
            Come, shake hands again, then,

377. **this quarrel:** i.e., that **this quarrel**

378. **prefixed:** appointed; **hold your course:** i.e., keep your promise to be **friends** (lines 371–72)

381. **usage like to:** treatment appropriate to

382. **who:** i.e., whoever, whichever of you; **settle here:** establish **here** in Athens (as a member of my court)

383. **yet:** nevertheless; or, perhaps, moreover; **bier:** tomb

The walled city of Athens. (5.1.64)
From Thucydides,
Eight bookes of the Peloponnesian warre . . . (1629).

And take heed, as you are gentlemen, this quarrel
Sleep till the hour prefixed, and hold your course.

PALAMON
We dare not fail thee, Theseus.

⌜*They shake hands again.*⌝

THESEUS   Come, I'll give you   380
Now usage like to princes and to friends.
When you return, who wins I'll settle here;
Who loses, yet I'll weep upon his bier.

They exit.

THE TWO
NOBLE KINSMEN

ACT 4

4.1 The jailer receives the news that he and his daughter have been pardoned for Palamon's escape, but that his daughter has gone mad. She enters and the others pacify her by going along with her delusions.

---

8. **both their pardons:** i.e., **pardons** for **both** Arcite and Palamon

10. **handsome:** magnanimous, gracious

11. **Methought:** it seemed to me; **staggering:** undecided, hesitating

16. **Half his own heart:** i.e., **his** (Theseus's) dearly loved friend; **that I hope:** so **that I hope**

17–18. **question / Of:** i.e., **question** about

19. **hold:** continue

Time with his wings, scythe, and hourglass. (2.2.114)
From August Casimir Redel, *Apophtegmata symbolica* ... [n.d.].

ACT 4

Scene 1

Enter Jailer and his Friend.

JAILER
⌜Heard⌝ you no more? Was nothing said of me
Concerning the escape of Palamon?
Good sir, remember!

FIRST FRIEND   Nothing that I heard,
For I came home before the business   5
Was fully ended. Yet I might perceive,
Ere I departed, a great likelihood
Of both their pardons; for Hippolyta
And fair-eyed Emily, upon their knees,
Begged with such handsome pity that the Duke, 10
Methought, stood staggering whether he should
 follow
His rash oath or the sweet compassion
Of those two ladies. And, to second them,
That truly noble prince, Pirithous—   15
Half his own heart—set in too, that I hope
All shall be well. Neither heard I one question
Of your name or his 'scape.

JAILER   Pray heaven it hold so.

Enter Second Friend.

22. **They:** i.e., the **news**
25. **discovered:** revealed
26. **means:** agency, intercession
29. **held:** considered, regarded as
36. **But they prevailed:** i.e., without prevailing;
suits: supplications, entreaties; **fairly:** fully

SPAANSSE CARAKEN

Carracks. (3.4.15)
From Cornelis van Yk,
De Nederlandsche scheeps-bouw-konst . . . (1697).

SECOND FRIEND
  Be of good comfort, man; I bring you news,   20
  Good news.
JAILER   They are welcome.
SECOND FRIEND   Palamon has cleared
      you
  And got your pardon, and discovered how   25
  And by whose means he escaped, which was your
      daughter's,
  Whose pardon is procured too; and the prisoner,
  Not to be held ungrateful to her goodness,
  Has given a sum of money to her marriage—   30
  A large one, I'll assure you.
JAILER   You are a good man
  And ever bring good news.
FIRST FRIEND   How was it ended?
SECOND FRIEND
  Why, as it should be: they that ne'er begged   35
  But they prevailed had their suits fairly granted;
  The prisoners have their lives.
FIRST FRIEND   I knew 'twould be so.
SECOND FRIEND
  But there be new conditions, which you'll hear of
  At better time.   40
JAILER   I hope they are good.
SECOND FRIEND   They are
      honorable;
  How good they'll prove I know not.
FIRST FRIEND   'Twill be known.   45

                Enter Wooer.

WOOER
  Alas, sir, where's your daughter?
JAILER   Why do you ask?
WOOER
  O, sir, when did you see her?

55. **mind:** think about, remember; **but . . . day:** i.e., only today

57. **what she was:** i.e., her usual self

59. **innocent:** simpleton; or, perhaps, young child

61. **Nothing but my pity:** perhaps, (1) I want to express **nothing** with regard to her **but my pity;** or, perhaps, (2) what I am about to say is said only with **pity**

65. **No, sir, not well:** For our placement of these words, see longer note, page 261.

74. **miscarrying:** perishing; **on his 'scape:** because of **his** escaping

78. **late:** recently

The death of Phaëthon, son of Phoebus Apollo.
(1.2.96–98; 5.1.98–100)
From Ovid, . . . *Metamorphoseos* . . . (1527).

SECOND FRIEND, ⌜*aside*⌝   How he looks!
JAILER
  This morning.   50
WOOER   Was she well? Was she in health?
  Sir, when did she sleep?
FIRST FRIEND, ⌜*aside*⌝   These are strange questions.
JAILER
  I do not think she was very well—for now
  You make me mind her; but this very day   55
  I asked her questions, and she answered me
  So far from what she was, so childishly,
  So sillily, as if she were a fool,
  An innocent, and I was very angry.
  But what of her, sir?   60
WOOER   Nothing but my pity;
  But you must know it, and as good by me
  As by another that less loves her.
JAILER   Well, sir?
WOOER
  No, sir, not well.   65
FIRST FRIEND   Not right?
SECOND FRIEND   Not well?
WOOER
  'Tis too true; she is mad.
FIRST FRIEND   It cannot be.
WOOER
  Believe you'll find it so.   70
JAILER   I half suspected
  What you told me. The gods comfort her!
  Either this was her love to Palamon,
  Or fear of my miscarrying on his 'scape,
  Or both.   75
WOOER   'Tis likely.
JAILER   But why all this haste, sir?
WOOER
  I'll tell you quickly. As I late was angling

82. **attending sport:** i.e., applying myself to this pastime

84. **gave my ear:** i.e., listened

85. **one that sung:** i.e., someone who sang; **smallness:** softness

86. **angle:** fishing rod

87. **To his own skill:** i.e., to fish by itself

89. **encompassed it:** i.e., surrounded the singer's location

91. **glade:** opening, open space

99. **betray him:** reveal his identity

100. **bevy:** company of ladies

101. **black-eyed maids:** dark-eyed maidens

102. **daffadillies:** daffodils

104. **antic:** grotesque dance

105. **beg his pardon:** i.e., entreat that Palamon be pardoned

108. **handsome:** i.e., tidy (literally, fitting)

111. **tall:** valiant; good-looking

112. **knee-deep:** i.e., knee-high in **rushes and reeds** (line 88)

In the great lake that lies behind the palace,
From the far shore—thick set with reeds and   80
    sedges—
As patiently I was attending sport,
I heard a voice, a shrill one; and, attentive,
I gave my ear, when I might well perceive
'Twas one that sung, and by the smallness of it   85
A boy or woman. I then left my angle
To his own skill, came near, but yet perceived not
Who made the sound, the rushes and the reeds
Had so encompassed it. I laid me down
And listened to the words she ⌜sung,⌝ for then,   90
Through a small glade cut by the fishermen,
I saw it was your daughter.

JAILER   Pray go on, sir.

WOOER
She sung much, but no sense; only I heard her
Repeat this often: "Palamon is gone,   95
Is gone to th' wood to gather mulberries;
I'll find him out tomorrow."

FIRST FRIEND   Pretty soul!

WOOER
"His shackles will betray him; he'll be taken,
And what shall I do then? I'll bring a bevy,   100
A hundred black-eyed maids that love as I do,
With chaplets on their heads of daffadillies,
With cherry lips and cheeks of damask roses,
And all we'll dance an antic 'fore the Duke,
And beg his pardon." Then she talked of you, sir—   105
That you must lose your head tomorrow morning,
And she must gather flowers to bury you,
And see the house made handsome. Then she sung
Nothing but "Willow, willow, willow," and between
Ever was "Palamon, fair Palamon,"   110
And "Palamon was a tall young man." The place
Was knee-deep where she sat; her careless tresses,

113. **wreath . . . rounded:** i.e., were encircled with **a wreath of bulrush; about her stuck:** i.e., on her were fastened

115. **fair nymph:** beautiful water spirit

116. **as Iris:** i.e., like the rainbow, Juno's messenger (See picture, below.)

117–18. **Rings . . . rushes:** Rush **rings** were used by those who could not buy **rings** of gold or silver.

119. **posies:** brief poetic sayings inscribed in gold and silver **rings** (line 117)

125. **made in to:** approached

126. **straight:** straightaway, at once; **sought the flood:** i.e., fell into the water

128. **presently:** at once

129. **to . . . made:** proceeded toward **the city**

132. **cross:** encounter

133. **your brother:** i.e., the Jailer's **brother; stayed:** stopped

134. **scarce:** barely

137. **etc.:** i.e., she sings the rest of the song

Iris, the rainbow. (4.1.116)
From Natale Conti, . . . *Mythologiae* . . . (1616).

A ⌜wreath⌝ of bulrush rounded; about her stuck
Thousand freshwater flowers of several colors,
That methought she appeared like the fair nymph   115
That feeds the lake with waters, or as Iris
Newly dropped down from heaven. Rings she made
Of rushes that grew by, and to 'em spoke
The prettiest posies: "Thus our true love's tied,"
"This you may lose, not me," and many a one;   120
And then she wept, and sung again, and sighed,
And with the same breath smiled and kissed her
    hand.

SECOND FRIEND
    Alas, what pity it is!

WOOER   I made in to her.   125
    She saw me, and straight sought the flood. I saved
        her
    And set her safe to land, when presently
    She slipped away, and to the city made
    With such a cry and swiftness that, believe me,   130
    She left me far behind her. Three or four
    I saw from far off cross her—one of 'em
    I knew to be your brother—where she stayed
    And fell, scarce to be got away. I left them with her
    And hither came to tell you.   135

Enter ⌜*Jailer's*⌝ *Brother,* ⌜*Jailer's*⌝ *Daughter, and others.*

                         Here they are.

DAUGHTER, ⌜*sings*⌝
        May you never more enjoy the light, etc.
    Is not this a fine song?

BROTHER   O, a very fine one.

DAUGHTER   I can sing twenty more.   140

BROTHER   I think you can.

DAUGHTER   Yes, truly can I. I can sing "The Broom"
    and "Bonny Robin." Are not you a tailor?

BROTHER   Yes.

147. **rarely:** early; **I . . . else:** otherwise I **must be** away from home

148. **call the maids:** summon the young girls

149. **by cocklight:** before dawn

149–50. **'Twill never thrive else:** i.e., otherwise it (perhaps the wedding night) will not turn out well

152. **e'en:** just; indeed

154. **Good e'en: good** evening

156. **wench:** familiar form of address to a young woman

159. **cross:** contradict, oppose

160. **distempered:** deranged, disturbed

161. **shows:** seems, appears

166. **for a trick:** i.e., because of **a trick** (The word *trick* had many meanings—stratagem, device, prank, contrivance, distinguishing trait, etc.—and it is here ambiguous.) **look to her:** take care of **her,** beware of what might happen **to her**

167. **gone:** lost, ruined (In Shakespeare's *Love's Labor's Lost,* a pregnant woman is described as "**gone,** . . . two months on her way" [5.2.745–46].) **done:** finished

168. **undone:** ruined (specifically, through seduction)

170. **let 'em all alone:** ignore them

173. **keep close:** i.e., stay quiet

174. **close as a cockle:** proverbial **cockle:** i.e., clam; **must be:** are inevitably

175. **trick on 't:** i.e., knack of begetting **boys**

176. **gelt for musicians:** i.e., castrated to preserve their soprano voices

DAUGHTER   Where's my wedding gown?   145
BROTHER   I'll bring it tomorrow.
DAUGHTER   Do, very rarely, I must be abroad else to
   call the maids and pay the minstrels, for I must
   lose my maidenhead by cocklight. 'Twill never
   thrive else.   150
  Sings.   O fair, O sweet, etc.
BROTHER, ⌜*to Jailer*⌝ You must e'en take it patiently.
JAILER   'Tis true.
DAUGHTER   Good e'en, good men. Pray, did you ever
   hear of one young Palamon?   155
JAILER   Yes, wench, we know him.
DAUGHTER   Is 't not a fine young gentleman?
JAILER   'Tis, love.
BROTHER, ⌜*aside to others*⌝ By no mean cross her; she
   is then distempered ⌜*far*⌝ worse than now she 160
   shows.
FIRST FRIEND, ⌜*to Daughter*⌝ Yes, he's a fine man.
DAUGHTER   O, is he so? You have a sister.
FIRST FRIEND   Yes.
DAUGHTER   But she shall never have him—tell her so— 165
   for a trick that I know; you'd best look to her, for
   if she see him once, she's gone, she's done and
   undone in an hour. All the young maids of our
   town are in love with him, but I laugh at 'em and
   let 'em all alone. Is 't not a wise course?   170
FIRST FRIEND   Yes.
DAUGHTER   There is at least two hundred now with
   child by him—there must be four; yet I keep close
   for all this, close as a cockle; and all these must be
   boys—he has the trick on 't—and at ten years old 175
   they must be all gelt for musicians and sing the
   wars of Theseus.
SECOND FRIEND   This is strange.
DAUGHTER   As ever you heard, but say nothing.
FIRST FRIEND   No.   180

182. **I'll warrant you:** i.e., I promise

183. **dispatch:** take care of and send away; **tickle 't up:** wordplay on "**tickle** it" (bring to an agreeable end) and "**tickle up**" (stir **up,** arouse by tickling)

184. **if his hand be in:** proverbial for "**if** he is in good form"

190. **would she:** i.e., I wish she

195. **Set . . . north:** i.e., use the mariner's **compass** to find magnetic **north**

197. **For . . . alone:** i.e., as **for the** ship's rigging, I'll take care of that; **weigh:** i.e., **weigh** anchor

198. **hearts:** i.e., men of courage (nautical language); **cheerly:** heartily (cry of encouragement among sailors)

199. **Owgh:** a grunting sound to accompany the (supposed) raising of the anchor

200. **fair:** favorable; **Top the bowline:** i.e., tighten the rope that holds the edge of the sail steady

202. **get her in:** i.e., **get** the ship to the land

203. **Up to the top:** i.e., climb to **the top** of the mast

206. **What kenn'st thou:** i.e., what can you see and recognize (Her use of **thou** in addressing the Second Friend suggests that he is pretending to play the part of the ship's **boy** [line 203].)

208. **Bear for it:** i.e., steer the boat toward the **wood** (line 207); **Tack about:** turn the ship's head to the wind

209. **Cynthia:** the moon

DAUGHTER   They come from all parts of the dukedom
  to him; I'll warrant you, he had not so few last
  night as twenty to dispatch. He'll tickle 't up in two
  hours, if his hand be in.

JAILER, ⌜*aside*⌝   She's lost past all cure.   185

BROTHER   Heaven forbid, man!

DAUGHTER, ⌜*to Jailer*⌝   Come hither; you are a wise
  man.

FIRST FRIEND, ⌜*aside*⌝   Does she know him?

⌜SECOND⌝ FRIEND   No; would she did.   190

DAUGHTER   You are master of a ship?

JAILER   Yes.

DAUGHTER   Where's your compass?

JAILER   Here.

DAUGHTER   Set it to th' north. And now direct your   195
  course to th' wood, where Palamon lies longing for
  me. For the tackling, let me alone.—Come, weigh,
  my hearts, cheerly.

ALL, ⌜*as if sailing a ship*⌝   Owgh, owgh, owgh!—'Tis up!
  The wind's fair!—Top the bowline!—Out with the   200
  main sail! Where's your whistle, master?

BROTHER   Let's get her in!

JAILER   Up to the top, boy!

BROTHER   Where's the pilot?

FIRST FRIEND   Here.   205

DAUGHTER   What kenn'st thou?

SECOND FRIEND   A fair wood.

DAUGHTER   Bear for it, master. ⌜*Tack*⌝ about!
  Sings.

> *When Cynthia with her borrowed light, etc.*

> *They exit.*

4.2 Emilia examines miniature portraits of Palamon and Arcite and is unable to choose between
them. Theseus, hearing descriptions of the knights
who have arrived from Thebes for the coming battle, is eager to see the men themselves.

───────────

0 SD. **pictures:** i.e., portrait miniatures of Palamon and Arcite

1. **Yet I may:** i.e., I could still

2. **else:** otherwise

4. **for me:** because of me

12. **coy:** i.e., modest (The word **coy** described
someone unresponsive to familiar advances.)

14. **quick:** lively

15. **Love:** Cupid, the boy-god of **Love** (frequently
described as sitting **smiling** in the lover's **eye** [line
13])

17. **such another:** i.e., **such** a smile; or, perhaps,
such an **eye; wanton:** perhaps, playful, flirtatious;
Ganymede: a beautiful boy kidnapped by **Jove** (See
picture, page 220.) **Ganymede** was made the gods'
cupbearer, and was later transformed into the **constellation** Aquarius (line 20).

18. **with:** It is unclear how this preposition functions here, but one possible reading of the sentence
is "**with such** a smile **wanton Ganymede set Jove
afire.**"

19. **goodly:** beautiful

20. **constellation:** See note to line 17, above.
brow: forehead

21. **carries:** exhibits, displays

(continued)

Scene 2

Enter Emilia alone, with two pictures.

EMILIA
Yet I may bind those wounds up that must open
And bleed to death for my sake else. I'll choose,
And end their strife. Two such young handsome men
Shall never fall for me; their weeping mothers,
Following the dead cold ashes of their sons,   5
Shall never curse my cruelty.
⌜*Looks at one of the pictures.*⌝
                    Good heaven,
What a sweet face has Arcite! If wise Nature,
With all her best endowments, all those beauties
She sows into the births of noble bodies,   10
Were here a mortal woman, and had in her
The coy denials of young maids, yet doubtless
She would run mad for this man. What an eye,
Of what a fiery sparkle and quick sweetness,
Has this young prince! Here Love himself sits   15
    smiling;
Just such another wanton Ganymede
Set ⌜Jove⌝ afire with, and enforced the god
Snatch up the goodly boy and set him by him,
A shining constellation. What a brow,   20
Of what a spacious majesty, he carries,
Arched like the great-eyed Juno's but far sweeter,
Smoother than Pelops' shoulder! Fame and Honor,
Methinks, from hence as from a promontory
Pointed in heaven, should clap their wings and sing   25
To all the under world the loves and fights
Of gods and such men near 'em.
                    ⌜*Looks at the other picture.*⌝
                    Palamon
Is but his foil, to him a mere dull shadow;
He's swart and meager, of an eye as heavy   30

23. **Smoother . . . shoulder:** i.e., **smoother than** ivory (The gods provided Pelops with an ivory **shoulder** to replace a missing one. See Ovid, *Metamorphoses* 6.403–11.)

24. **hence:** i.e., Arcite's **brow** (line 20)

25. **Pointed:** i.e., reaching its peak

26. **under world:** i.e., the earth below them

27. **near 'em:** i.e., like **gods**

29. **his foil:** i.e., that which sets him off to advantage (as if Arcite were a precious jewel on the **dull** background provided by Palamon); **to him:** i.e., in comparison to Arcite

30. **swart:** swarthy; **meager:** thin, emaciated; **heavy:** doleful, gloomy

31. **still:** i.e., lethargic; **temper:** temperament

32. **stirring:** excitement, passion

33. **this:** i.e., Arcite's; **sharpness:** intellectual acuteness; **smile:** perhaps, trace

34. **errors:** flaws; **become:** look well on, suit

35. **Narcissus:** See note to 2.2.136–37. **sad:** serious, sorrowful; **heavenly:** i.e., divinely beautiful

36. **bent:** direction; **fancy:** amorous inclination

38. **choice:** power of choosing; **lewdly:** vilely

39. **On my knees:** She may or may not kneel at this point.

40–41. **alone / And only:** solely, uniquely

43. **maid:** maiden; **cross:** oppose, go counter to

46. **brown:** dark

47. **is complexion:** i.e., is the (only) appearance (that appeals to me)

48. **a changeling:** i.e., an ugly child left by the

(continued)

178

As if he had lost his mother; a still temper,
No stirring in him, no alacrity;
Of all this sprightly sharpness not a smile.
Yet these that we count errors may become him;
Narcissus was a sad boy but a heavenly.   35
O, who can find the bent of woman's fancy?
I am a fool; my reason is lost in me;
I have no choice, and I have lied so lewdly
That women ought to beat me. On my knees
I ask thy pardon: Palamon, thou art alone   40
And only beautiful, and these the eyes,
These the bright lamps of beauty, that command
And threaten love, and what young maid dare cross
   'em?
What a bold gravity, and yet inviting,   45
Has this brown manly face! O Love, this only
From this hour is complexion. Lie there, Arcite.
                    ⌜*She puts aside his picture.*⌝
Thou art a changeling to him, a mere gypsy,
And this the noble body. I am sotted,
Utterly lost. My virgin's faith has fled me.   50
For if my brother but even now had asked me
Whether I loved, I had run mad for Arcite.
Now, if my sister, more for Palamon.
Stand both together. Now, come ask me, brother.
Alas, I know not! Ask me now, sweet sister.   55
I may go look! What a mere child is Fancy,
That, having two fair gauds of equal sweetness,
Cannot distinguish, but must cry for both.

                Enter ⌜*a*⌝ *Gentleman.*

How now, sir?
GENTLEMAN   From the noble duke, your brother,   60
   Madam, I bring you news: the knights are come.
EMILIA
To end the quarrel?

fairies in exchange for a stolen child; **to him:** i.e., in comparison with him; **gypsy:** dark-skinned person (See longer note, page 262.)

49. **this:** i.e., Palamon; **sotted:** besotted, rendered stupid

50. **faith:** i.e., constancy

51. **my brother:** i.e., Theseus; **but even now:** i.e., only this moment

52. **Whether:** which of the two; **had:** i.e., would have

53. **sister:** i.e., **sister had asked** (line 51); **more:** i.e., (**I had run mad** [line 52]) even **more**

54. **both:** i.e., **both** pictures

56. **may go look:** i.e., have no answer; **Fancy:** the personification here of amorous inclination

57. **fair gauds:** pretty playthings; **sweetness:** delightfulness

58. **distinguish:** i.e., prefer (one to the other)

59. **How now:** a question about the person's well-being or intentions

65. **Diana:** See note to 2.5.71.

66. **unspotted:** unblemished

70. **joy:** rejoice

71. **unhappy:** misfortune-causing, unlucky

73. **by any means: by all means**

79. **both:** i.e., **love both**

80. **So:** in order that

82. **awhile:** (for) a short time

87. **speak:** i.e., tell us, declare

90. **braver:** finer

GENTLEMAN   Yes.
EMILIA   Would I might end first!
  What sins have I committed, chaste Diana,   65
  That my unspotted youth must now be soiled
  With blood of princes, and my chastity
  Be made the altar where the lives of lovers—
  Two greater and two better never yet
  Made mothers joy—must be the sacrifice   70
  To my unhappy beauty?

Enter Theseus, Hippolyta, Pirithous and Attendants.

THESEUS, ⌜*to Attendant*⌝ Bring 'em in
  Quickly, by any means; I long to see 'em.
  ⌜*To Emilia.*⌝ Your two contending lovers are
    returned,   75
  And with them their fair knights. Now, my fair
    sister,
  You must love one of them.
EMILIA   I had rather both,
  So neither for my sake should fall untimely.   80
THESEUS
  Who saw 'em?
PIRITHOUS   I awhile.
GENTLEMAN   And I.

Enter ⌜a⌝ Messenger.

THESEUS
  From whence come you, sir?
MESSENGER   From the knights.   85
THESEUS   Pray
    speak,
  You that have seen them, what they are.
MESSENGER   I will, sir,
  And truly what I think. Six braver spirits   90
  Than these they have brought, if we judge by the
    outside,

94. **seeming:** appearance
95. **stout:** formidable; valiant
96. **say:** declare
98. **proud of:** pleased with, gratified by
100. **as:** like; **heated:** angry
104. **curious:** beautifully made
104–5. **when . . . with:** i.e., **with** which to ratify his intentions **when** he is displeased (as if affixing a seal to a document)
105. **Better:** i.e., a **better sword** (line 103)
108. **Yet a:** i.e., **yet** he is a
111. **speak:** describe
113. **greater:** of higher social rank; **show:** appearance (with possible wordplay on "spectacle" or "display" [of weapons and other military accoutrements])
114. **ornament:** trappings
115. **he spoke:** i.e., the messenger **spoke**
118. **what he fights for:** i.e., love; **so apter:** i.e., therefore readier
124. **temper:** temperament; **yellow:** blond
125. **Hard-haired:** of uncertain meaning; **tods:** bushes
126. **to undo:** i.e., to be untwined (if the reference is to the hair); or, to be destroyed (if the reference is to the knight); **with thunder:** i.e., even with a thunderbolt
127. **livery:** distinctive badge; **the warlike maid:** perhaps, the goddess Athena; or, perhaps, the goddess Bellona (both of whom are pictured in Roman art wearing a helmet and armor) See pictures, pages 154 and 248.

I never saw nor read of. He that stands
In the first place with Arcite, by his seeming,
Should be a stout man, by his face a prince—   95
His very looks so say him; his complexion
Nearer a brown than black—stern and yet noble—
Which shows him hardy, fearless, proud of dangers;
The circles of his eyes show ⌜fire⌝ within him,
And as a heated lion, so he looks.   100
His hair hangs long behind him, black and shining
Like ravens' wings; his shoulders broad and strong,
Armed long and round; and on his thigh a sword
Hung by a curious baldric, when he frowns
To seal his will with. Better, o' my conscience,   105
Was never soldier's friend.

THESEUS   Thou hast well described him.

PIRITHOUS   Yet a great
   deal short,
Methinks, of him that's first with Palamon.   110

THESEUS
   Pray speak him, friend.

PIRITHOUS   I guess he is a prince too,
   And, if it may be, greater; for his show
   Has all the ornament of honor in 't:
   He's somewhat bigger than the knight he spoke of,   115
   But of a face far sweeter; his complexion
   Is, as a ripe grape, ruddy. He has felt
   Without doubt what he fights for, and so apter
   To make this cause his own. In 's face appears
   All the fair hopes of what he undertakes,   120
   And when he's angry, then a settled valor,
   Not tainted with extremes, runs through his body
   And guides his arm to brave things. Fear he cannot;
   He shows no such soft temper. His head's yellow,
   Hard-haired and curled, thick-twined like ivy ⌜tods,⌝   125
   Not to undo with thunder. In his face
   The livery of the warlike maid appears,

128. **red and white:** considered the colors of the beautiful female complexion

129. **rolling:** rapidly moving

130. **ever:** throughout all time

131. **character:** distinctive sign

132. **fit:** i.e., appropriate

135. **Sounds:** resounds

145. **they:** i.e., the freckles (See longer note, page 262.) **sweet:** charming

148. **disposed:** placed, arranged

149. **white-haired:** blond

150. **wanton white:** perhaps, like the blond hair of children

151. **auburn:** yellowish or brownish; **nimble-set:** i.e., agile

153. **Lined:** strengthened, reinforced

154. **new-conceived:** newly pregnant

155. **labor:** with wordplay on childbearing (from **new-conceived,** line 154)

156. **still:** (1) always; (2) not in motion

157. **stirs:** moves

Pure red and white, for yet no beard has blessed him.
And in his rolling eyes sits Victory,
As if she ever meant to ⌜crown⌝ his valor.   130
His nose stands high, a character of honor;
His red lips, after fights, are fit for ladies.

EMILIA
Must these men die too?

PIRITHOUS   When he speaks, his tongue
Sounds like a trumpet. All his lineaments   135
Are as a man would wish 'em, strong and clean.
He wears a well-steeled axe, the staff of gold;
His age some five-and-twenty.

MESSENGER   There's another—
A little man, but of a tough soul, seeming   140
As great as any; fairer promises
In such a body yet I never looked on.

PIRITHOUS
O, he that's freckle-faced?

MESSENGER   The same, my lord.
Are they not sweet ones?   145

PIRITHOUS   Yes, they are well.

MESSENGER   Methinks,
Being so few, and well disposed, they show
Great and fine art in nature. He's white-haired—
Not wanton white, but such a manly color   150
Next to an auburn; tough and nimble-set,
Which shows an active soul. His arms are brawny,
Lined with strong sinews—to the shoulder-piece
Gently they swell, like women new-conceived,
Which speaks him prone to labor, never fainting   155
Under the weight of arms; stout-hearted still,
But when he stirs, a tiger. He's grey-eyed,
Which yields compassion where he conquers; sharp
To spy advantages, and where he finds 'em,
He's swift to make 'em his. He does no wrongs,   160

161. **takes:** submits to, undergoes

163. **shows:** appears, looks like

164. **oak:** i.e., the garland of **oak** awarded for valor in battle (See picture, below.)

165. **favor:** gift from a **lady** to her knight to be worn conspicuously

167. **charging-staff:** presumably a lance used by a horseman in battle

171. **men:** i.e., real **men,** heroes

174. **Bravely about:** i.e., splendidly (if they were) fighting about

178. **steeled 'em:** nerved or strengthened them

180. **the field:** i.e., management of **the field** of honor (the place on which the combat will be held); **order:** prepare

183. **stay:** wait

184. **Their fame:** i.e., the reports (I have just heard) about them

185. **royal:** generous, munificent

186. **want no bravery:** lack **no** splendor

An oak garland. (4.2.164)
From Claude Guichard,
Funerailles et diverses manieres . . . (1581).

Nor takes none. He's round-faced, and when he
   smiles
He shows a lover; when he frowns, a soldier.
About his head he wears the winner's oak,
And in it stuck the favor of his lady.   165
His age some six-and-thirty. In his hand
He bears a charging-staff embossed with silver.

THESEUS
Are they all thus?

PIRITHOUS   They are all the sons of honor.

THESEUS
Now, as I have a soul, I long to see 'em.—   170
Lady, you shall see men fight now.

HIPPOLYTA   I wish it,
But not the cause, my lord. They would show
Bravely about the titles of two kingdoms;
'Tis pity love should be so tyrannous.—   175
O, my soft-hearted sister, what think you?
Weep not till they weep blood. Wench, it must be.

THESEUS, ⌜*to Emilia*⌝
You have steeled 'em with your beauty. (⌜*To
   Pirithous.*⌝) Honored friend,
To you I give the field; pray order it   180
Fitting the persons that must use it.

PIRITHOUS   Yes, sir.

THESEUS
Come, I'll go visit 'em. I cannot stay—
Their fame has fired me so—till they appear.
Good friend, be royal.   185

PIRITHOUS   There shall want no bravery.
                  ⌜*All but Emilia*⌝ *exit.*

EMILIA
Poor wench, go weep, for whosoever wins
Loses a noble cousin for thy sins.

                         She exits.

4.3 The jailer's daughter is diagnosed by the doctor as suffering from love melancholy. He prescribes that the daughter's wooer, who still wishes to marry her, begin to court her, pretending to be Palamon.

---

1. **distraction:** mental derangement, insanity

1–2. **time of the moon:** Lunacy, or intermittent insanity, was thought to be brought about by changes **of the moon.**

2. **other some:** others

3. **continually:** i.e., not intermittently; **harmless distemper:** i.e., derangement causing no harm to others

5. **drinking:** See 3.2.26–27: "Food took I none . . . ; / Sipped some water."

6. **what . . . she's about:** i.e., whatever disjointed **matter** she talks about

7. **lards it:** is inserted into it; **that she farces:** i.e., so **that she** stuffs

8. **withal:** with it; **fits it to:** i.e., makes it fit; **question:** subject of discussion

11. **burden on 't:** i.e., refrain of the song

12. **down-a:** a common refrain

13–14. **fantastical:** fanciful

14. **as ever . . . legs:** Proverbial: "**As** good a man **as ever** went **upon legs.**"

15–16. **Dido, Aeneas:** In Shakespeare's accounts of **Dido** and **Aeneas,** their spirits live together in Elysium, the abode of the blessed in the next world. (See longer note, page 262.)

19. **E'en thus:** exactly this way

(continued)

Scene 3

Enter Jailer, Wooer, Doctor.

DOCTOR Her distraction is more at some time of the
moon than at other some, is it not?

JAILER She is continually in a harmless distemper,
sleeps little, altogether without appetite, save often
drinking, dreaming of another world, and a better;   5
and what broken piece of matter soe'er she's about,
the name *Palamon* lards it, that she farces ev'ry
business withal, fits it to every question.

Enter ⌜Jailer's⌝ Daughter.

Look where she comes; you shall perceive her
behavior.   ⌜*They stand aside.*⌝   10

DAUGHTER I have forgot it quite. The burden on 't was
"down-a down-a," and penned by no worse man
than Geraldo, Emilia's schoolmaster. He's as fantastical, too, as ever he may go upon 's legs, for in
the next world will Dido see Palamon, and then   15
will she be out of love with Aeneas.

DOCTOR, ⌜*aside to Jailer and Wooer*⌝ What stuff's here?
Poor soul.

JAILER E'en thus all day long.

DAUGHTER Now for this charm that I told you of, you   20
must bring a piece of silver on the tip of your
tongue, or no ferry; then if it be your chance to
come where the blessed spirits ⌜are,⌝ there's a
sight now! We maids that have our livers perished,
cracked to pieces with love, we shall come there,   25
and do nothing all day long but pick flowers with
Proserpine. Then will I make Palamon a nosegay;
then let him mark me then.

DOCTOR How prettily she's amiss! Note her a little
further.   30

DAUGHTER Faith, I'll tell you, sometime we go to

20. **charm:** magic spell

21–22. **bring . . . ferry:** In ancient Rome, **a piece of silver** was placed **on the tongue** of a corpse to pay the ferryman at the river Styx in the Underworld.

22. **chance:** fortune

23. **where the blessed spirits are:** i.e., Elysium

24. **maids:** maidens; **perished:** destroyed

27. **Proserpine:** i.e., Proserpina, abducted by the king of the Underworld while she was "**pick**[ing] **flowers**"

28. **mark:** pay attention to, notice

29. **Note:** observe

32. **barley-break:** a game played by couples in which the couple in the middle (called "hell") tried to catch the others; **sore:** oppressively severe

33. **i' th' other place:** i.e., hell

35. **shrewd:** harsh; **measure:** i.e., punishment (literally, treatment meted out, allotted); **one:** someone

37. **Jupiter:** i.e., Jove (See picture, page 150.)

39. **cutpurses:** i.e., pickpockets

40. **enough:** perhaps, cooked sufficiently

41. **coins:** invents, fabricates

42–43. **got . . . child:** impregnated young women

46. **in troth:** truly

48. **to be rid on 't:** i.e., **to be** free of that **punishment** (line 46)

50. **this fancy:** i.e., the fiction that she is in hell

50–51. **engraffed:** implanted (in the mind)

52. **melancholy:** melancholia, an illness thought to result from an excess of black bile in the body

(continued)

barley-break, we of the blessed. Alas, 'tis a sore life
they have i' th' other place—such burning, frying,
boiling, hissing, howling, chatt'ring, cursing—O,
they have shrewd measure, take heed! If one be   35
mad, or hang or drown themselves, thither they
go, Jupiter bless us, and there shall we be put in
a cauldron of lead and usurers' grease, amongst a
whole million of cutpurses, and there boil like a
gammon of bacon that will never be enough.   40

DOCTOR   How her brains coins!

DAUGHTER   Lords and courtiers that have got maids
with child, they are in this place. They shall stand
in fire up to the navel and in ice up to th' heart, and
there th' offending part burns and the deceiving   45
part freezes: in troth, a very grievous punishment,
as one would think, for such a trifle. Believe me,
one would marry a leprous witch to be rid on 't, I'll
assure you.

DOCTOR   How she continues this fancy! 'Tis not an en-   50
graffed madness, but a most thick and profound
melancholy.

DAUGHTER   To hear there a proud lady and a proud city
wife howl together—I were a beast an I'd call it
good sport. One cries "O this smoke!" ⌜th' other,⌝   55
"This fire!"; one cries, "O, that ever I did it behind
the arras!" and then howls; th' other curses a suing
fellow and her garden house.

   Sings.

      I will be true, my stars, my fate, etc.
                              Daughter exits.

JAILER   What think you of her, sir?   60

DOCTOR   I think she has a perturbed mind, which I
cannot minister to.

JAILER   Alas, what then?

DOCTOR   Understand you she ever affected any man
ere she beheld Palamon?   65

53. **there:** i.e., in hell

53–54. **city wife:** wife of a **city** merchant (The **lady,** married to a lord, would be appalled at being **together** with **a city wife.**)

54. **were a beast an:** would be **a beast** if

55. **good sport:** i.e., amusing, entertaining

57. **arras:** hanging tapestry; **suing:** i.e., seductive

58. **garden house:** a building in a **garden,** often associated with assignations

62. **minister:** give aid

64. **affected:** felt affection for, was attracted to

68–69. **would ... on 't:** **would** think I made a good bargain **penn'orth:** pennyworth, bargain

69. **to give:** i.e., if I gave; **state:** estate

70. **stood unfeignedly:** were genuinely

72. **That ... eye:** i.e., **her** overindulgence in gazing (at Palamon)

72–73. **distempered:** disturbed, disordered

74. **execute ... faculties:** i.e., carry out their destined functions

75. **vagary:** wandering state

78. **her friend:** i.e., **you** who are **her friend**

80. **commune:** talk

83. **pranks and friskins:** i.e., playthings

84. **green:** youthful

85–86. **stuck in:** adorned with, covered with

86. **is mistress of:** possesses

87. **thereto:** in addition; **make ... of:** i.e., add

87–88. **compounded odors:** i.e., perfumes

88. **grateful:** pleasing; **sense:** i.e., **sense** of smell

89. **become:** be appropriate to

90. **sweet:** fragrant

(continued)

JAILER I was once, sir, in great hope she had fixed her
liking on this gentleman, my friend.

WOOER I did think so, too, and would account I had a
great penn'orth on 't to give half my state that both
she and I, at this present, stood unfeignedly on the   70
same terms.

DOCTOR That intemp'rate surfeit of her eye hath distempered the other senses. They may return and
settle again to execute their preordained faculties,
but they are now in a most extravagant vagary.   75
This you must do: confine her to a place where
the light may rather seem to steal in than be
permitted.—Take upon you, young sir, her friend,
the name of Palamon; say you come to eat with
her, and to commune of love. This will catch her   80
attention, for this her mind beats upon; other
objects that are inserted 'tween her mind and eye
become the pranks and friskins of her madness.
Sing to her such green songs of love as she says
Palamon hath sung in prison. Come to her stuck   85
in as sweet flowers as the season is mistress of,
and thereto make an addition of some other compounded odors which are grateful to the sense.
All this shall become Palamon, for Palamon can
sing, and Palamon is sweet and ev'ry good thing.   90
Desire to eat with her, ⌜carve⌝ her, drink to her, and
still among intermingle your petition of grace and
acceptance into her favor. Learn what maids have
been her companions and playferes, and let them
repair to her with *Palamon* in their mouths, and   95
appear with tokens, as if they suggested for him.—
It is a falsehood she is in, which is with falsehoods to be combated. This may bring her to eat,
to sleep, and reduce what's now out of square in
her into their former law and regiment. I have seen   100
it approved, how many times I know not, but to

91. **Desire:** express a wish; **carve her:** i.e., **carve to her,** serve food to **her** at table

92. **among:** all the while; **petition of:** supplication for; **grace:** good opinion

94. **playferes:** playmates

95. **repair:** go

96. **tokens:** love tokens, keepsakes; **suggested for him:** i.e., tempted her on his behalf

97. **falsehood:** i.e., delusion

97–98. **falsehoods:** lies, deceptions

99. **reduce:** bring back; **out of square:** disordered

100. **regiment:** rule

101. **it approved:** i.e., this method demonstrated; **how . . . know not:** i.e., countless **times**

103. **passages:** proceedings, transactions

103–4. **come in:** intervene

104. **appliance:** treatment (It is unclear what treatment the Doctor has in mind.)

105. **success:** final result, outcome; **doubt:** fear

106. **comfort:** relief, satisfaction

A conjurer. (3.5.99)
From Laurentius Wolffgang Woyt, . . .
Emblematischer Parnassus . . . (1728–30).

make the number more, I have great hope in this.
I will between the passages of this project come
in with my appliance. Let us put it in execution
and hasten the success, which doubt not will bring   105
forth comfort.

                                                They exit.

THE TWO NOBLE KINSMEN

ACT 5

5.1 In preparation for the coming confrontation, Arcite and his companion knights pray for victory at the altar of Mars; Palamon and his knights pray to Venus to win the love of Emilia; and Emilia and her women pray to Diana that she might remain a virgin in Diana's service.

---

2. **Tender:** offer, proffer
4. **commend:** present
5. **no due be wanting:** i.e., nothing owed (**to those above us**) **be** lacking
6. **They:** Arcite, Palamon, and their knights; **in hand:** in process; **will honor:** i.e., that **will honor**
10. **german foes: foes** who are kinsmen
11. **nearness:** kinship, close friendship, intimacy
12. **dove-like:** gently, in peace
16. **help be:** i.e., support should or must **be**
17. **regard:** watch over; or, perhaps, observe

Mars, the god of war. (1.1.68; 1.2.21;
2.2.24; 5.1.42, 68; 5.4.127)
From Vincenzo Cartari, *Le imagini de i dei de gli antichi* . . . (1587).

ACT 5

Scene 1

Flourish. Enter Theseus, Pirithous, Hippolyta,
⌐*and*¬ *Attendants.* ⌐*Three altars set up onstage.*¬

THESEUS
  Now let 'em enter and before the gods
  Tender their holy prayers. Let the temples
  Burn bright with sacred fires, and the altars
  In hallowed clouds commend their swelling incense
  To those above us. Let no due be wanting.   5
  They have a noble work in hand will honor
  The very powers that love 'em.
PIRITHOUS   Sir, they enter.

*Flourish of cornets. Enter Palamon and Arcite
and their Knights.*

THESEUS
  You valiant and strong-hearted enemies,
  You royal german foes, that this day come   10
  To blow that nearness out that flames between you,
  Lay by your anger for an hour and, dove-like,
  Before the holy altars of your helpers,
  The all-feared gods, bow down your stubborn
    bodies.   15
  Your ire is more than mortal; so your help be.
  And as the gods regard you, fight with justice.

19. **part:** divide

21. **glass is running:** i.e., an irreversible process is in motion (literally, sand **is running** through the hourglass)

23. **show:** appear, seem

25. **another:** i.e., the other **eye** (line 24)

27. **parcel:** a part

28. **tender:** regard, value

29. **in labor:** laboring (as in childbirth)

30. **ancient:** former, bygone; **kindred:** kinship

32. **confound:** destroy

33. **port:** bring to port

34. **Limiter:** i.e., the One who sets bounds

36. **turn:** i.e., leave

41. **lovers:** i.e., dear friends, those who love me and whom I love; **my sacrifices:** i.e., those who may be sacrificed in my cause

43. **apprehension:** anticipation

44. **still:** always; **of it:** i.e., **of fear** (line 43)

45. **profession:** (military) calling

46. **Require:** ask, request

47. **breath:** i.e., endurance (literally, power of breathing)

48. **go on:** advance

I'll leave you to your prayers, and betwixt you
I part my wishes.

PIRITHOUS   Honor crown the worthiest!   20
                              Theseus and his train exit.

PALAMON
The glass is running now that cannot finish
Till one of us expire. Think you but thus,
That were there aught in me which strove to show
Mine enemy in this business, were 't one eye
Against another, arm oppressed by arm,   25
I would destroy th' offender, coz—I would
Though parcel of myself. Then from this gather
How I should tender you.

ARCITE   I am in labor
To push your name, your ancient love, our kindred   30
Out of my memory, and i' th' selfsame place
To seat something I would confound. So hoist we
The sails that must these vessels port even where
The heavenly Limiter pleases.

PALAMON   You speak well.   35
Before I turn, let me embrace thee, cousin.

                              ⌜*They embrace.*⌝

This I shall never do again.

ARCITE   One farewell.

PALAMON
Why, let it be so. Farewell, coz.

ARCITE   Farewell, sir.   40
                              Palamon and his Knights exit.

Knights, kinsmen, lovers, yea, my sacrifices,
True worshippers of Mars, whose spirit in you
Expels the seeds of fear and th' apprehension
Which still is ⌜father of⌝ it, go with me
Before the god of our profession. There   45
Require of him the hearts of lions and
The breath of tigers, yea, the fierceness too,
Yea, the speed also—to go on, I mean;

50. **feat:** deeds

51. **sticks:** i.e., is fastened, adheres

52. **The queen of flowers:** perhaps, the rose (long associated with virgins such as Emilia [See note to line 171 SD, below.]) **intercession:** prayer

53. **camp:** i.e., military **camp; cistern:** vessel

54. **Brimmed:** filled to the brim

57. **Green Neptune:** i.e., the ocean (**Neptune** is the Roman god of the sea.) **purple:** crimson

58. **prewarn:** warn of in advance, forecast

59. **Unearthèd:** unburied

61. **The . . . foison:** i.e., fields of grain **teeming:** prolific **foison:** plentiful harvest (Ceres is the Roman goddess of grain.)

62. **armipotent:** mighty; **blue clouds:** perhaps, **clouds** of smoke from battle

63. **masoned:** i.e., stone

64. **girths:** i.e., walls (For a picture of the walled city of Athens, see page 158.) **pupil:** disciple

65. **thy drum:** See note to 1.1.211. **instruct:** furnish, equip

66. **laud:** praise

67. **streamer:** flag, banner

68. **styled:** named, called

69 SD. **as formerly:** See 55 SD, above. **as the burst:** i.e., **as** if it were the violent outbreak

70. **enormous:** monstrous, disordered

71. **o'er-rank:** excessively large; or, rotten

72. **titles:** claims, rights; **that:** i.e., who

74. **pleurisy:** i.e., superabundance (literally, an illness thought to be caused by an excess of humors)

76. **design:** goal, purpose, intent

Else wish we to be snails. You know my prize
Must be dragged out of blood; force and great feat   50
Must put my garland on, where she sticks,
The queen of flowers. Our intercession, then,
Must be to him that makes the camp a cistern
Brimmed with the blood of men. Give me your aid,
And bend your spirits towards him.   55
> *They ⌐go to Mars's altar, fall on*
> *their faces before it, and then⌐ kneel.*

Thou mighty one, that with thy power hast turned
Green Neptune into purple, ⌐whose approach⌐
Comets prewarn, whose havoc in vast field
Unearthèd skulls proclaim, whose breath blows
   down   60
The teeming Ceres' foison, who dost pluck
With hand armipotent from forth blue clouds
The masoned turrets, that both mak'st and break'st
The stony girths of cities; me thy pupil,
Youngest follower of thy drum, instruct this day   65
With military skill, that to thy laud
I may advance my streamer, and by thee
Be styled the lord o' th' day. Give me, great Mars,
Some token of thy pleasure.
> *Here they fall on their faces as formerly, and*
> *there is heard clanging of armor, with a short*
> *thunder, as the burst of a battle, whereupon*
> *they all rise and bow to the altar.*

O, great corrector of enormous times,   70
Shaker of o'er-rank states, thou grand decider
Of dusty and old titles, that heal'st with blood
The earth when it is sick, and ⌐cur'st⌐ the world
O' th' pleurisy of people, I do take
Thy signs auspiciously, and in thy name   75
To my design march boldly.—Let us go.   *They exit.*

76 SD. the former observance: i.e., the same rituals as performed by Arcite and his knights

77–78. Our stars . . . extinct: i.e., we **must today** be victorious or die   **stars:** i.e., fates   **glister:** sparkle   **extinct:** extinguished

78. argument: subject of contention

79. goddess of it: i.e., **Venus, goddess of love** (See picture, page 156.)

81. free: generous, magnanimous

82. hazard: peril, risk of loss or harm

84. our party: our side (in the coming battle)

87. weep: i.e., make him **weep** for love

88. choke . . . drum: i.e., silence threats of war

89. alarm: call to arms

90. flourish with: i.e., brandish

91. Before: i.e., more quickly than; **Apollo:** See note to 1.4.53. **the king:** i.e., a king

93. Stale gravity: aged seriousness, i.e., old men; **polled:** i.e., bald

94. Whose youth: i.e., who in his **youth; wanton:** naughty

95. skipped: escaped; **flame:** wordplay on **flame** as a bonfire and as the passion of love

96. scorn: mockery

97. young . . . love: i.e., youthful **love** songs

98. Phoebus: **Phoebus** Apollo, the sun god

99. flames: See note to **flame,** line 95 above.

99–100. heavenly fires . . . thine him: For the two myths alluded to here, see longer note, page 263.

100. The huntress: the goddess Diana

101. moist: Diana was goddess of the moon, which, in *Hamlet* 1.1.130, is called "the **moist** star." **cold:** chaste

(continued)

204

Enter Palamon and his Knights,
with the former observance.

PALAMON

　Our stars must glister with new fire, or be
　Today extinct. Our argument is love,
　Which, if the goddess of it grant, she gives
　Victory too. Then blend your spirits with mine,　　80
　You whose free nobleness do make my cause
　Your personal hazard. To the goddess Venus
　Commend we our proceeding, and implore
　Her power unto our party.

　　　　　　Here they ⌜*go to Venus's altar, fall on*
　　　　　　their faces before it, and then ⌝ *kneel.*

　Hail, sovereign queen of secrets, who hast power　　85
　To call the fiercest tyrant from his rage
　And weep unto a girl; that hast the might
　Even with an eye-glance to choke Mars's drum
　And turn th' alarm to whispers; that canst make
　A cripple flourish with his crutch, and cure him　　90
　Before Apollo; that mayst force the king
　To be his subject's vassal, and induce
　Stale gravity to dance. The polled bachelor,
　Whose youth, like wanton boys through bonfires,
　Have skipped thy flame, at seventy thou canst catch,　　95
　And make him, to the scorn of his hoarse throat,
　Abuse young lays of love. What godlike power
　Hast thou not power upon? To Phoebus thou
　Add'st flames hotter than his; the heavenly fires
　Did scorch his mortal son, thine him. The huntress,　　100
　All moist and cold, some say, began to throw
　Her bow away and sigh. Take to thy grace
　Me, thy vowed soldier, who do bear thy yoke
　As 'twere a wreath of roses, yet is heavier
　Than lead itself, stings more than nettles.　　105
　I have never been foul-mouthed against thy law,

102. **sigh:** i.e., **sigh** for love (Diana, in an earlier form—the Titan moon goddess Selene—fell desperately in love with the shepherd boy Endymion.) **to thy grace:** i.e., into your favor

107. **not:** i.e., **not** have **revealed** them

108. **kenned:** known; **were:** existed

108–9. **practiced / Upon:** i.e., seduced

110. **liberal:** licentious; **wits:** clever persons

111. **betray:** i.e., reveal (the indiscretions of)

112. **simp'ring:** affected, smirking

113. **large confessors:** i.e., those who boast of their gross sins (presumably of sexual conquests)

117. **brided:** married; **thy:** Venus's

118. **dust:** (1) flesh; (2) dead or decayed matter

119. **screwed:** twisted; **square:** sturdy; **round:** around (with wordplay on **round** and **square**)

121–22. **from his . . . their spheres:** i.e., **had almost** pulled the sockets away **from his** protuberant **eyes globy:** globular **spheres:** positions

123. **anatomy:** (1) withered, emaciated creature; (2) corpse dried to skin and bone

124. **fair fere:** beautiful spouse

126. **Brief:** i.e., in **brief,** in short

127. **prate:** boast; **done:** i.e., seduced women

128. **have not:** i.e., **have not** done what they boasted of

129. **would:** i.e., want to (love / or seduce a woman); **rejoicer:** perhaps, comforter

130. **that tells close offices:** who reveals secrets

131. **concealments:** things hidden

132. **Such a one:** i.e., **such a** person as I have described myself (lines 106–15, 126–29)

(continued)

Ne'er revealed secret, for I knew none—would not,
Had I kenned all that were. I never practiced
Upon man's wife, nor would the libels read
Of liberal wits. I never at great feasts   110
Sought to betray a beauty, but have blushed
At simp'ring sirs that did. I have been harsh
To large confessors, and have hotly asked them
If they had mothers—I had one, a woman,
And women 'twere they wronged. I knew a man   115
Of eighty winters—this I told them—who
A lass of fourteen brided; 'twas thy power
To put life into dust. The agèd cramp
Had screwed his square foot round;
The gout had knit his fingers into knots;   120
Torturing convulsions from his globy eyes
Had almost drawn their spheres, that what was life
In him seemed torture. This anatomy
Had by his young fair fere a boy, and I
Believed it was his, for she swore it was,   125
And who would not believe her? Brief, I am
To those that prate and have done, no companion;
To those that boast and have not, a defier;
To those that would and cannot, a rejoicer.
Yea, him I do not love that tells close offices   130
The foulest way, nor names concealments in
The boldest language. Such a one I am,
And vow that lover never yet made sigh
Truer than I. O, then, most soft sweet goddess,
Give me the victory of this question, which   135
Is true love's merit, and bless me with a sign
Of thy great pleasure.

> *Here music is heard; doves are*
> *seen to flutter. They fall again upon*
> *their faces, then on their knees.*

O thou that from eleven to ninety reign'st
In mortal bosoms, whose chase is this world

135. **question:** i.e., battle; **which:** i.e., **victory**
136. **merit:** due reward
137 SD. **doves:** sacred to Venus
138. **eleven:** age **eleven**
139. **chase:** hunting ground
141. **laid unto:** applied to (as if medicinally)
145 SD. **Still:** subdued, soft; **hair . . . wreath:** See note to 1.1.0 SD. **stuck:** adorned; **hind:** a symbol of Diana as goddess of the hunt; **aloof:** at a distance
147. **Abandoner:** forsaker; **revels:** festivities
148. **white:** i.e., as **white**
150. **blood:** (1) bloodshed (appropriate to **knights** [line 149]); (2) passion, sexual desire
151. **Which:** i.e., the **blush** [line 150] as a sign of both modesty and shame
152. **humbled:** i.e., kneeling, bent
153. **green:** youthful, innocent
154. **maculate:** defiled
155. **silver mistress:** Diana, as goddess of the moon, is described in terms of the metal associated with the moon (**silver**).
156. **scurrile:** scurrilous, coarse; **port:** gateway
157. **wanton:** lewd, lascivious
159. **vestal office:** religious observance as a virgin serving Diana; **bride-habited:** dressed as a bride
160. **'pointed:** i.e., who is appointed (for me)
163. **election:** i.e., having chosen
164. **equal:** equally
165. **doom:** condemn

And we in herds thy game, I give thee thanks   140
For this fair token, which being laid unto
Mine innocent true heart, arms in assurance
My body to this business.—Let us rise
And bow before the goddess.   *They ⌜rise and⌝ bow.*
                                    Time comes on.   145
                                            They exit.

*Still music of ⌜recorders.⌝ Enter Emilia in white, her
hair about her shoulders, ⌜wearing⌝ a wheaten wreath;
one in white holding up her train, her hair stuck with
flowers; one before her carrying a silver hind, in which
is conveyed incense and sweet odors, which being
set upon the altar ⌜of Diana,⌝ her maids standing
aloof, she sets fire to it. Then they curtsy and kneel.*

EMILIA
  O sacred, shadowy, cold, and constant queen,
  Abandoner of revels, mute contemplative,
  Sweet, solitary, white as chaste, and pure
  As wind-fanned snow, who to thy female knights
  Allow'st no more blood than will make a blush,   150
  Which is their order's robe, I here, thy priest,
  Am humbled 'fore thine altar. O, vouchsafe
  With that thy rare green eye, which never yet
  Beheld thing maculate, look on thy virgin,
  And, sacred silver mistress, lend thine ear—   155
  Which ne'er heard scurrile term, into whose port
  Ne'er entered wanton sound—to my petition,
  Seasoned with holy fear. This is my last
  Of vestal office. I am bride-habited
  But maiden-hearted. A husband I have 'pointed,   160
  But do not know him. Out of two I should
  Choose one, and pray for his success, but I
  Am guiltless of election. Of mine eyes,
  Were I to lose one—they are equal precious—
  I could doom neither; that which perished should   165

166. **Go to 't:** i.e., **go to** its destruction
167. **pretenders:** claimants, suitors
168. **truest title:** i.e., most legitimate claim
169. **grant:** i.e., may you **grant**
170. **file and quality:** i.e., rank and condition (as a virgin); **hold:** possess
171. **band:** company, troop
171 SD. **rose tree:** i.e., **rose** bush (At 2.2.168 the **rose** is called "the very emblem" of a virgin.)
172. **our . . . flows:** i.e., goddess of the moon, which controls the **ebbs and flows** of the tides
173. **bowels:** center, interior
174. **but one rose:** i.e., a single **rose**
175. **If well inspired:** i.e., **if** I interpret correctly; **confound:** destroy
177 SD. **twang:** sharp ringing sound
179. **dischargest me:** i.e., release me from service; **gathered:** picked, plucked
181. **Unclasp:** open up; **mystery:** hidden intents
182. **gracious:** favorable (Perhaps another sign is granted Emilia [line 181]. Otherwise, her claim that the **signs were gracious** is hard to explain.)

5.2 The doctor observes the jailer's daughter with the wooer pretending to be Palamon, and declares that she will soon be cured. Over her father's protest, the doctor encourages the wooer to go along with her desire that they sleep together.

———————

0 SD. **in the habit of:** dressed like
2. **maids:** young women

Go to 't unsentenced. Therefore, most modest queen,
He of the two pretenders that best loves me
And has the truest title in 't, let him
Take off my wheaten garland, or else grant
The file and quality I hold I may   170
Continue in thy band.

> *Here the hind vanishes under the*
> *altar, and in the place ascends a rose*
> *tree, having one rose upon it.*

See what our general of ebbs and flows
Out from the bowels of her holy altar
With sacred act advances: but one rose.
If well inspired, this battle shall confound   175
Both these brave knights, and I, a virgin flower,
Must grow alone unplucked.

> *Here is heard a sudden twang of instruments,*
> *and the rose falls from the tree.*

The flower is fall'n, the tree descends. O mistress,
Thou here dischargest me. I shall be gathered;
I think so, but I know not thine own will.   180
Unclasp thy mystery!—I hope she's pleased;
Her signs were gracious.

> *They curtsy and exit.*

Scene 2

Enter Doctor, Jailer, and Wooer in
⌜*the*⌝ *habit of Palamon.*

DOCTOR
  Has this advice I told you done any good upon her?
WOOER
  O, very much. The maids that kept her company
  Have half-persuaded her that I am Palamon;
  Within this half-hour she came smiling to me,

7. **Presently:** now, at once
9. **mainly:** entirely
11. **watch:** stay awake, sit up
12. **fit:** illness; inclination; **take:** attack, seize, affect
14. **fit her home:** i.e., satisfy her thoroughly
15. **presently:** without any delay
16. **would have me:** wanted me to
19. **ill:** badly, faultily
20. **observe:** gratify, humor
22. **confirm:** convince
23. **That's . . . if:** i.e., that doesn't matter so long as
27. **in the way of:** as a means of producing a
29. **I' . . . honesty:** (1) under honorable conditions; (2) with a view to chastity (**Honesty** meant "chastity" when applied to women.)
30. **niceness:** fastidiousness; i.e., trivial detail
32. **honest:** chaste

And asked me what I would eat, and when I would   5
  kiss her.
I told her "Presently," and kissed her twice.
DOCTOR
  'Twas well done; twenty times had been far better,
  For there the cure lies mainly.
WOOER   Then she told me   10
  She would watch with me tonight, for well she knew
  What hour my fit would take me.
DOCTOR   Let her do so,
  And when your fit comes, fit her home,
  And presently.   15
WOOER   She would have me sing.
DOCTOR
  You did so?
WOOER   No.
DOCTOR   'Twas very ill done, then.
  You should observe her ev'ry way.   20
WOOER   Alas,
  I have no voice, sir, to confirm her that way.
DOCTOR
  That's all one, if you make a noise.
  If she entreat again, do anything.
  Lie with her, if she ask you.   25
JAILER   Ho there, doctor!
DOCTOR
  Yes, in the way of cure.
JAILER   But first, by your leave,
  I' th' way of honesty.
DOCTOR   That's but a niceness.   30
  Ne'er cast your child away for honesty.
  Cure her first this way; then if she will be honest,
  She has the path before her.
JAILER
  Thank you, doctor.

38. **stays:** waits

42. **physic:** medical treatment

46. **may be:** i.e., **may be** chaste

47. **all one:** irrelevant

50. **Videlicet:** namely, that is to say (Latin); **have:** understand

53. **home:** thoroughly, effectively; **it cures her:** i.e., **it cures; ipso facto:** i.e., through the act itself (Latin)

54. **melancholy humor:** i.e., love-sickness (To be in a **melancholy humor** was to suffer from an excess of black bile, as was characteristic of love-sickness.)

A hornbook. (2.3.48)
From Andrew White Tuer, *History of the horn-book . . .* (1896).

DOCTOR   Pray bring her in   35
  And let's see how she is.
JAILER   I will, and tell her
  Her Palamon stays for her. But, doctor,
  Methinks you are i' th' wrong still.   *Jailer exits.*
DOCTOR   Go, go.   40
  You fathers are fine fools. Her honesty?
  And we should give her physic till we find that!
WOOER
  Why, do you think she is not honest, sir?
DOCTOR
  How old is she?
WOOER   She's eighteen.   45
DOCTOR   She may be.
  But that's all one; 'tis nothing to our purpose.
  Whate'er her father says, if you perceive
  Her mood inclining that way that I spoke of,
  Videlicet, the way of flesh—you have me?   50
WOOER
  ⌈Yes,⌉ very well, sir.
DOCTOR   Please her appetite,
  And do it home; it cures her, *ipso facto*,
  The melancholy humor that infects her.
WOOER
  I am of your mind, doctor.   55
DOCTOR   You'll find it so.

    Enter Jailer, Daughter, ⌈and⌉ Maid.

  She comes; pray ⌈humor⌉ her.
                    ⌈*Wooer and Doctor stand aside.*⌉
JAILER, ⌈*to Daughter*⌉
  Come, your love Palamon stays for you, child,
  And has done this long hour, to visit you.
DAUGHTER
  I thank him for his gentle patience.   60

66. **fair:** good-looking
67. **saw him:** i.e., **saw the horse** (line 63)
70. **comely:** handsomely (See picture, page 218.)
71. **jig:** lively kind of dance; **come cut and long tail:** proverbial for "whatever happens" (**Cut** is a dog or horse with a docked tail and **long tail** is one whose tail is not docked.)
72. **turns you:** i.e., **turns** (**You** is the ethic dative.)
75. **will founder the best hobbyhorse:** i.e., would cause **the best hobbyhorse** to go lame **hobbyhorse:** character in the **morris** dance (played by a man dressed as a horse), but used here as if referring to an actual horse
76. **If I have any skill:** i.e., **if I** know anything about this
77. **gallops:** he (**the horse** [line 63]) **gallops**
79. **virtues:** unusual abilities, accomplishments
83. **A very fair hand:** i.e., his handwriting is clear and legible; **casts:** adds up, reckons; **accounts:** bills, statements of what is owed (with possible wordplay on the phrase "to **cast accounts**" ["to make calculations"])
84. **Of:** for; **provender:** fodder
84–85. **That hostler . . . cozens him:** i.e., any **hostler** who cheats him **must** get up early
89. **his master:** i.e., Palamon

He's a kind gentleman, and I am much bound to
  him.
Did you ne'er see the horse he gave me?
JAILER   Yes.
DAUGHTER
How do you like him?   65
JAILER   He's a very fair one.
DAUGHTER
You never saw him dance?
JAILER   No.
DAUGHTER   I have, often.
He dances very finely, very comely,   70
And for a jig, come cut and long tail to him,
He turns you like a top.
JAILER   That's fine indeed.
DAUGHTER
He'll dance the morris twenty mile an hour,
And that will founder the best hobbyhorse,   75
If I have any skill, in all the parish,
And gallops to the ⌜tune⌝ of "Light o' love."
What think you of this horse?
JAILER   Having these virtues,
I think he might be brought to play at tennis.   80
DAUGHTER
Alas, that's nothing.
JAILER   Can he write and read too?
DAUGHTER
A very fair hand, and casts himself th' accounts
Of all his hay and provender. That hostler
Must rise betime that cozens him. You know   85
The chestnut mare the Duke has?
JAILER   Very well.
DAUGHTER
She is horribly in love with him, poor beast,
But he is like his master, coy and scornful.

91. **bottles:** bundles of hay

92. **strike:** bundles; **ne'er have her:** never couple with her (or, in the Daughter's anthropomorphized account, "never marry her")

100. **Yours . . . honesty:** i.e., I will do whatever you **command,** so long as it accords with chastity

105–6. **stool-ball:** a country game reminiscent of cricket, usually played by girls and women

109. **keep:** celebrate, solemnize

113. **nice:** fastidious, difficult to please

115. **blot:** blemish, disgrace

A dancing horse from 1595. (5.2.70)
From Robert Chambers, *The book of days* . . . [1869].

JAILER
  What dowry has she?   90
DAUGHTER   Some two hundred bottles,
  And twenty strike of oats, but he'll ne'er have her.
  He lisps in 's neighing able to entice
  A miller's mare. He'll be the death of her.
DOCTOR, ⌈*aside*⌉ What stuff she utters!   95

        ⌈*Wooer and Doctor come forward.*⌉

JAILER
  Make curtsy; here your love comes.
WOOER   Pretty soul,
  How do you?   ⌈*Daughter curtsies.*⌉
              That's a fine maid; there's a curtsy!
DAUGHTER
  Yours to command i' th' way of honesty.—   100
  How far is 't now to th' end o' th' world, my masters?
DOCTOR
  Why, a day's journey, wench.
DAUGHTER, ⌈*to Wooer*⌉   Will you go with me?
WOOER
  What shall we do there, wench?
DAUGHTER   Why, play at stool-   105
    ball.
  What is there else to do?
WOOER   I am content,
  If we shall keep our wedding there.
DAUGHTER   'Tis true,   110
  For there, I will assure you, we shall find
  Some blind priest for the purpose, that will venture
  To marry us; for here they are nice and foolish.
  Besides, my father must be hanged tomorrow,
  And that would be a blot i' th' business.   115
  Are not you Palamon?
WOOER   Do not you know me?

119. **petticoat:** skirt; **smocks:** loose shirtlike undergarments

120. **That's all one:** i.e., that doesn't matter

121. **surely:** truly, indeed

124. **E'en when you will:** i.e., whenever you wish

125. **fain:** gladly

128. **sweet:** fragrant

129. **against:** in preparation for

142. **kept down:** perhaps, prevented from growing; **hard meat:** rough or unpleasant food; **ill:** bad

Jove as an eagle "snatch[ing] up" Ganymede. (4.2.17–19)
From Gabriele Simeoni, *La vita . . .* (1559).

DAUGHTER
Yes, but you care not for me; I have nothing
But this poor petticoat and two coarse smocks.

WOOER
That's all one; I will have you.   120

DAUGHTER   Will you surely?

WOOER, ⌐*taking her hand*⌐
Yes, by this fair hand, will I.

DAUGHTER   We'll to bed then.

WOOER
E'en when you will.   ⌐*He kisses her.*⌐

DAUGHTER, ⌐*wiping her face*⌐ O, sir, you would fain 125
be nibbling.

WOOER
Why do you rub my kiss off?

DAUGHTER   'Tis a sweet one,
And will perfume me finely against the wedding.
Is not this your cousin Arcite? ⌐*She indicates Doctor.*⌐ 130

DOCTOR   Yes, sweetheart,
And I am glad my cousin Palamon
Has made so fair a choice.

DAUGHTER   Do you think he'll have me?

DOCTOR
Yes, without doubt.   135

DAUGHTER, ⌐*to Jailer*⌐ Do you think so too?

JAILER   Yes.

DAUGHTER
We shall have many children. (⌐*To Doctor.*⌐) Lord,
how you're grown!
My Palamon, I hope, will grow too, finely, 140
Now he's at liberty. Alas, poor chicken,
He was kept down with hard meat and ill lodging,
But I'll kiss him up again.

                    Enter a Messenger.

148. **bear a charge:** i.e., have responsibilities
149. **straight:** at once
150. **e'en:** just now
154. **I'll warrant you:** i.e., I promise that
156. **from her:** i.e., leave her side
157. **still preserve her:** i.e., continue to take care of her
168. **marry:** i.e., indeed

"Tott'ring Fortune." (5.4.22)
From [Robert Recorde,] *The castle of knowledge . . .* [1556].

MESSENGER
  What do you here? You'll lose the noblest sight
  That e'er was seen.   145
JAILER   Are they i' th' field?
MESSENGER   They are.
  You bear a charge there too.
JAILER   I'll away straight.—
  I must e'en leave you here.   150
DOCTOR   Nay, we'll go with you.
  I will not lose the ⌜sight.⌝
JAILER, ⌜aside to Doctor⌝   How did you like her?
DOCTOR
  I'll warrant you, within these three or four days
  I'll make her right again. ⌜Jailer and Messenger exit.⌝ 155
  (⌜To Wooer.⌝)   You must not from her,
  But still preserve her in this way.
WOOER   I will.
DOCTOR
  Let's get her in.
WOOER   Come, sweet, we'll go to dinner   160
  And then we'll play at cards.
DAUGHTER   And shall we kiss too?
WOOER
  A hundred times.
DAUGHTER   And twenty.
WOOER   Ay, and twenty.   165
DAUGHTER
  And then we'll sleep together.
DOCTOR, ⌜to Wooer⌝   Take her offer.
WOOER
  Yes, marry, will we.
DAUGHTER   But you shall not hurt me.
WOOER
  I will not, sweet.   170
DAUGHTER   If you do, love, I'll cry.
                                        They exit.

5.3 Emilia listens to the sounds of the combat as first one contestant and then the other seems to be winning. When Arcite is finally declared the victor, she is told that he will be her husband and that Palamon and his knights will immediately be executed.

————————

3. **hawk at:** i.e., attack
4. **decision:** judgment, i.e., trial by combat
5. **Threats:** threatens; **brave:** worthy; **each stroke:** i.e., the sword of **each** combatant
7. **bell:** i.e., passing **bell** (sounded to announce a death)
10. **deafing:** i.e., deafening myself
15. **in their kind:** i.e., in reality, in nature
16. **penciled:** i.e., (when) painted, or (when) depicted in words
17. **make:** create; **the belief:** i.e., its credibility
18. **Both sealed with:** i.e., confirmed **with both**
19. **meed:** recompense; **price:** trophy; **garland:** victor's wreath
20. **the question's title:** i.e., the one who wins the right (to you) in this dispute
21. **Pardon me:** i.e., please excuse me (from attending)
22. **wink:** close my eyes
24. **as 'twere:** as if it were
26. **extinct:** extinguished, no longer burning
27. **envy:** malice; **shows:** reveals
28. **The one:** i.e., **one** combatant to
29. **dam:** mother
30. **Of:** i.e., by

Scene 3

Flourish. Enter Theseus, Hippolyta,
Emilia, Pirithous, and some Attendants.

EMILIA
  I'll no step further.

PIRITHOUS   Will you lose this sight?

EMILIA
  I had rather see a wren hawk at a fly
  Than this decision; ev'ry blow that falls
  Threats a brave life; each stroke laments   5
  The place whereon it falls, and sounds more like
  A bell than blade. I will stay here.
  It is enough my hearing shall be punished
  With what shall happen, 'gainst the which there is
  No deafing but to hear; not taint mine eye   10
  With dread sights it may shun.

PIRITHOUS, ⌜*to Theseus*⌝   Sir, my good lord,
  Your sister will no further.

THESEUS   O, she must.
  She shall see deeds of honor in their kind,   15
  Which sometime show well, penciled. Nature now
  Shall make and act the story, the belief
  Both sealed with eye and ear.—You must be present;
  You are the victor's meed, the price and garland
  To crown the question's title.   20

EMILIA   Pardon me.
  If I were there, I'd wink.

THESEUS   You must be there;
  This trial is as 'twere i' th' night, and you
  The only star to shine.   25

EMILIA   I am extinct;
  There is but envy in that light which shows
  The one the other. Darkness, which ever was
  The dam of horror, who does stand accursed
  Of many mortal millions, may even now,   30

34. **Set off:** take away, remove; **whereto:** i.e., of which

36. **In faith:** a mild oath

39. **must needs:** must necessarily; **by:** i.e., present

40. **give the service pay:** i.e., reward **the service** of the victor

42. **title of:** rights to; **tried:** determined

43. **Out of itself:** i.e., in a place outside of the **kingdom** (line 42)

44. **at your pleasure:** i.e., as you choose

45. **office:** duty, attendance

48. **like:** likely

49. **start:** i.e., moment (but also "advantage, priority in a competitive undertaking")

50. **of the two know best:** i.e., **know** to be the better **of the two**

51. **lot:** destiny, gift (of **the gods** [line 49])

52. **gently visaged:** i.e., (1) has a kind or tender face; and (2) has the face of a nobleman

53. **engine bent:** weapon, like a bow, ready to shoot

57. **graved:** i.e., furrowed (literally, engraved); **bury:** wordplay on **graved** as "buried"

By casting her black mantle over both,
That neither could find other, get herself
Some part of a good name, and many a murder
Set off whereto she's guilty.

HIPPOLYTA   You must go.   35

EMILIA
In faith, I will not.

THESEUS   Why, the knights must kindle
Their valor at your eye. Know, of this war
You are the treasure, and must needs be by
To give the service pay.   40

EMILIA   Sir, pardon me.
The title of a kingdom may be tried
Out of itself.

THESEUS   Well, well, then; at your pleasure.
Those that remain with you could wish their office   45
To any of their enemies.

HIPPOLYTA   Farewell, sister.
I am like to know your husband 'fore yourself
By some small start of time. He whom the gods
Do of the two know best, I pray them he   50
Be made your lot.

                    Theseus, Hippolyta, Pirithous, ⌜and others,⌝
                        exit. ⌜Emilia remains, comparing again
                        the pictures of Arcite and Palamon.⌝

EMILIA
Arcite is gently visaged, yet his eye
Is like an engine bent, or a sharp weapon
In a soft sheath; mercy and manly courage
Are bedfellows in his visage. Palamon   55
Has a most menacing aspect; his brow
Is graved, and seems to bury what it frowns on;
Yet sometimes 'tis not so, but alters to
The quality of his thoughts. Long time his eye
Will dwell upon his object. Melancholy   60
Becomes him nobly; so does Arcite's mirth;

64. **humors:** dispositions, temperaments

65. **Stick misbecomingly on:** adhere or cleave unbecomingly to; **them:** Palamon and Arcite

67. **spurs to spirit:** i.e., **trumpets** (line 66 SD) **spirit:** courage

68. **proof:** trial

69–70. **to . . . figure:** i.e., so that he is mutilated **spoiling:** marring **figure:** form; appearance

71. **chance:** mishap, unfortunate event; **by:** i.e., present

74. **Omit:** fail to use; **ward:** defensive posture (a fencing term); **forfeit:** give up; **offense:** attack, assault

75. **craved:** demanded, required; **time:** opportunity, right moment

75 SD. **À Palamon:** a war cry of support and acclamation

78. **minister:** render aid

79. **What is the chance:** i.e., **what** has happened

83. **prim'st:** chiefest, most excellent

87. **Poor servant:** See longer note to 2.5.71–72, page 257

89. **still:** always

But Palamon's sadness is a kind of mirth,
So mingled, as if mirth did make him sad
And sadness merry. Those darker humors that
Stick misbecomingly on others, on them   65
Live in fair dwelling.
            Cornets. Trumpets sound as to a charge.
Hark how yon spurs to spirit do incite
The princes to their proof! Arcite may win me,
And yet may Palamon wound Arcite to
The spoiling of his figure. O, what pity   70
Enough for such a chance? If I were by,
I might do hurt, for they would glance their eyes
Towards my seat, and in that motion might
Omit a ward or forfeit an offense
Which craved that very time.   75
            Cornets. A great cry and noise
                within crying "À Palamon!"
                    It is much better
I am not there. O, better never born
Than minister to such harm!

            Enter Servant.

                    What is the chance?
SERVANT   The cry's "À Palamon."   80
EMILIA   Then he has won. 'Twas ever likely.
He looked all grace and success, and he is
Doubtless the prim'st of men. I prithee run
And tell me how it goes.
            Shout and cornets, crying "À Palamon!"
SERVANT   Still "Palamon."   85
EMILIA
Run and inquire.   ⌜*Servant exits.*⌝
⌜*Addressing Arcite's picture.*⌝ Poor servant, thou hast
    lost.
Upon my right side still I wore thy picture,
Palamon's on the left—why so, I know not.   90

91. **end in 't:** i.e., purpose in doing so

92. **sinister:** left

93. **best-boding:** i.e., most promising

97. **Within . . . pyramid:** For the terms of victory in the combat, see 3.6.363–67. **that:** i.e., so **that**

98. **anon:** instantly

99. **Th' assistants:** i.e., Arcite's companion knights; **redemption:** deliverance, recovery

100. **titlers:** claimants for the title

101. **Hand to hand at it:** fighting **hand to hand**

102. **Were they:** i.e., if only **they were;** or, perhaps, if **they were**

104. **composed:** composite, compound; **Their single share:** i.e., (even) **their** individual **share** (of **nobleness** [line 105])

105. **peculiar to them:** i.e., that they possess individually

105–7. **gives . . . breathing:** i.e., damages **any lady breathing** with the **disparity** (between her worth and theirs), her deficiency in value **prejudice:** injury, damage

115. **consummation:** conclusion

116. **wind instruments: cornets** (line 112 SD)

117. **Half-sights saw:** i.e., eyes almost blind could see

118. **God's lid:** a strong oath, "by **God's** eyelid"

119. **looked:** showed

I had no end in 't else; chance would have it so.
On the sinister side the heart lies; Palamon
Had the best-boding chance.
                    Another cry, and shout within, and cornets.
                              This burst of clamor
Is sure th' end o' th' combat.   95

                    Enter Servant.

SERVANT
    They said that Palamon had Arcite's body
    Within an inch o' th' pyramid, that the cry
    Was general "À Palamon." But anon,
    Th' assistants made a brave redemption, and
    The two bold titlers at this instant are   100
    Hand to hand at it.

EMILIA   Were they metamorphosed
    Both into one—O, why, there were no woman
    Worth so composed a man! Their single share,
    Their nobleness peculiar to them, gives   105
    The prejudice of disparity, value's shortness,
    To any lady breathing.
                    Cornets. Cry within, "Arcite, Arcite."
                    More exulting?
    "Palamon" still?

SERVANT   Nay, now the sound is "Arcite."   110

EMILIA
    I prithee lay attention to the cry;
    Set both thine ears to th' business.
            Cornets. A great shout, and cry "Arcite, victory!"

SERVANT   The cry is "Arcite"
    And "Victory! Hark, Arcite, victory!"
    The combat's consummation is proclaimed   115
    By the wind instruments.

EMILIA   Half-sights saw
    That Arcite was no babe. God's lid, his richness
    And costliness of spirit looked through him; it could

121. **humble:** low-lying; **go to law with:** i.e., resist, take action against

122. **drift-winds:** driving winds

123. **miscarry:** come to harm or misfortune

125. **coming off:** leaving the field of combat

129. **arbitrament:** absolute decision

130. **a good one:** i.e., as **good a one**

131. **struck at head:** i.e., fought; **your hands:** The joining of **hands,** or "handfasting," constituted a formal betrothal.

132. **plighted:** bound by pledge, engaged

133. **decay:** i.e., grow older, lose health and strength

136–37. **cheaply . . . rate:** i.e., at a low cost in comparison to my appraisal of

141. **race:** lineage

143. **methought:** it seemed to me; **Alcides:** Hercules (See note to 1.1.73, and picture, page xvii.)

144. **To him:** i.e., in comparison **to him; sow of lead:** large mass **of** solidified **lead; If:** i.e., but even **if**

145. **to th' all I have spoke:** i.e., in the way **I have** praised **him** generally

146. **Did:** would

148. **emulous:** rivalrous; **Philomels:** nightingales (called **Philomels** because, in mythology, the much-tormented Philomela was transformed into a nightingale)

149. **throats:** i.e., songs

150. **Anon:** at once

151. **by-and-by:** immediately; **out-breasted:** i.e., outsung

No more be hid in him than fire in flax, 120
Than humble banks can go to law with waters
That drift-winds force to raging. I did think
Good Palamon would miscarry, yet I knew not
Why I did think so. Our reasons are not prophets
When oft our fancies are. They are coming off. 125
Alas, poor Palamon!

Cornets. Enter Theseus, Hippolyta, Pirithous,
Arcite as victor, and Attendants ⌈and others.⌉

THESEUS
Lo, where our sister is in expectation,
Yet quaking and unsettled.—Fairest Emily,
The gods by their divine arbitrament
Have given you this knight; he is a good one 130
As ever struck at head.—Give me your hands.
Receive you her, you him. Be plighted with
A love that grows as you decay.
ARCITE   Emily,
To buy you I have lost what's dearest to me 135
Save what is bought, and yet I purchase cheaply,
As I do rate your value.
THESEUS   O loved sister,
He speaks now of as brave a knight as e'er
Did spur a noble steed. Surely the gods 140
Would have him die a bachelor, lest his race
Should show i' th' world too godlike. His behavior
So charmed me that methought Alcides was
To him a sow of lead. If I could praise
Each part of him to th' all I have spoke, your Arcite 145
Did not lose by 't, for he that was thus good
Encountered yet his better. I have heard
Two emulous Philomels beat the ear o' th' night
With their contentious throats, now one the higher,
Anon the other, then again the first, 150
And by-and-by out-breasted, that the sense

153. **Good space:** for a long time

154. **Make hardly one:** perhaps, **make one** by a very little; or, perhaps, with difficulty **make one; garland:** wreath of victory

155. **For the subdued:** i.e., as **for** those defeated

156. **our present justice:** i.e., immediate execution

157. **pinch:** torment

159. **Arm:** i.e., give your arm to

160. **lose her:** (1) be deprived of her; (2) loose her, let her go

166. **charge me live:** command **me** to **live**

171. **one:** i.e., **one** person

172. **two:** i.e., **two eyes** (line 171)

5.4 As Palamon puts his head on the block for his beheading, word comes that Arcite has been crushed by his falling horse. Mortally wounded, Arcite confesses that he was wrong to pursue Emilia after Palamon had already declared his love for her. He gives his right in Emilia to Palamon, and then dies. Theseus declares that the court will spend some days in mourning for Arcite and then turn to the celebration of Palamon's marriage to Emilia.

---

0 SD. **block:** wooden **block** for beheading the condemned (See picture, page 238.)

2. **state:** situation, condition

5–6. **To live . . . wishes:** i.e., we **have men's good wishes** that we might continue **to live**

Could not be judge between 'em. So it fared
Good space between these kinsmen, till heavens did
Make hardly one the winner.—Wear the garland
With joy that you have won.—For the subdued,   155
Give them our present justice, since I know
Their lives but pinch 'em. Let it here be done.
The scene's not for our seeing. Go we hence
Right joyful, with some sorrow.—Arm your prize;
I know you will not lose her.—Hippolyta,   160
I see one eye of yours conceives a tear,
The which it will deliver.

EMILIA   Is this winning?
O all you heavenly powers, where is your mercy?
But that your wills have said it must be so,   165
And charge me live to comfort this unfriended,
This miserable prince, that cuts away
A life more worthy from him than all women,
I should and would die too.

HIPPOLYTA   Infinite pity   170
That four such eyes should be so fixed on one
That two must needs be blind for 't.

THESEUS   So it is.
                                Flourish. They exit.

Scene 4

Enter Guard ⌈with⌉ Palamon and his Knights,
pinioned; Jailer, Executioner ⌈and Others,
carrying a block and an ax.⌉

⌈PALAMON⌉
There's many a man alive that hath outlived
The love o' th' people; yea, i' th' selfsame state
Stands many a father with his child. Some comfort
We have by so considering. We expire,
And not without men's pity. To live still,   5

7. **beguile:** disappoint, cheat

8. **rheum:** catarrh, i.e., inflammation of mucous membranes; **lag:** last; **attend:** are in store

9. **gray approachers:** i.e., those who approach death when old

10. **unwappered:** i.e., hearty; **halting:** limping; **crimes:** offenses

11. **sure:** surely

12. **Sooner than such:** i.e., in preference to **gray approachers** (line 9); **nectar:** drink of **the gods** (line 11)

13. **clear:** pure, unclouded

14. **this poor comfort:** See line 3, above.

17. **content:** satisfaction

18. **Fortune:** i.e., good **fortune; whose title:** i.e., the possession of which

19. **grain:** smallest unit of weight

20. **o'er-weigh:** outweigh

22. **patience:** calm acceptance; **tott'ring:** wavering; **Fortune:** goddess Fortuna, sometimes pictured standing on a rolling ball (See picture, page 222.)

23. **certain'st:** most fixed; **reels:** sways unsteadily

24. **begins:** i.e., will be first executed

25. **E'en he that:** i.e., the very person who

26. **Taste to:** i.e., act as taster to; test the **banquet** (line 25) by being the first to **taste** it

29. **see 't done:** i.e., give **me freedom** (through death)

30. **her kind of ill:** i.e., the nature of **her** illness

34. **By my short life:** wordplay on the mild oath "(I swear) **by my life**"

(continued)

Have their good wishes; we prevent
The loathsome misery of age, beguile
The gout and rheum that in lag hours attend
For gray approachers; we come towards the gods
Young and unwappered, not halting under crimes   10
Many and stale. That sure shall please the gods
Sooner than such, to give us nectar with 'em,
For we are more clear spirits. My dear kinsmen,
Whose lives for this poor comfort are laid down,
You have sold 'em too too cheap.   15

FIRST KNIGHT   What ending could be
Of more content? O'er us the victors have
Fortune, whose title is as momentary
As to us death is certain. A grain of honor
They not o'er-weigh us.   20

SECOND KNIGHT   Let us bid farewell;
And with our patience anger tott'ring Fortune,
Who at her certain'st reels.

THIRD KNIGHT   Come, who begins?

PALAMON
E'en he that led you to this banquet shall   25
Taste to you all. ⌜*To Jailer.*⌝ Ah ha, my friend, my
    friend,
Your gentle daughter gave me freedom once;
You'll see 't done now forever. Pray, how does she?
I heard she was not well; her kind of ill   30
Gave me some sorrow.

JAILER   Sir, she's well restored,
And to be married shortly.

PALAMON   By my short life,
I am most glad on 't. 'Tis the latest thing   35
I shall be glad of; prithee, tell her so.
Commend me to her, and to piece her portion,
Tender her this.   ⌜*He gives his purse to Jailer.*⌝

FIRST KNIGHT   Nay, let's be offerers all.

35. **latest:** last, final
36. **prithee:** i.e., I pray you
37. **Commend me to her:** i.e., give her my best wishes; **piece:** i.e., **piece** out, enlarge; **portion:** dowry
38. **Tender:** offer
40. **maid:** virgin
42. **right:** very; **more to me deserving:** winning more for me
43. **quit:** requite, repay
49 SD. **within:** offstage; **Hold:** stop
52. **done:** finished (i.e., executed Palamon)
53. **will:** i.e., are determined to
56. **false:** faithless, treacherous
59. **dearly:** deeply, keenly
62. **List:** listen

A beheading on the executioner's block. (5.4.0 SD)
From [Richard Verstegen,] *Théatre des cruautéz . . .* (1607).

SECOND KNIGHT
Is it a maid? 40
PALAMON   Verily, I think so.
A right good creature, more to me deserving
Than I can quit or speak of.
ALL KNIGHTS   Commend us to her.
                              They give their purses.
JAILER
The gods requite you all and make her thankful! 45
PALAMON
Adieu, and let my life be now as short
As my leave-taking.   ⌜*Lays his head*⌝ *on the block.*
FIRST KNIGHT   Lead, courageous cousin.
SECOND ⌜and THIRD⌝ KNIGHTS   We'll follow cheerfully.

A great noise within crying "Run!" "Save!" "Hold!"
Enter in haste a Messenger.

MESSENGER
Hold, hold! O, hold, hold, hold! 50

Enter Pirithous in haste.

PIRITHOUS
Hold, ho! It is a cursèd haste you made
If you have done so quickly!—Noble Palamon,
The gods will show their glory in a life
That thou art yet to lead.
PALAMON   Can that be, 55
When Venus, I have said, is false? How do things
  fare?
PIRITHOUS
Arise, great sir, and give the tidings ear
That are most ⌜dearly⌝ sweet and bitter.
PALAMON, ⌜*rising*⌝   What 60
Hath waked us from our dream?
PIRITHOUS   List then: your
  cousin,

65. **owing:** possessing

66. **a hair worth:** i.e., **a** single **hair**

67. **Weakens his price:** reduces its worth

68. **His goodness:** i.e., an otherwise good horse; **note:** mark, distinguishing feature

69. **finds allowance:** is acknowledged (as true)

70. **calkins:** i.e., horseshoes (literally, turned-down ends or edges of horseshoes)

71. **tell:** count

72. **length:** i.e., stride

73. **pride:** mettle, spirit

76. **envious:** malicious; **flint:** stone that gives off sparks when struck with iron

77. **Saturn:** a Roman god, characterized as **old** and as **cold** (See picture, page 249.)

79. **Or what . . . else:** i.e., **or else what fierce sulphur** (**Sulphur,** also known as "brimstone," is highly flammable; it was associated with lightning, gunpowder, devils, and the fires of hell.) **to this end made:** i.e., **made** for this purpose

80. **hot:** eager, excited

81. **Took toy: took** fright, shied

82. **comes on end: comes** forward

83. **school-doing:** conduct taught in riding school

84. **kind:** proper, appropriate; **manage:** training to good paces; **whines:** cries in pain

85. **rowel:** i.e., spur

87. **jadery:** behavior of a jade or ill-tempered horse; **disseat:** unseat

88. **kept it:** i.e., **kept** his seat; **bravely:** skillfully; splendidly

(continued)

Mounted upon a steed that Emily
Did first bestow on him—a black one, owing   65
Not a hair worth of white, which some will say
Weakens his price, and many will not buy
His goodness with this note, which superstition
Here finds allowance—on this horse is Arcite
Trotting the stones of Athens—which the calkins   70
Did rather tell than trample, for the horse
Would make his length a mile, if 't pleased his rider
To put pride in him. As he thus went counting
The flinty pavement, dancing, as 'twere, to th' music
His own hooves made—for, as they say, from iron   75
Came music's origin—what envious flint,
Cold as old Saturn, and like him possessed
With fire malevolent, darted a spark,
Or what fierce sulphur else, to this end made,
I comment not; the hot horse, hot as fire,   80
Took toy at this and fell to what disorder
His power could give his will; bounds, comes on end,
Forgets school-doing, being therein trained
And of kind manage. Pig-like he whines
At the sharp rowel, which he frets at rather   85
Than any jot obeys; seeks all foul means
Of boist'rous and rough jadery to disseat
His lord that kept it bravely. When naught served,
When neither curb would crack, girth break, nor
    diff'ring plunges   90
Disroot his rider whence he grew, but that
He kept him 'tween his legs, on his hind hoofs
On end he stands
That Arcite's legs, being higher than his head,
Seemed with strange art to hang. His victor's wreath 95
Even then fell off his head, and presently
Backward the jade comes o'er, and his full poise
Becomes the rider's load. Yet is he living,
But such a vessel 'tis that floats but for

89. **curb:** chain or strap under the horse's lower jaw; **crack:** split into pieces; **girth:** strap around the horse's body securing the saddle

90. **diff'ring:** varying, diverse

91. **Disroot:** dislodge; **whence he grew:** i.e., from the place he was fixed

92. **He:** i.e., the **rider** (line 91)

93. **he stands:** i.e., **the horse** (line 80) **stands**

94. **That:** so **that**

95. **art:** skill

97. **jade:** contemptuous word for a horse; **poise:** weight

98. **Yet is he living:** i.e., Arcite **is** still **living**

99. **but for:** i.e., only awaiting

102. **alliance:** kinship; friendship

109. **told:** counted, reckoned up; **false:** wrong

112. **done:** finished

114. **Elysium:** the abode of the blessed in the afterlife

118. **This day:** i.e., the anniversary of **this day**

119. **honor:** i.e., honoring (the memory of Arcite)

120–21. **In this place . . . sundered you:** See Act 3, scene 6, and note to 3.6.175 SD.

125. **arrouse:** bedew, sprinkle

126. **graced her altar:** perhaps, gratified worshippers at **her altar**

127. **Our:** perhaps, my (the royal plural); or, perhaps, Theseus includes the other knights who, as soldiers, follow **Mars**

128. **vouched:** upheld; affirmed

The surge that next approaches. He much desires   100
To have some speech with you. Lo, he appears.

Enter Theseus, Hippolyta, Emilia,
⌜*and*⌝ *Arcite* ⌜*carried*⌝ *in a chair.*

PALAMON
O, miserable end of our alliance!
The gods are mighty, Arcite. If thy heart,
Thy worthy, manly heart, be yet unbroken,
Give me thy last words. I am Palamon,   105
One that yet loves thee dying.

ARCITE   Take Emilia
And with her all the world's joy. Reach thy hand;
Farewell. I have told my last hour. I was false,
Yet never treacherous. Forgive me, cousin.   110
One kiss from fair Emilia.   ⌜*She kisses him.*⌝
'Tis done.
Take her. I die.   ⌜*He dies.*⌝

PALAMON   Thy brave soul seek Elysium!

EMILIA
I'll close thine eyes, prince. Blessed souls be with   115
    thee!
Thou art a right good man, and while I live,
This day I give to tears.

PALAMON   And I to honor.

THESEUS
In this place first you fought; e'en very here   120
I sundered you. Acknowledge to the gods
Our thanks that you are living.
His part is played, and though it were too short,
He did it well. Your day is lengthened, and
The blissful dew of heaven does arrouse you.   125
The powerful Venus well hath graced her altar,
And given you your love. Our master, Mars,
⌜Hath⌝ vouched his oracle, and to Arcite gave

129. **grace:** i.e., victory (literally, favor)

130. **this:** i.e., Arcite's body

133. **of our desire:** i.e., **of things we** (also) **desire** (line 132)

137. **passage:** perhaps, (1) combat, **passage** at arms; or, (2) progress of events

138. **equal:** equitable

141. **fancy:** love

142. **desired:** requested, entreated

143. **justice:** legal power to execute an offender

146. **lovers:** See note to 5.1.41.

147. **adopt:** i.e., **adopt** as

148. **grace:** favor

149. **in whose end:** i.e., at the **end** of which

152. **But one hour since:** i.e., only **one hour** ago

154. **As for him sorry:** i.e., **as** I am **sorry for** Arcite; **charmers:** workers of magic and enchantment (i.e., **the gods** [line 143])

156. **still:** always

157. **kind:** fashion, way

158. **with you leave dispute:** i.e., cease to argue with you

159. **That are above our question:** i.e., who do not condescend to be questioned by mortals

160. **bear us:** conduct ourselves, behave; **like the time:** i.e., in a manner appropriate to the situation

The grace of the contention. So the deities
Have showed due justice.—Bear this hence.   130
PALAMON   O cousin,
  That we should things desire which do cost us
  The loss of our desire, that naught could buy
  Dear love but loss of dear love.
                    ⌜*Arcite's body is carried out.*⌝
THESEUS   Never Fortune   135
  Did play a subtler game. The conquered triumphs;
  The victor has the loss; yet in the passage
  The gods have been most equal.—Palamon,
  Your kinsman hath confessed the right o' th' lady
  Did lie in you, for you first saw her and   140
  Even then proclaimed your fancy. He restored her
  As your stol'n jewel and desired your spirit
  To send him hence forgiven. The gods my justice
  Take from my hand and they themselves become
  The executioners. Lead your lady off,   145
  And call your lovers from the stage of death,
  Whom I adopt my friends. A day or two
  Let us look sadly, and give grace unto
  The funeral of Arcite, in whose end
  The visages of bridegrooms we'll put on   150
  And smile with Palamon—for whom an hour,
  But one hour since, I was as dearly sorry
  As glad of Arcite, and am now as glad
  As for him sorry. O you heavenly charmers,
  What things you make of us! For what we lack   155
  We laugh, for what we have are sorry, still
  Are children in some kind. Let us be thankful
  For that which is, and with you leave dispute
  That are above our question. Let's go off
  And bear us like the time.   160
                    Flourish. They exit.

Epilogue   The speaker bids the audience farewell, hoping that the play has pleased them.

———————————

2. **cannot say: cannot** speak, am tongue-tied

3. **cruel fearful:** exceedingly timid or nervous; **stay a while:** "i.e., wait a bit before you applaud or hiss" (Evans)

5. **hard:** badly

6. **wench:** woman, girl

9. **conscience:** internal conviction

9–10. **kill / Our market:** spoil our trade

10. **stay you:** hold you back

11. **Have at ... can come:** i.e., bring on your **worst**

14. **We ... cause:** perhaps, (1) **we have no** grounds for being **bold** (line 13); or, (2) being **bold** is not our intention; **tale:** alluding to the "Knight's **Tale**" in Chaucer and to the make-believe nature of tales

16. **meant you:** i.e., intended

17. **have our end:** i.e.; **have** achieved **our** goal

18. **many a better:** i.e., **many better** plays

18–19. **to prolong ... to us:** i.e., **to** cause **your** long-standing support of **us to** continue

20. **Rest at your service:** a formula for saying farewell   **Rest:** remain

246

⌜*Enter Epilogue.*⌝

EPILOGUE
I would now ask you how you like the play,
But, as it is with schoolboys, cannot say.
I am cruel fearful! Pray yet, stay a while,
And let me look upon you. No man smile?
Then it goes hard, I see. He that has   5
Loved a young handsome wench, then, show his
    face—
'Tis strange if none be here—and, if he will,
Against his conscience let him hiss and kill
Our market. 'Tis in vain, I see, to stay you.   10
Have at the worst can come, then! Now what say
    you?
And yet mistake me not: I am not bold.
We have no such cause. If the tale we have told—
For 'tis no other—any way content you—   15
For to that honest purpose it was meant you—
We have our end; and you shall have ere long,
I dare say, many a better, to prolong
Your old loves to us. We, and all our might,
Rest at your service. Gentlemen, good night.   20
                    Flourish. ⌜*He exits.*⌝

Bellona, goddess of war. (1.1.84; 1.3.16)
From Giovanni Battista Cavalleriis,
Antiquarum statuarum . . . (1585–94).

The god Saturn. (5.4.77)
From Abu Ma'shar, *De magnis coniunctionibus* . . . [1515].

Hymen. (1.1.0 SD)
From Vincenzo Cartari, *Imagines deorum* . . . (1581).

Longer Notes

1.1.44. Creon: The dialogue here places the action of the play shortly after the end of the war known as "the Theban War" or "the Seven against Thebes." In this civil war, the two sons of Oedipus battled for the kingdom after his death: Polyneices and six other leaders ("the Seven") fought against Eteocles and the Theban army. Both brothers were killed in the war, and their uncle **Creon** assumed the throne. This myth was treated in a number of great Greek tragedies—including Aeschylus's *Seven against Thebes*, Sophocles' *Antigone* and *Oedipus at Colonus*, and Euripides' *The Suppliants* and *The Phoenician Women*—many of which were well known in the early modern period (some through Latin versions written by Seneca). *Antigone* focuses on Creon's proclamation that no one be allowed to bury Polyneices' body; because Polyneices' sister Antigone defies this edict, Creon sentences her to death.

1.1.52. purger: Some scholars have explained the phrase **purger of the earth** as referring to Theseus's modeling himself on his cousin Hercules and seeking out monsters to destroy; others see the phrase as an allusion to Theseus's service to Mars, the god of war. Lois Potter (Arden 3 edition) suggests that as "purger of the earth," Theseus is here imaged as Mars himself.

1.1.68. Mars's altar . . . that time fair: Potter (Arden 3 edition) argues that this line should be punctuated in such a way that "by Mars's altar" appears as a mild oath instead of as a designation of a meeting place. In her edition, therefore, lines 67–68 appear as follows: "I met your groom. / By Mars's altar, you were that time fair!" In support of her argument, she notes Theseus's later oath "By th' helm of Mars" (1.4.20).

1.1.120–21. so sorrow . . . matter: Other possible readings are (1) in the same way, **sorrow,** which lacks **form,** becomes even more formless under the pressure of **deeper matter;** or (2) in the same way, **sorrow,** lacking formal expression, is oppressed or burdened with matters more profound or grave.

1.2.23. her ancient fit of jealousy: In classical mythology, the **jealousy** of the Roman goddess Juno (identified with the Greek Hera) was the cause of many wars. Most famously it lay behind the Trojan War and her fury at "the judgment of Paris"—his choice of Aphrodite (Venus) as the most beautiful of the goddesses (see *Iliad* 24.25–30). In the *Aeneid,* Virgil writes memorably of Juno's use of war to pursue the Trojans even after the war ended in their defeat.

> Unable to stop Aeneas despite her power,
> Her hideous presence heads for earth,
> And from the home of the appalling Furies
> And hellish darkness she calls up the dread
> Alecto, in whose heart are gruesome wars
> And violence and fraud and injuries.

To this spirit of vengeance she says "break this settled peace; / Sow war and crime; let sudden quarrel spur / Young men to want, demand, and seize the sword" (7.323–26, 339–40, trans. Allen Mandelbaum [Bantam, 1961]).

Palamon's desire that Juno once again stir up war may allude as well to the Theban War, whose legends also include a jealous Juno. She hated the city and its citizens because Jove, her brother and husband, had seduced two Theban women, Alcmene and Semele. In opening his epic *Thebaid* (from which Chaucer derived "The Knight's Tale," by way of Boccaccio's *Teseida*), Statius notes that "Far backward runs the story" that leads to the war for Thebes, including the "deed fierce Juno wrought" in her fury against the city that was home to Alcmene and Semele (1.7–12, trans. H. Mozley [Loeb Classical Library, 1928]).

1.2.24–25. **purge . . . repletion:** It was an accepted idea that prolonged peace was unhealthy for a nation. Potter (Arden 3 edition) notes that peace was often "seen as a time of literal and figurative over-eating." She also points out that the idea expressed in lines 25–27, that peace is made not only healthier but also kinder through war, finds expression in the anonymous *Histriomastix* (1610), which depicts "the cycle in which Peace leads to Plenty, then to Pride, Envy, War, Poverty, and again to Peace."

1.3.83. **haply:** Like much of this speech, line 83, as it appears in the 1634 Quarto, presents severe challenges to editors and other readers today. The Quarto reading is "happely, her careles, were." *Happely* can mean either "perhaps" ("haply") or "happily"—the words were used almost interchangeably at the time—and "were" and "wear" were interchangeable spellings. Many editors write these words not as "**haply hers careless were,**" as we do, but instead as "happily her careless wear." Our choice of spellings and punctuation gives what we consider the most intelligible reading, but not necessarily the "correct" one. A similar problem occurs at line 85, which the Quarto gives as "humm'd on." Because "on" and "one" were used interchangeably, we (and other editors) print "hummed one," which in context seems to make the most sense—though it has been suggested that "on" might have meant "on and on." Since "on" and "one" were variant spellings not distinguished in Shakespeare's day, we do not use half-brackets to mark "one" as an emendation of the Quarto's "on," but we do record such choices in the textual notes.

1.3.93. **in sex individual:** Since 1750, editors have changed "sex individual" to "sex dividual," on the assumption that the word *individual* has only one possible meaning—namely, "single." Assuming that Emilia is contrasting the love between two girls with that of a heterosexual couple, and assuming that "sex individual" would have meant "single or same sex" and thus have made nonsense of her argument, editors have replaced "individual" with "dividual." But *individual* was originally used to refer to the three persons of the Christian trinity, which were one and "individual"—i.e., in-dividual, indivisible—and as has recently been noted (on the basis of evidence readily available in the *OED* and discoverable elsewhere), it retained that meaning until the second decade of the seventeenth century. Moreover, it was used to describe the union that defines marriage ("man and wife is one flesh"): Henry Cockerham (*The English Dictionarie*, 1623) includes the entry "Indiuiduall, not to bee parted, as man and wife."

We have been persuaded that *individual* here may carry its original meaning—in other words, that the Quarto's "sex individual" may mean "a man and a woman joined indissolubly (in marriage)." We also see that *individual* may instead carry its newer meaning of "single," in which case Emilia might be saying that the love between two maidens may well rest on more than their sharing the same sex; or she might be playing on the antithetical meanings of *individual* and saying at the same time that the two girls are inseparable, indivisible, in more than in their shared sex (in the many ways she points out in lines 69–93).

None of these readings is certain, but any one of them is possible. For that reason, the traditional emendation of "individual" to "dividual" seems unnecessary—indeed, unjustified. For the most complete discussion of this phrase, see Peter Stallybrass, "Shakespeare, the Individual, and the Text," in *Cultural Studies*, ed. Lawrence Grossberg, Cary Nelson, and Paula A. Treichler (New York: Routledge, 1991), pp. 593–610, esp. 595, 602–6. See also Jeffrey Masten, *Textual Intercourse: Collaboration, Authorship, and Sexualities in Renaissance Drama* (New York: Cambridge University Press, 1997), pp. 50–55.

1.4.0 SD. **Cornets:** These wind instruments have no resemblance to the brass instruments used today that are called by the same name. Instead, early modern cornets (also called *cornetts* and *cornettos*) look like slightly curved recorders; they have stops for the fingers and thumb and a small trumpetlike mouthpiece. They are capable of a wide variety of musical tones, from a sound much like the trumpet's to one approximating the violin's. They are employed in most major music of the period (as in Monteverdi's 1610 *Vespers*) and were popular stage instruments; in this play, they are called for a dozen times.

2.2.54. **Flies like a Parthian quiver:** Our gloss reflects a reading of this phrase as a simple comparison of the fleeing boar to the swift flight of a quiverful of arrows, but some editors link it to the Parthians' reputation for shooting backward toward the enemy while fleeing or pretending to flee. In that reading, the **quiver** is the actual case of arrows worn by the Parthian archer: "the Bristles and Darts sticking on [the boar's] back" resemble "the Arrows on the Archer's Shoulder, and the frequent and furious Turnings of the

Boar" resemble "the Parthian's turning to shoot as he flies" (T. Seward, 1750).

2.2.98–99. **envy . . . acquaintance:** This puzzling clause is often emended by substituting another word for **crave,** though none of the emendations is especially helpful. The puzzle arises in part because the words **envy, ill,** and **crave** all have multiple plausible meanings, and the syntax can be read in many ways. Potter, for example, glosses the clause as "Arcite fears . . . his and Palamon's succumbing to (becoming acquainted with) the vice of envying or imitating despicable people." Waith's note reads "either (1) we might suffer from coming to know the malice of evil men, or (2) we might come to envy them." And Evans glosses **envy** as "malice," **ill** as "evil," and "**Crave** our acquaintance" as "intrude upon us [?]." In context, the clause is one in a sequence of clauses pointing out the ways in which Arcite and Palamon might be severed or destroyed "were [they] at liberty" (line 96).

2.2.110–14. **all those pleasures . . . him:** Chapters 1 and 2 of Ecclesiastes spell out the **pleasures that woo the wills of men to** delight in the world or in themselves, but which are of no value (because transitory). In those chapters, Solomon declares each gift of the world to be nothing but "vanity and vexation of the spirit." See, e.g., 1.14: "I have considered all the works that are done under the sun, and behold, all is **vanity,** and vexation of the spirit." The marginal notes in the Geneva Bible interpret the message of these chapters as follows: "Solomon doth not condemn man's labor or diligence, but showeth that there is no full contentation [i.e., contentment] in anything under the heavens or in any creature [i.e., anything created] forasmuch as all things are transitory."

2.2.175. leaves . . . briers: While many editors read
briers in this line as referring to the thorns on a garden
rose bush (and thus gloss "leaves him to base briers" as,
e.g., "shows him only her thorns"), both Shakespeare
and Fletcher regularly use "brier" and "briers" to refer
to the wild rose bush, a plant represented as "base" in
comparison to the garden rose.

2.2.190–91. That's . . . then: These lines mean, perhaps, (1) "That depends on how I **bargain** with that
someone." "**Well,** the two of you **agree.**" Or, perhaps,
(2) "That depends on how you and I **bargain.**" "We'll
agree then." (The second reading assumes that "Well"
is an error for "Wele"—i.e., "We'll.")

2.3.19. Come what can come: Potter (Arden 3 edition) makes the interesting suggestion that these
words, which, in the Quarto, are crowded into the line
above, were perhaps intended to replace the phrase
that follows ("The worst is death"), which is essentially
repeated in line 25 ("I'll . . . be near her, or no more").
Making the substitution suggested here would make
line 20 read "Come what can come, I will not leave the
kingdom." We would add that removing "the worst is
death" also avoids the concurrence of two four-word
clichés—one a proverb, the second ("the worst is
death") found in Shakespeare's *Richard II* 3.2.105.

2.5.71–72. Wait . . . mistress: Theseus uses the word
mistress here (as does Emilia at line 78) to character-
ize Emilia as the person whom Arcite serves (i.e., as the
female equivalent to *master*). As the dialogue between
Arcite and Palamon at 2.2.192–280 makes clear, for
Arcite she is (according to the medieval fashion of
"courtly love") also his **mistress** in the sense that she
is the woman whom he adores, who has control over

his heart. The same duality applies to Arcite as Emilia's **servant** (2.5.56), a term used both for one who serves at another's command and for a man who dedicates himself to love of a woman.

3.1.36–37. I . . . traitor: Trials by combat were used in medieval and even later times to determine the guilty party in a dispute or to prove that someone, accused by the challenger, is a traitor. In this play, Palamon challenges Arcite to such a trial in order to establish his right to Emilia and to prove that Arcite, in loving Emilia, is a traitor to him. As in a formal trial by combat, the cousins assume that the one who is not entitled to her love will be slain, thereby confirming the legitimacy of the other's claim. Because their combat is carried out in secret—neither sanctioned by the ruler nor fought in the presence of "officers of arms" (3.6.179) serving as spectators/judges—theirs is not a legitimate trial by combat, as Theseus makes clear (3.6.176–79); it is thus illegal and, if discovered, punishable by the death of both participants. Nevertheless, they follow all the rules and procedures of the formal trial by combat, and their language here and in 3.6 is that of the formal challenge, acceptance, and preparation for it.

3.3.16. Do: Potter (Arden 3 edition) suggests that Palamon may here be responding sarcastically to some stage action performed by Arcite. In the 1634 Quarto, the words "To your health" (line 15) are followed by "&", which might indicate some drinking ritual or other stage business.

3.5.16–17. do you . . . comely out: Ovid makes it clear that the Calydonian **boar** killed by **Meleager** was far from **comely** as he breaks out of hiding: "From hence [i.e., the marsh of osiers, rushes, and reeds where the boar was concealed] the boar was roused

out, and fiercely forth he flies / Among the thickest of
his foes like thunder from the skies" (*Metamorphoses*
8.336–39).

3.5.70. The George Alow: The Jailer's Daughter
sings many popular English songs and alludes to yet
more. For details about these songs, see Ross W. Duf-
fin, *Shakespeare's Songbook* (New York: Norton, 2004);
see also Potter (Arden 3 edition), Appendix 6, "The
Music," pp. 360–64.

3.5.132. dismal: This is a dangerously ambiguous
word for the Schoolmaster to apply to Duke Theseus,
since its original meaning, stemming from *dies mali*
(evil days), is "sinister, malign, fatal."

3.5.143. Lord of May and Lady: There is considerable evidence that the presentation before Theseus
and his court in this scene is taken from the very popular second anti-masque in Francis Beaumont's *The
Masque of the Inner Temple and Gray's Inn*, presented
before King James I and his court in February 1613.
In the printed version of this *Masque* (ca. 1613), after
Iris introduces the second anti-masque with the words
"Send hither all the rural company, / Which deck the
May-games with their country sports," we find the following description of the stage action:

> *The second anti-masque rush in, dance their mea-
> sure, and as rudely depart, consisting of*
> A Pedant.

May Lord,	*May Lady,*
Servingman,	*Chambermaid,*
A Country Clown, or Shepherd,	*Country Wench,*
An Host,	*Hostess,*
A He-Baboon,	*She-Baboon,*
A He-Fool,	*She-Fool, . . .*

After this "cast of characters" list, the _Masque_ goes on to report that these actors were "appareled to the life," that "the music was extremely well fitted, having . . . a spirit of country jollity," and that "the dancers, or rather actors, expressed every one their part . . . naturally and aptly." King James, it continues, was so taken with this anti-masque that he requested it be performed again at the end of the masque. (Potter includes Beaumont's _Masque of the Inner Temple and Gray's Inn_ as Appendix 3 in her Arden 3 edition [pages 340–49].)

In the version of the anti-masque performed in _The Two Noble Kinsmen_, the Schoolmaster plays the role of "The Pedant," and he names nine characters that exactly parallel nine of those named in the anti-masque. The three he does not name—the "She-Baboon," the "She-Fool," and the "Country Wench"—he mentions as _"multis aliis,"_ "many others" (line 151). The Schoolmaster's six pairs of dancers would be composed of the six Countrymen, the five Country Wenches, and the Jailer's Daughter.

3.5.146. **welcomes to their cost:** If these words mean, as we suggest, "gives them a costly welcome," the word **their** refers to "the gallèd traveler" (147). If **their** instead refers to "mine Host / And his fat Spouse" (145–46), the words **welcomes to their cost** might mean "invites them to have a drink at the expense of the Host and his wife." Such a reading would affect the meaning of lines 147–48, "with a beck'ning / Informs the tapster to inflame the reck'ning," which would probably mean "gestures to **the tapster** to inflate the (final) statement of charges."

3.6.79. **grand guard:** It has been suggested that the **grand guard** is a very heavy piece of armor used only for tournaments on horseback. Palamon's response (line 80) supports this suggestion. If this is correct, Arcite's question about Palamon wearing **a grand guard** might be said jokingly.

3.6.299. **their lives:** Potter (Arden 3 edition) proposes, attractively, that the short, perhaps incomplete, line 297 be filled out with the words "Tell me not." With this addition, Emilia would be reminding Theseus of his argument (at lines 276–80) that if the cousins remained alive, they would damage Emilia's reputation: "Tell me not . . . how their lives / Might breed the ruin of my name."

4.1.65. **No, sir, not well:** In the 1634 Quarto (Q), our lines 4.1.64–68 are printed as follows:

Iay.	Well Sir.
I.Fr.	Not right?
2.Fr.	Not well?——————*Wooer*, No Sir not well.
Woo.	Tis too true, she is mad.

Where in a modern edition to place the Wooer's "No Sir not well" is a problem. The long dash that precedes it raises questions, as does the repetition of its speech prefix in the following line. Most editors combine the two speeches that Q assigns the Wooer, removing the second of the two speech prefixes and printing the lines as follows:

Jailer.
      Well, sir?
First Friend.   Not right?
Second Friend.   Not well?
Wooer.   No, sir, not well.
      'Tis too true: she is mad.

Lois Potter (Arden 3 edition), while printing the lines in this traditional way, notes that the Wooer's "No Sir not well," preceded as it is by the long dash, "may have been written in the margin [of the manuscript] and misplaced by the compositor, the more so, as the speech prefix is repeated before his next line."

Agreeing with Potter that the Wooer's half-line may well, for whatever reason, be misplaced in the Quarto, and noting an apparent gap in meaning between the Jailer's "Well, sir?" and the First Friend's "Not right?," we have placed the Wooer's "No, sir, not well" so that it responds to the Jailer's question and thus fills a seeming lacuna.

4.2.48. gypsy: This may or may not refer to Arcite's actual skin color. Only a few lines earlier, Emilia had referred to Palamon as "swart." Since at the time this play was written fair skin was defined as beautiful, either "swart" or "gypsy" might have been used not as descriptive of skin color but as a general term of disparagement.

4.2.145. they: The details of this description, including the freckles, are based on Chaucer's "Knight's Tale." The earlier descriptions (lines 93–106 and 115–32) are also essentially drawn from Chaucer.

4.3.14–16. in the next world . . . Aeneas: In his *Antony and Cleopatra* (4.14.63), Shakespeare has Antony represent Aeneas and Dido together in the Elysian fields, just as the Jailer's Daughter is made to do here— at least until she imagines Dido preferring Palamon to Aeneas. Such representation is at odds with Virgil's *Aeneid*, the major source of the story of Aeneas and Dido for Shakespeare's culture and for ours. There, in book 6 Aeneas meets the shade of Dido in his journey to the Underworld: she had committed suicide after the gods forced him to desert her. When he addresses her in the Fields of Mourning where the shades of unhappy lovers dwell, she is hostile and shuns him, seeking instead the embrace of her former husband, Sichaeus (*Aeneid* 6.450–74).

5.1.99–100. **heavenly fires . . . thine him:** In the first myth alluded to in these lines, Phoebus Apollo's **son** Phaëthon, attempting to drive the chariot of the sun, loses control of the chariot, comes close to destroying the earth with the sun's scorching fires, and is destroyed himself by Jove's lightning bolt. In the second myth, Phoebus mocks Cupid, son of Venus, for playing with a bow and arrow, weapons designed for men. Cupid punishes him by shooting him with an arrow that inflames him, making him fall hopelessly in love.

Textual Notes

The reading of the present text appears to the left of the square bracket. Unless otherwise noted, the reading to the left of the bracket is from **Q**, the First Quarto text of 1634 (upon which this edition is based). The earliest sources of readings not in Q are indicated as follows: **F** is the version of the play in the Beaumont and Fletcher Second Folio *Fifty Comedies and Tragedies. Written by Francis Beaumont and John Fletcher, Gentlemen* of 1679 (*The Two Noble Kinsmen* was not included in the Beaumont and Fletcher First Folio of 1647, which collected only previously unpublished plays); **Ed.** is an edition of the play from the eighteenth century or later, the first such edition being *The Works of Mr. Francis Beaumont, and Mr. John Fletcher* (1711). No sources are given for emendations of punctuation or for corrections of obvious typographical errors, like turned letters that produce no known word. **SD** means stage direction; **SP** means speech prefix; ***uncorr.*** means the first or uncorrected state of the First Quarto; ***corr.*** means a second or corrected state of the First Quarto; ~ stands in place of a word already quoted before the square bracket; ∧ indicates the omission of a punctuation mark.

Prologue 0 SD. *Flourish*] *1 line later in* Q; 27. tack] Q (take)

1.1 0. SD *Music. Enter . . . The Song*] Ed.; *Enter . . . The Song, Musike* Q; 0. SD *Pirithous*] Ed.; *Theseus* Q; 6. *thyme*] Q (*Time*); 13–14. *sweet | Lie*] Q (*sweete-| Ly*); 16. *angel*] Q (*angle*); 20. *chough*] Ed.; *Clough* Q; 20. *hoar*] Ed.; *hee* Q; 65. lord.] ~∧ Q; 68. Mars's] Q (Marsis); 76. Nemean] Ed.; Nenuan Q; 88. hast] Q (ha'st); 89. scythe] Q (Sith); 100. thy] Ed.; the Q; 100. speech,]

265

~. Q; 118. was] Ed.; was *kneele to Emilia* Q; 127. peb-
bles] Q (peobles); 127. glassy] Ed.; glasse Q; 147, 172.
to th'] Q (to'th); 150. longer] Ed.; long Q; 152. Knolls]
Q (Knowles); 153. more∧] ~. Q; 156. move] F; mooves
Q; 156. ospreys] Q (Asprayes); 161. for th'] Q (for'th);
164. human] Q (humaine); 183. Artesius] *Artesuis* Q;
186. levy] Q *corr.;* l evy Q *uncorr.;* 190. hands.] ~∧ Q;
203. neglected∧] ~, Q; 206. twinning] Q (twyning); 211.
drum] Q (Drom); 232. now!] ~∧ Q; 246. before,] ~)∧
Q; 248. Aulis] Ed.; Anly Q; 255. SD *exit*] Ed.; *Exeunt*
Q; 265. dost] Q (do'st); 273. do;] ~, Q; 274. human] Q
(humane); 275. SD *Flourish*] *1 line earlier in* Q

　　1.2　20. fought.] ~, Q; 43. every] Q (eve'ry); 59. scis-
sored] Q (Cizard); 78. glory;] ~∧ Q; 78. one∧] on∧ Q
uncorr.; on; Q *corr.;* 92. not∧] ~: Q; 93. SD *Enter Valerius.*] *1 line earlier in* Q; 94. Valerius.] ~∧ Q

　　1.3　31. SD *Pirithous*] Q (*Pir.*); 37. one] Ed; ore Q;
42. for 't] Q (fort); 63. Flavina] Ed.; *Flauia* Q; 68–74. Q
sets in left margin: "2. Hearses ready with Palamon: and
Arcite: the 3. Queenes. Theseus: and his Lordes ready."
83. hers] This ed.; her Q; 85. one] Q (on); 86. musical]
misicall Q; 94. out] ont Q

　　1.4　0. SD *within*] *withim* Q; 7. herd] Q (Heard); 11.
supply 't] Q (suppl'it); 14. haste] Q (hast); 20. By th']
Q (By'th); 21. smeared] Q *corr.* (smeard); succard Q
uncorr.; 26. Wi'] Ed.; We Q; 31–32. Q *sets in left margin:*
"3. *Hearses ready.*" 38. waste] Q (wast); 47. friends'] ~,
Q; 48. Love's∧] Loves, Q; 52. O'er-] Ed.; Or Q; 56. 'fore]
Ed.; for Q; 56. SD *Flourish*] *1 line earlier in* Q

　　1.5　10. *naught . . . woes*] Q (&c)

　　2.1　15. SD *Enter . . . rushes.*] *1 line earlier in* Q; 19.
that∧] ~. Q; 19. now;] ~, Q; 29. SP DAUGHTER] Q *corr.*
(*Daugh.*); *Dœugh.* Q *uncorr.;* 43. sometimes] Q (sometime); 44. them—] ~. Q; 50. SD *Enter . . . above.*] *1 line
earlier in* Q

　　2.2　0. SD *Palamon . . . above.*] Ed.; *Enter Palamon,*

and Arcite in prison. Q; 4. war; yet∧] ~∧ ~, Q; 24. wore]
Ed.; were Q; 25. Ravished] Bravishd Q; 115. been,] ~∧
Q; 133. SP EMILIA This] Ed.; This Q; 134. What] Ed.;
Emil. What Q; 154. Will 't] Q (wilt); 157. Cousin] Gosen
Q; 207. SP PALAMON] *Pal.* Q *corr.; Pal:* Q *uncorr.;* 208.
her∧] ~; Q; 235. your blood] F; you blood Q; 273. 'twere]
Q (tw'er); 280. SD *Enter . . . above.*] *1 line earlier in* Q;
280, 290, 310, 358. SD *Jailer*] Q (*Keeper*); 284 *and here-
after in this scene.* SP JAILER] Ed.; *Keeper.* Q; 286. to th']
Q (to'th); 298. ne'er] Q (ne're); 302. you,] ~. Q; 337.
Prithee] Q (pre'thee); 344. you] F; yon Q

   2.3 6. sins] Q *corr.;* fins Q *uncorr.;* 8. hast] Q (ha'st);
25. SD garland] Q *corr.* (garlond); Garlon Q *uncorr.;* 32.
tickle 't] Q (tick'lt); 45. you] Ed.; yet Q; 59. means;] ~∧
Q; 60. says] Ed.; sees Q; 62. to th'] Q (to'th); 94. plum]
Q (plumb)

   2.5 0. Scene 5] Ed.; Scæna 4. Q; 0. SD *This . . .
within.*] *in small type in the left margin in* Q; 0. SD
Attendants, and others] Ed.; *&c.* Q; 40. For] Fo Q; 88.
SD *Flourish.*] *1 line earlier in* Q

   2.6 3. him;] ~∧ Q; 15. dirge∧] ~. Q; 24. free man]
Q (Freeman); 31. no man] Q (no-man); 35. hubbub] Q
(whoobub)

   3.1 0. SD *Cornets . . . Maying.*] *in small type in the
right margin of* Q *opposite* "Actus Tertius"; 2. laund]
Q (land); 2. rite] Q (Right); 11. presence.] ~, Q; 38.
looked,] ~∧ Q; 38. void'st] Ed.; voydes Q; 38. honor∧]
~. Q; 92. house.] ~, Q; 96. prison.] ~, Q; 108. SD *Wind
. . . cornets.*] *1 line earlier in* Q; 108. SD *off*] Q (*of*); 110.
muset] Ed.; Musicke Q; 110. lest] Q (least); 111. ere] Q
(er); 116. pour] Q (powre); 121. language.] ~, Q; 122.
not] F; nor Q; 123. SD *Wind horns.*] *2 lines earlier in* Q;
130. 'Tis] Ed.; If Q

   3.2 1. mistook∧] ~; Q; 1. brake] Ed.; Beake Q; 3.
matter;] ~, Q; 7. reck] Q (wreake); 14. gyves] Q (Gives);
19. fed] F; feed Q; 25. dozens] Q (dussons); 25. moped]

Q (mop't); 28. brine] bine Q; 35–36. screech owl] Schreichowl Q *uncorr.;* Schreichowle Q *corr.*

3.3 4. here's] Q (her'es); 4. SD *Enter Palamon.*] *3 lines earlier in* Q; 15. SD *He drinks.*] Ed.; , &c. Q; 19. 'twill] Q (t'will); 36. them] F; then Q; 66. 'tis] Q (t'is); 82. perfumes] per | (fumes Q *uncorr.;* per-| (fumes Q *corr.*

3.4 9. Open] Ed.; Vpon Q; 10. tack] Q (take)

3.5 0. Scene 5] Ed.; Scæna 6. Q; 0. SD *Enter . . . Bavian*] Ed.; *Enter a Schoole master .4. Countrymen: and Baum .2. or 3 wenches, with a Taborer* Q *corr.;* Baumʌ Q *uncorr.;* 7. coarse] Q (course); 7. jean] Ed.; jave Q; 17. boar—] ~ʌ Q; 19. figure,] ~ʌ Q; 24. SD *Enter the Taborer.*] *See note to 3.5.0 SD above.* 58. by th'] Q (by'th); 75–76. *In small type in the left margin of* Q: "Chaire and stooles out"; 77. *Till I*] Ed.; *till* Q; 79. *he*] Ed.; *not in* Q; 83–84. master] Q (Mʳ.); 100. *Chi passa*] Ed.; *Quípassa* Q; 107. SD *Wind horns.*] ~ ~: Q *uncorr.;* ~ ~ʌ Q *corr.; 2 lines earlier in* Q; 109. SD *All . . . exit.*] Ed.; *Ex. all but Schoolemaster. 2 lines earlier in* Q; 110. SD *Enter . . . train.*] Ed.; *Enter Thes. Pir. Hip. Emil. Arcite:and traine.* Q; 115. SP THESEUS] F; *Per.* Q; 116. SD *Chairs . . . out.*] *See note to 3.5.75–76 above.* 120. favor,] ~; Q; 149. beest] Q (beast); 155. SD *Music . . . dance.*] Ed.; *Musicke Dance. 1 line earlier in* Q. (*In small type in the left margin of* Q: Knocke for Schoole. Enter The Dance.); 157. ye] Ed.; thee Q; 160. thee] F; three Q; 170. you] F; yon Q; 178. *deaeque*] Q (*Deaq*)

3.6 0. Scene 6] Ed.; Scæna 7 Q; 17. SD *Enter . . . swords.*] *1/2 line later in* Q; 38. upbraidings] Q (obbraidings); 41. Will 't] Q (wilt); 58. soldier,] ~. Q; 98. armor's] Q (Armo'rs); 128. hopes.] ~: Q; 129. SD *They . . . stand.*] *in small type in the left margin in* Q *opposite lines 129–33* (*with an asterisk in the text to mark where the stage action should happen*); 190. thine own] Ed.; this owne Q; 223. us;] ~, Q; 224. valiant,] ~; Q; 239. 'em,] ~; Q; 239. ruin.] ~, Q; 242. to th'] Q (to'th); 243. sister;] ~, Q;

244. us.] ~, Q; 279. They'd] Q (The'yld); 283. by th'] Q
(by'th); 286. anger;] ~, Q; 287. it.] ~, Q; 289. Besides]
Q (Beside); 296. now;] ~, Q; 296. fail] Ed.; fall Q; 300.
Opinion!] ~, Q; 302. prune] Q (proyne); 329. He's] Q
(H'es); 355. excellent.] ~∧ Q; 383. bier] Q (Beere)

4.1 1. Heard] Ed.; Heare Q; 13. oath] Q (o'th); 19.
SD *Enter . . . Friend.*] *1 line earlier in* Q; 38. 'twould] Q
(t'would); 45. 'Twill] Q (T'will); 45. SD *Enter Wooer.*] *1
line earlier in* Q; 64–68. sir. . . . WOOER] Ed.; Sir. | I *Fr.*
Not right? | 2 *Fr.* Not well?—*Wooer,* No Sir not well. |
Woo. Q; 85. 'Twas] Q (T'was); 90. sung] F; song Q; 96. to
th'] Q (to'th); 104. antic] Q (Antique); 113. wreath] Ed.;
wreake Q; 135. SD *Enter . . . others.*] *1 line earlier in* Q;
137, 151, 209. *etc.*] Ed.; &c. Q; 151. SD *Sings.*] *moved
from end of line in* Q *to beginning of line;* 154. Good] Q
(Good'); 160. far] Ed.; For Q; 190. SP SECOND FRIEND] F;
I. *Fr.* Q; 195. to th'] Q (too'th); 196. course] conrse Q;
196. to th'] Q (to'th); 200. bowline] Q (Bowling); 208.
Tack] Q (take)

4.2 18. Jove] Ed.; Love Q; 21. carries,] ~? Q; 27.
such] sueh Q; 44. 'em?] ~∧ Q; 50. Utterly∧] Q *corr.*
(Vtterly); Vtterly. Q *uncorr.;* 58. SD *Enter a Gentleman.*]
Ed.; *Enter Emil. and Gent:* Q; 59. How] Ed.; *Emil.* How
Q; 83. SD *Enter a Messenger.*] Ed.; *Enter Messengers.
Curtis.* (*3 lines earlier in* Q); 94. first] fitst Q; 99. fire]
Ed.; faire Q; 107. hast] Q (ha'st); 125. tods] Ed.; tops
Q; 130. crown] Ed.; corect Q; 151. auburn] Q (aborne);
184. so—] ~; Q; 184. appear.] ~, Q; 186. SD *All . . . exit.*]
See note to 4.2.188 below. 188. SD *She exits*] *Exeunt* Q

4.3 6. soe'er] Q (so'ere); 11. on 't] Q (o'nt); 19. SP
JAILER] *Ioy.* Q; 23. spirits∧ are,] Ed.; spirits, as∧ Q; 33. i'
th' other] F; i'th Thother Q; 40. enough.] Ed.; enough.
Exit. Q; 44. navel] Q (Nav'le); 44. to th'] Q (to'th); 46.
punishment] Q *corr.;* punishuent Q *uncorr.;* 54. were]
Q *corr.;* weare Q *uncorr.;* 54. I'd] Q (il'd); 55. th' other]
Ed.; another Q; 56. behind] Q *corr.;* behold Q *uncorr.;*

59. *etc.*] Ed.; & *c.* Q; 71. same] Q *corr.* (Same); Saue Q *uncorr.;* 90. sweet∧] Q *uncorr.;* ~, Q *corr.;* 91. carve] F; crave Q

5.1   0. SD *Flourish.*] *1 line earlier in* Q *before "Exe-unt" at the end of Act 4;* 8. SD *Flourish of cornets.*] *3 lines earlier in* Q; 8. SD *Enter . . . Knights.*] *1 line earlier in* Q; 40. SD *Palamon . . . exit.*] *1 line earlier in* Q; 44. father of] Ed.; farther off Q; 50. blood;] ~, Q; 53. cistern] Q (Cestron); 57. whose approach] Ed.; *omit* Q; 62. armipotent] Q (armenypotent); 73. cur'st] Ed.; curst Q; 76. boldly.] ~∧ Q *uncorr.;* ~, Q *corr.;* 84. Her] Q *corr.;* His Q *uncorr.;* 84. SD kneel] Ed.; kneele *as formerly* Q; 87. hast] Q (ha'st); 94. wanton] Q *corr.;* wonton Q *uncorr.;* 99. his;] ~∧ Q; 104, 115. 'twere] Q (t'wer); 127. done, no companion;] ~; ~ ~∧ Q; 128. not, a defier;] ~; ~ ~∧ Q; 129. cannot, a rejoicer.] ~; ~ ~, Q; 132. language.] ~, Q; 138. O] Ed.; *Pal.* O Q; 144. SD *They . . . bow.*] *2 lines earlier in* Q; 145. SD *recorders*] *Records* Q; 157. Ne'er] Q (Ne're); 161. him.] ~∧ Q; 163. election.] ~∧ Q

5.2   2. kept] hept Q; 51. Yes] F; Yet Q; 56. SD *Enter . . . Maid.*] *1 line earlier in* Q; 57. humor] Ed.; honour Q; 77. tune] Ed.; turne Q; 77. o'] Q (*a'*); 92. ne'er] Q (ne're); 101. to th'] Q (to'th); 119. two] Q (too); 152. sight] Ed.; fight Q

5.3   0. SD *Flourish.*] *1 line earlier in* Q *before "Exe-unt" at the end of 5.2;* 0. SD *Attendants.*] Ed.; *Attendants, T. Tucke: Curtis.* Q; 4. decision; ev'ry∧] ~∧ ~; Q; 22. I'd] Q (I'ld); 24. 'twere] Q (t'wer); 51. SD *and others*] Q (&c.); 58. sometimes] Q (sometime); 83, 111. prithee] Q (pre'thee); 91. in 't else;] ~ ~; ~∧ Q; 93. SD *Another . . . cornets*] *2 lines earlier in* Q; 112, 145. to th'] Q (to'th); 112. SD *Cornets . . . victory*] *1 line earlier in* Q; 126. SD *and Others*] Q (&c.); 145. all∧] ~; Q; 164. your] F; you Q; 173. SD *Flourish*] *11 lines earlier in* Q

5.4   0. SD *Enter . . . ax.*] Ed.; *Enter Palamon and his Knightes pyniond: Iaylor, Executioner &c. Gard.* Q; 1. SP

PALAMON] Ed.; *omit* Q; 10. unwappered, notʌ] ~ʌ ~, Q;
20. o'er-weigh] Q (ore'-weigh); 29. does] Q (do'es); 36.
prithee] Q (pre'thee); 43. quit] Q (quight); 47. SD *Lays
his head*] Ed.; *Lies* Q; 48. courageous] couragiour Q;
49. SP SECOND and THIRD] Ed.; I.2. Q; 59. dearly] Ed.;
early Q; 74. 'twere] Q (t'wer); 74. to th'] Q (to'th); 95.
victor's] Q *corr.;* victoros Q *uncorr.;* 103. Arcite.] ~, Q;
104. unbroken,] ~: Q; 128. Hath] Ed.; Hast Q; 156.
sorry, stillʌ] ~ʌ ~, Q

The Two Noble Kinsmen: A Modern Perspective

Dieter Mehl

The Two Noble Kinsmen, though not included in the First Folio of 1623, has for about the past fifty years been generally accepted as a play in which Shakespeare had at least a large share, and it has been included in practically all major editions of his works.[1] The play was first published in 1634, with the title page stating that it was "written by the memorable Worthies of their time; Mr. John Fletcher, and Mr. William Shakespeare" and that it had been "Presented at the Blackfriers by the Kings Maiesties servants, with great applause."[2] A large part of the critical commentary has therefore been concerned with the question of authorship. Most modern scholars agree with the title page's statement that the play was the product of collaboration, and there also seems to be almost unanimous agreement that the relative shares of the two dramatists can be determined with some confidence.[3]

The subject of the play, as the Prologue declares, is taken from Geoffrey Chaucer; in fact, *The Two Noble Kinsmen* "represents Shakespeare's most direct and unquestionable use of a Chaucerian source."[4] No other play in the canon acknowledges its ancestry so openly:

> I am sure
> It has a noble breeder and a pure,
> A learnèd, and a poet never went
> More famous yet 'twixt Po and silver Trent.

John Fletcher.
From the frontispiece to *Comedies and tragedies . . .
by Francis Beaumont and John Fletcher* (1647).

The true portraiture of GEFFREY CHAUCER
the famous English poet, as by THOMAS
OCCLEUE is described who liued in his
time, and was his Scholar.

"Chaucer, of all admired." (Pro. 13)
From the title page of the Thomas Speght edition
of Chaucer's *Works* (1602).

Chaucer, of all admired, the story gives;
There, constant to eternity, it lives.

(Prologue 9–14)

The work in question is "The Knight's Tale," the
first of the *Canterbury Tales* (c. 1387–1400), Chaucer's
celebrated collection of stories, a unique miscellany
of contrasting narrative genres and subjects. The tale
offered by the Knight, who is the first in social status
among the pilgrims on their way to the Shrine of Saint
Thomas in Canterbury, is, apart from two prose tracts,
the longest and most ambitious contribution to the sto-
rytelling contest. "The Knight's Tale," itself a drastically
condensed version of Giovanni Boccaccio's *Il Teseida*
(written before 1341), proved to be one of Chaucer's
most popular works; the story was apparently dramatized by a series of Elizabethan playwrights, though
none of their texts has survived. It has many of the traditional elements of medieval romance that appealed
to Elizabethan and Jacobean poets and dramatists in
search of new material and that evidently were popular
with audiences as well: old-fashioned chivalry, ceremonial tournament, rivalry in love and friendship, and the
unpredictable whims of Fortune and Fate. Chaucer's
poem, a highly stylized and beautifully balanced narrative of some 2,250 lines in rhyming couplets, is set in
classical Greece in the city-states of Athens and Thebes,
within a cosmos governed by the planets and gods who
were familiar to educated Englishmen from Greek
mythology. Yet the two protagonists, Palamon and
Arcite, are medieval knights aspiring to the ideals of the
traditional chivalric code—as exemplified by Chaucer's
Knight, who is described as loving "chivalrie / Trouthe
and honour, fredom and curteisie" (A.45–46).[5] His tale
places the two knights in a situation that tests their
moral qualities in a series of trials in love, friendship,

loyalty, and valor. Several of these themes had been explored by Shakespeare earlier in his comedies, and *A Midsummer Night's Dream* in particular has a number of incidental borrowings from "The Knight's Tale."[6] *The Two Noble Kinsmen*, however, keeps much closer to the action and to the general spirit of its source.[7]

Chaucer's "Knight's Tale" has been described as a philosophical romance: a traditional story of love and adventure that urgently probes the nature of providence and the justice of individual suffering and destiny. After simultaneously falling in love with the same woman, the two kinsmen, separated from one another and unable to be near the object of their sudden passion, reflect on the instability of fortune and the unfathomable ways of providence: "What governance is in this prescience, / That giltelees tormenteth innocence?" laments the imprisoned Palamon (A.1313–14). And toward the poem's end Arcite, cut down at his moment of triumph by a seemingly indiscriminate fate in the guise of a whimsical planet-god, asks in heroic despair: "What is this world? What asketh men to have?" (A.2777). The narrator's interest, above all, is in "the dominant role of chance in determining the course of human life."[8] There is no suggestion that men are masters of their fate; rather, in the face of inexplicable chance, they have to make the best of what they are powerless to influence. As Chaucer's Theseus tells the survivors: "Thanne is it wysdom, as it thynketh me, / To maken vertu of necessitee" (A.3041–42). Of course, this is not Chaucer's last word in the *Canterbury Tales*. Indeed, "The Knight's Tale" is immediately followed (and put into question) by the outrageous farce of "The Miller's Tale," with two lovers whose rivalry ends in undignified burlesque. Taken all together, the collection's broad range of humorous, tragic, philosophical, and religious interpretations of human affairs forestalls any conclusion that the author endorsed the Knight's implied stoic fatalism.

It was evidently the dramatic and moral dilemma posed by the story's action that intrigued the two dramatists; but it appears from the text of the play that they did not wholly agree on details of character and dramatic method. Such differences may account for some of the more puzzling aspects of the play's moral and philosophical attitudes, as well as its not entirely satisfactory final form.

The playwrights took over the main outline of Chaucer's story, with its teasing tragicomic conclusion. An unmistakable element of trickery and moral equivocation is softened in the poem by the indefinite passage of time and by the narrative's somewhat digressive pace. In the play, however, as in *Troilus and Cressida* and *Romeo and Juliet*, "speed is the medium of fate."[9] Shakespeare and Fletcher have drastically altered Chaucer's time scheme: the events follow one another with breathless haste and no perceptible lapse of time.[10] The most striking compression of the action occurs in the last act, where Arcite's death is immediately followed by Theseus's public sanction of Palamon's union, blessed earlier by his rival's final words: "Take her. I die" (5.4.113). In "The Knight's Tale," the pace is considerably more relaxed and unhurried. Arcite in his dying speech warmly recommends his friend to Emily and concludes: "And if that evere ye shul ben a wyf, / Foryet nat Palamon, the gentil man" (A.2796–97).[11] An elaborate description of the funeral ceremonies follows, before the narrator proceeds with the conclusion of his tale:

> By processe and by lengthe of certeyn yeres,
> Al stynted is the moornynge and the teres
> Of Grekes, by oon general assent.

> (A.2967–69)

Only then, and after a meeting of the parliament, is peace established between Athens and Thebes. Palamon and Emily are sent for and, after a solemn philosophical oration by Theseus, joined together in marriage.

Shakespeare opens the play with an elaborate pageant: a ceremonial procession to Theseus's wedding, which is looked forward to with such impatience in the first scene of *A Midsummer Night's Dream* (written some fifteen years earlier). Here, the revels are halted by an unexpected challenge that turns out to be a choice between two moral duties. At first, the wedding seems more important to Theseus than any of his heroic achievements, but the plea of Hippolyta, supported by Emilia, persuades him that the widowed queens have a higher claim to his humanity. The ceremony is accordingly postponed:

> As we are men,
> Thus should we do; being sensually subdued,
> We lose our human title.
>
> (1.1.272–74)

Chaucer's couple are already married by the time they are confronted with the mourning widows, and Theseus is immediately overwhelmed by compassion; there is no moral dilemma, nor are Hippolyta and Emilia included in the debate. In *The Two Noble Kinsmen*, significantly, Emilia from the very beginning is associated with the theme of virginity by her threat never to take a husband if Theseus should refuse Hippolyta's plea (1.1.238–39; see also the Third Queen's address to her, 1.1.31–33).

The second scene, which has no equivalent in Chaucer's tale, then introduces the two kinsmen. The dramatist (most probably Shakespeare) evidently wanted to present the protagonists, before their interactions

with Theseus, as nobly united in friendship and broth-
erly affection. They are resolved to leave Creon's corrupt court, but when he is threatened by Theseus they
feel honor bound to join him and "stand to the mercy
of our fate" (1.2.116). Arcite's lines that end the scene
confirm their reliance on fate and submission to the
rule of fortune:

> Let th' event,
> That never-erring arbitrator, tell us
> When we know all ourselves, and let us follow
> The becking of our chance.
>
> (1.2.132–35)

The theme is again taken up when Theseus, returning
as victor to the grateful praises of the three queens,
credits the gods with his triumph:

> Th' impartial gods, who from the mounted heavens
> View us their mortal herd, behold who err
> And, in their time, chastise.
>
> (1.4.6–8)

It is an aspect of Chaucer's tale that Shakespeare clearly
found significant and worth exploring.[12]

The scene inserted before Theseus's campaign is
also an addition to Chaucer's narrative, introduc-
ing the theme of love in a way that casts an ominous
and rather un-Chaucerian light on the action that follows. When Hippolyta, her wedding delayed by the
war against Creon, wonders whom Theseus loves best,
herself or his friend Pirithous, Emilia recalls her own
affection for a girl who died at eleven. Her assertion
that "the true love 'tween maid and maid may be /
More than in sex individual" (1.3.92–93) attests that
she will never be able to love "any that's called man"

(97) with the same certainty. Her speech, unparalleled in Chaucer, has been compared with Helena's pathetic appeal to Hermia after Robin Goodfellow's mischievous magic has confounded the pairs of lovers (*A Midsummer Night's Dream* 3.2.206–22), but Helena's plaint is forgotten as soon as the spell has been lifted and order restored; Emilia's desire for a single life, or companionship with a partner of her own sex, has a very different resonance. Nothing that is said in *The Two Noble Kinsmen* seems more genuinely sincere than Emilia's final word in this first dialogue: "I am not / Against your faith, yet I continue mine" (1.3.110–11). She never explicitly swerves from her conviction that virginity is preferable to conventional marriage.

The first act, ending with the funeral of the three kings, concludes the introductory section of the story. N. W. Bawcutt remarks, with some justice, "If Shakespeare had gone on to write the whole of *The Two Noble Kinsmen* the first act would probably have received more praise and attention than it has."[13] It has introduced a lively panorama of romance, chivalry, and classical ideals, with a teasing invitation to moral and philosophical debate. Regrettably, these elements receive little development in the succeeding acts until the play's tragicomic finale, which returns to some of the moral and poetic intensity of the first scenes.

One can hardly escape the impression that this change has to do with the different minds at work at different stages of the story. Many scholars agree that Shakespeare's coauthor took over after 2.1, which introduces the Jailer, his Daughter, and her Wooer and includes the Daughter's characteristic line: "It is a holiday to look on them. Lord, the diff'rence of men!" (2.1.58–59).[14]

The addition of the subplot is the dramatists' most original contribution to the play's structure. It has no

basis in "The Knight's Tale," where Palamon's escape
from prison, after seven years, is achieved by "helpyng
of a freend" (A.1468); he drugs the jailer with a narcotic
brew of sweet wine and opium. The Jailer's Daughter,
her pathetic infatuation with Palamon, and her part in
his escape are a brilliant new addition to the dramatic
action. Her madness and its cure by sex add a subdued
note of comic harmony to an otherwise problematic
and not entirely satisfactory tragicomic ending; they
also provide a dramatically effective commentary
on the main action, with its disturbing exhibition of
perverse human obsession.[15] The part of the Jailer's
Daughter has proved particularly successful on stage
in several recent revivals.[16] The two dramatists skillfully use this subplot and the more realistic scenes of
rustic entertainment to extend the social range of the
play, at the same time creating a somewhat more opti-
mistic alternative to the sinister trick played on Arcite
in Chaucer's tale by Saturn, who consoles Venus, weeping for the defeat of her knight Palamon, by sending a
fury out of hell to spook Arcite's horse.

The second act, after the first scene, and most of
the following two acts are written in a noticeably different idiom. The crucial moment in the story, when
the two friends catch sight of Emilia and fall in love
simultaneously, is presented with heroic pathos, without any comic innuendo. One can hardly avoid the
suspicion that Shakespeare at this point might have
remembered his earlier comedy *As You Like It*, with its
gently mocking quotation from Marlowe: "Who ever
loved that loved not at first sight?" (3.5.87). But the
conflict presented here (most likely by John Fletcher),
is more conventional, with an abrupt transition from
emphatic mutual protestation of eternal friendship to
deadly enmity. Chaucer's tone is much more distant
and faintly humorous: even during the first quarrel of

the kinsmen, his Arcite points out the absurdity of the situation, remembering the fable of two dogs fighting over a bone that a kite snatches out from under their noses while they are still squabbling (A.1177–80).

Elsewhere—notably, in *Love's Labor's Lost* and *As You Like It*—Shakespeare, too, presents the conventions and pretensions of "courtly" love with satiric skepticism. The eye for love's absurdities is no less sharp and no more blinkered by romantic idealism in Chaucer's "The Knight's Tale" than in any Shakespearean comedy. When the two rivals are surprised in the open grove, fighting like wild boars (A.1699), Theseus points to the spectacle as a demonstration of love's madness:

> Now looketh, is nat that an heigh folye?
> Who may been a fool but if he love?
> . . . .
> But this is yet the beste game [joke] of alle,
> That she for whom they han this jolitee
> Kan hem therfore as muche thank as me.
> She woot namoore of al this hoote fare,
> By God, than woot a cokkow or an hare!
>
> (A.1798–99, 1806–10)

Little of this ironic detachment has found its way into *The Two Noble Kinsmen*, though the two playwrights could hardly have failed to notice Chaucer's skepticism regarding immature illusion and some ridiculous aspects of literary convention.

Fletcher, however, was evidently less interested in subtle mockery of literary cliché or persuasive consistency of characterization than in local dramatic effects. He is a master of surprising twists of plot and unusual theatrical situations. His preferred method is to confront his characters with some agonizing dilemma for the sake of sensational dramatic novelty. Theseus's arbitrary

verdict of death for the loser in the combat between
the two rivals, not found in Chaucer's story, seems a
characteristic Fletcherian twist, adding an element of
willful cruelty not demanded by the plot.[17] It makes
Emilia's position needlessly unpleasant and highlights
the superior subtlety of Shakespeare's characterization
in the first part and the conclusion. One can hardly
disagree with Talbot Donaldson's impression that the
"silly scene" in which Emilia compares the two pictures
(4.2) is "so much at variance with her earlier and later
Shakespearean appearances as to make Shakespeare's
authorship impossible."[18]

The dilemma forced on Emilia as the unwilling
object of male desire is far more painful in the play
than in Chaucer's narrative, where she is primarily the
target of a more conventional courtly love worship and
lacks a sharply drawn personality. Her own preference
seems to be no vital part of the story, though; in *The Two
Noble Kinsmen*, as in the poem, she prays for virginity
and sincerely laments over Arcite's sudden death. What
is particularly characteristic of Shakespeare's Emilia is
that she appears to enjoy neither her power as the prize
desired by the two most worthy knights nor the prospect of marriage to either of them. Her anxiety over
the life and health of the two knights is more intense
and sincere than any personal attachment or inclination, and when Theseus hands her over to Arcite after
his victory she responds with an eloquence that almost
matches her relation of her adolescent friendship in
the first act:

> Is this winning?
> O all you heavenly powers, where is your mercy?
> But that your wills have said it must be so,
> And charge me live to comfort this unfriended,

This miserable prince, that cuts away
A life more worthy from him than all women,
I should and would die too.

(5.3.163–69)

She clearly believes that Arcite has lost more than
any woman will ever be able to give him, whatever he
may feel himself at this moment. After her last farewell to Arcite—"while I live, / This day I give to tears"
(5.4.117–18)—there is not another word from her. In
all Shakespearean comedy or romance, no marriage
is entered into with less enthusiasm or joyful expectation. Chaucer's tale, in contrast, offers the traditional
promise of a happy ending:

And Emelye hym loveth so tendrely,
And he hire serveth so gentilly,
That nevere was ther no word hem bitwene
Of jalousie or any oother teene [vexation].

(A.3103–6)

In the tragicomedy of *The Two Noble Kinsmen*, the successful wooer of the Jailer's Daughter—the victim of a
benevolent deception—may well be the luckier of the
two bridegrooms in the end.

Gain and loss are apportioned more equally in Chaucer's tale. His Arcite has achieved what in his prayer to
Mars he asked for, as is explicitly confirmed after his
death. Following some general reflections on the divine
ordering of the universe, Theseus observes

And certeinly a man hath moost honour
To dyen in his excellence and flour,
Whan he is siker of his goode name.

(A.3047–49)

In the play, after Arcite's sudden death, such honor is treated almost like a consolation prize, further cheapened by Theseus's verdict that Arcite has "restored" Emilia as a "stol'n jewel" (5.4.141–42). This explanation, accepted by the dying Arcite but absent from Chaucer's tale, reduces the painful moral dilemma to a simple juvenile quarrel, tidily resolved. With remarkable and hardly sensitive promptness Theseus transfers his favor and the hand of his sister-in-law to Palamon, without a moment's consideration for Emilia's emotional state of mind. She has been, throughout, no more than a passive object of his godlike power, though at the end he admits that "The gods my justice / Take from my hand and they themselves become / The executioners" (5.4.143–45). Even in *Hamlet*, the change from funeral to "visages of bridegrooms" (5.4.150) is less sudden.

Piero Boitani justly points out the great difference between the Theseus in *The Two Noble Kinsmen* and his Chaucerian namesake, whose comment reveals humble trust in the regiment of the divine powers:

> "What may I conclude of this longe serye
> [argument],
> But after wo I rede [advise] us to be merye
> And thanken Juppiter of al his grace?"
>
> (A.3067–9)

Shakespeare's Theseus appears somewhat glib and sententious in comparison:

>   O you heavenly charmers,
> What things you make of us! For what we lack
> We laugh, for what we have are sorry, still
> Are children in some kind. Let us be thankful
> For that which is, and with you leave dispute
> That are above our question.
>
> (5.4.154–59)

Whether we ultimately agree with Boitani's verdict that "Shakespeare and Fletcher have 'perverted' their Chaucer"[19] depends on our own reading of Chaucer and of the two dramatists. The brevity of the play's close (thirty-five lines against Chaucer's three hundred) certainly seems to scant the potentially tragic conflict, and the conclusion lacks much of the philosophical depth and seriousness of "The Knight's Tale."

Most of the play's subplot scenes appear to be the work of John Fletcher, though Shakespeare may well have contributed some ideas. Unfortunately, we know nothing about their collaboration—the practical details, their discussions during composition, the general ideas or ground plan they agreed on before beginning to write. Nor can we be certain about how they read and interpreted Chaucer's text, though it is difficult to believe that they were unaware of the narrator's distanced and occasionally humorous attitude toward his characters and their old-fashioned ideas of love and chivalry.

At several points in the story the Knight explicitly addresses the audience (and readers), drawing attention to an emotional crisis or a particular philosophical problem. One such appeal occurs at the end of Part One:

> Yow loveres axe I now this questioun:
> Who hath the worse, Arcite or Palamoun?
> That oon may seen his lady day by day,
> But in prison he moot dwelle alway;
> That oother wher hym list may ride or go,
> But seen his lady shal he nevere mo.
> Now demeth as yow liste, ye that kan,
> For I wol telle forth as I bigan.

(A.1347–54)

It is the kind of love problem treated by medieval romances but sidestepped in *The Two Noble Kinsmen*—

presumably in the interest of dramatic economy—by Palamon's forced removal from the room where he can enjoy the view of Emilia and by radically shortening Arcite's period of banishment and omitting his departure from Athens. Only in the Epilogue are the lovers in the audience directly addressed, though the voice of Chaucer's narrator, intrigued yet faintly amused by the spectacle of chivalric heroism, seems occasionally to be echoed in the playwrights' rhetoric.

Judging by the reception of "The Knight's Tale" in the generations succeeding Chaucer, most of his readers have agreed with the Canterbury pilgrims that it was "a noble storie / And worthy for to drawen to memorie" (A.3111–12); yet Fletcher seems to have been attracted primarily by the opportunity it offered for sensational effects and novel dramatic situations. It is, of course, idle to speculate what *The Two Noble Kinsmen* would have been like if Shakespeare, more alive to the story's rich philosophical and moral potential, had written all of it. Given the achievement of the first and last acts, it might have been a quite different play.

---

1. E.g., the play is printed in the Riverside, Oxford, Norton, and Bevington one-volume collections, as well as in such series as the Arden, New Cambridge, Oxford, Penguin, and Pelican.

2. See the facsimile of the first edition of 1634 at http://internetshakespeare.uvic.ca/Library/facsimile/bookplay/BL_Q1_TNK/TNK/ (accessed July 2009). It is worth noting that the play was entered in the Stationers' Register on April 8, 1634, as "TragiComedy," a term not used in that register for almost twenty years. The first performance, by Shakespeare and Fletcher's company, the King's Men, probably took place in 1613 or early 1614.

3. Details of the apportionment are discussed later in this essay. Shakespeare is generally agreed to have written 1.1–5 (with some uncertainty about 1.4–5), 2.1, 3.1, 5.1, and 5.3–4. Fletcher is generally assigned the Prologue and Epilogue and the rest. The most thorough treatment is Brian Vickers, *Shakespeare, Co-Author: A Historical Study of Five Collaborative Plays* (Oxford: Oxford University Press, 2002).

4. E. Talbot Donaldson, *The Swan at the Well: Shakespeare Reading Chaucer* (New Haven: Yale University Press, 1985), p. 51. A good modern interlinear translation of "The Knights Tale" is available at www.courses .fas.harvard.edu/~chaucer/ (accessed July 2009). For a close comparative reading, see also Ann Thompson, *Shakespeare's Chaucer: A Study in Literary Origins* (Liverpool: Liverpool University Press, 1978).

5. All quotations are from *The Riverside Chaucer*, general editor Larry D. Benson, 3rd ed. (Boston: Houghton and Mifflin, 1987).

6. See the approaching marriage of Theseus and Hippolyta in the first scene and the celebrations in the last act.

7. There were several editions of Chaucer's works printed during the sixteenth century: *The Workes of Geffray Chaucer*, ed. William Thynne (1532, 1542, 1550); ed. J. Stowe (1561); ed. Thomas Speght (1598, 1602). For details of these editions, see *Chaucer's Fame in England*, ed. Jackson Campbell Boswell and Sylvia Wallace Holton, STC Chauceriana, 1475–1640 (New York: Modern Language Association, 2004).

Speght's edition of 1598 contains a long biography of Chaucer and brief "arguments" of each work. Of "The Knight's Tale" it says, "Palamon and Arcite, a paire of friends and fellow prisoners, fight a combat before Duke Theseus, for the lady Emeli, sister to the Queene Ipolita wife of Theseus. A Tale fitting for the person of the Knight, for that it discourseth of the deeds of Armes, and loue of Ladies."

8. Donaldson, *The Swan at the Well*, p. 51.

9. Brian Gibbons, ed., *Romeo and Juliet*, Arden Edition (London: Methuen, 1980), p. 76.

10. Chaucer's knights languish in prison "yeer by yeer" (A.1033); Arcite, when released from prison, spends "a yeer or two" in Thebes before returning to Athens (A.1381), where he serves another "yeer or two" (A.1426) as a page; Palamon's escape succeeds "in the seventhe yer" (A.1462).

11. Derek Pearsall calls this "the most moving line of the poem"; see *The Canterbury Tales* (London: George Allen and Unwin, 1985), p. 136.

12. The repeated references to fate, chance, and divine providence in "The Knight's Tale" make clear that this was a central element in Chaucer's retelling of Boccaccio's story.

13. N. W. Bawcutt, ed., *The Two Noble Kinsmen*, New Penguin Shakespeare (Harmondsworth: Penguin, 1977), p. 27.

14. See the Oxford Edition, ed. Eugene M. Waith (Oxford: Clarendon Press, 1989), pp. 108–9 and note.

15. Other subplots in Shakespearean and Fletcherian drama function similarly. Critics have pointed out the evident influence of Shakespeare's Ophelia on the Jailer's Daughter's madness.

16. In the Royal Shakespeare Company's 1986 production of *Two Noble Kinsmen*—which opened the new Swan Theatre at Stratford-upon-Avon—many found Imogen Stubbs's portrayal of the Jailer's Daughter to be the most memorable feature of the performance. For photographs of this production, see www.rsc.org.uk/ searcharchives/search/text?text=two+noble+kinsmen (accessed July 2009).

The subplot, completely independent of Chaucer,

includes Arcite's encounter with the rustics and the grotesque morris dance prepared by the Schoolmaster in honor of the newly married Theseus, in which the Jailer's Daughter is made to join involuntarily as "a dainty madwoman" to complete the necessary set of dancers with her "rarest gambols" (3.5.83, 86). The entertainment is clearly influenced by *The Masque of the Inner Temple and Gray's Inn*, contributed by Fletcher's close friend and coauthor Francis Beaumont in 1613 for the celebrations around the marriage of King James's daughter Elizabeth to Frederick, Prince Palatine. (See longer note to 3.5.143, p. 259, above.)

17. It is significant in this context that the dramatists have omitted Chaucer's insistence on Theseus's decree that any bloodshed should be avoided, forbidding sharp weapons and the infliction of lethal wounds. This is loudly praised by the people: "God save swich a lord, that is so good / He wilneth no destruccion of blood!" (A.2563–64). Fletcher's Theseus has no such scruples. On Fletcher's characteristic dramatic style, see Clifford Leech, *The John Fletcher Plays* (London: Chatto and Windus, 1962), esp. pp. 144–50.

18. Donaldson, *The Swan at the Well*, pp. 63, 147 n. 13. The Emilia presented at the end of the scene, however, is more consistent with Shakespeare's conception of her, as she concludes: "Poor wench, go weep, for whosoever wins / Loses a noble cousin for thy sins" (4.2.187–88).

19. See Piero Boitani, "The Genius to Improve and Invention: Transformations of the 'Knight's Tale,'" in *Chaucer Traditions: Studies in Honour of Derek Brewer*, ed. Ruth Morse and Barry Windeatt (Cambridge: Cambridge University Press, 1990), pp. 185–98; quotation, 195.

Further Reading

The Two Noble Kinsmen

Abbreviations: *Cym.* = *Cymbeline; H8* = *Henry VIII; KT* = "The Knight's Tale"; *MND* = *A Midsummer Night's Dream; Per.* = *Pericles; Tmp.* = *The Tempest; Tit.* = *Titus Andronicus; Tim.* = *Timon of Athens; Tro.* = *Troilus and Cressida; TNK* = *The Two Noble Kinsmen; WT* = *The Winter's Tale*

Bertram, Paul. *Shakespeare and "The Two Noble Kinsmen."* New Brunswick, N.J.: Rutgers University Press, 1965.
Bertram's study of *TNK* provides separate chapters on the authorship question, the manuscript behind the 1634 Quarto, critical views, and dramatic design. In his critical analysis, the author addresses the play's relationship to Chaucer, the arrangement of the story, wedding symbolism, the Doctor's scenes, and the characterization and thematic significance of the "two bold titlers" (5.3.100). Dividing *TNK* into three movements—the war against Creon (Act 1), the May Day contests (Acts 2 and 3), and the final tournament (Acts 4 and 5)—Bertram claims that the "controlling organization" of the action demonstrates "a single imagination at work," namely, Shakespeare's. The quarrel between Palamon and Arcite moves from being simply a question of "title" to Emilia to a "contest embracing every chivalric virtue." By 5.3, the two kinsmen come to embody "[t]hose best affections that the heavens infuse / In their best-tempered pieces" (1.3.11–12) and prove their "title" to "the name of men." The meaning of their contest

"consists of the viewer's sense of the heroic and human values arising from all the lesser conflicts and confrontations in the preceding acts . . . [and] of the cumulative gathering of these values" as they come together in Act 5. The book concludes with two appendices, one dealing with the play's compositional date and the other providing a checklist of editions. Bertram's claim that bibliographical, historical, and critical analysis supports the argument for Shakespeare's sole authorship is a rarity in *TNK* scholarship; most critics regard the play as a collaboration between Shakespeare and Fletcher.

Donaldson, E. Talbot. "Love, War, and the Cost of Winning: *The Knight's Tale* and *The Two Noble Kinsmen*." In *The Swan at the Well: Shakespeare Reading Chaucer*, pp. 50–73. New Haven: Yale University Press, 1985.

Calling *TNK* a "very unpleasant" play, Donaldson argues that Shakespeare was "fulsomely reexpress[ing]" the dark side of *KT* that he had first observed when writing *MND*: "[N]o play in the canon contains more horrid images than [*TNK*]." Confining himself for the most part to the scenes commonly assigned to Shakespeare, Donaldson makes the following points: (1) the gods in Chaucer (namely Mars, Venus, and Diana) have "an objective existence" missing from the play, where, as "human impulses objectified only in a poetic image," they manipulate human behavior not from above but from within the human heart; (2) the differences between Palamon and Arcite, however slight in Chaucer, are eliminated in the play, whose "design assimilates Arcite to Palamon," the former's "ego . . . inflated to match" the latter's; (3) in contrast to Chaucer's Emily ("hardly more than a poetic image"), Shakespeare's Emilia is more developed, her wish to remain a virgin "not just a girlish whim but a sincere womanly desire"; and (4) Shakespeare's Theseus—"harsher, more remote, more prideful, more bullheaded" than Chaucer's—is even less justified in asserting "the existence of a principle of divine justice that neither work sanctions." Compared with *KT*, *TNK* "has no . . . moral, except that the world dominated by Mars and Venus is a messy one": in short, Emilia's question "Is this winning?" (5.3.163) serves as "an excellent if oblique commentary on the play." Although a collaboration with Fletcher, *TNK* remains Shakespeare's "most direct and unquestionable use of a Chaucerian source."

Edwards, Philip. "On the Design of *The Two Noble Kinsmen*." *Review of English Literature* 5 (October 1964): 89–105.
Edwards argues for a unity of design and a subtlety of theme in *TNK* that reflect the craftsmanship of Shakespeare's hand, especially in Acts 1 and 5, which are generally assigned to him, with the middle acts attributed to Fletcher. The overall design marks a progression from innocence to experience, from the freedom of youthful friendship to the restriction of marriage: 1.1 and 1.3 provide "the clearest presentation of three people [Theseus, Hippolyta, and Emilia] conscious of the two major ways of life it is necessary to tread, innocence and experience, the impulsive life of youth . . . and the more contained life of marriage." Taken together, the first three scenes depict the thwarting of desire when helpless human agents are confronted by forces beyond their control. In a reading that posits "consistency" rather than "contradiction" between the first and final acts, " 'mature' love means abandoning something more worthwhile." This dark vision of love and desire informs the relationship of Theseus and Hippolyta, Emilia's initial vow never to marry, the subplot of the Jailer's Daughter, the facility with which

both Emilia and the Jailer's Daughter accept substitute suitors, and, most notably, the lives of Palamon and Arcite. As their broken bonds of youthful friendship attest, "to gain the new love [of Emilia] is to destroy the old," a theme first suggested in the " 'rivalry' between Pirithous and Hippolyta for Theseus' affection" (1.3). Edwards locates the play's center in Palamon's address to Venus (5.1.85–137), a speech more realistic than romantic in its focus on love's clandestine ways and power to deform. *TNK* rejects the idea of sexual love as "the natural and beautiful fulfillment of an otherwise immature innocence" and charts a movement away from joy to the misery of loss, thus emerging as Shakespeare's "most cynical assessment of the progress of life since the writing of *Tro.*" Edwards concludes that "we really need not be ashamed of" a play having such "purposeful" thematic design.

Frey, Charles H., ed. *Shakespeare, Fletcher and "The Two Noble Kinsmen."* Columbia: University of Missouri Press, 1989.

Frey's anthology consists of ten essays, a brief intro-duction, and an annotated bibliography. The essays cover the following topics: the textual provenance and compositorial attribution of the 1634 Quarto (Paul Werstine), the problem of authorial attribution (Charles H. Frey, Donald K. Hedrick, and Michael D. Bristol), traditions of male friendship (Barry Weller), gender anxiety (Charles H. Frey and Susan Green), the figure of the Amazon in male Western tradition and "crises of male self-definition" (Jeanne Addison Rob-erts), *TNK* as "bourgeois drama" (Richard Abrams), and performance history (Hugh Richmond). Rounding out the volume is Will Hamlin's bibliographical guide to the play's critical and scholarly history. The "emer-gent theme" of the collection is that *TNK*, "a superb dramatic work . . . [whose] time is now," presents "not only rivalrous personalities but also rivalrous systems of identity and value for artistic merit, gender relations, and social class [that] oppose and mingle in curiously self-subverting ways."

Lief, Madelon, and Nicholas F. Radel. "Linguistic Subversion and the Artifice of Rhetoric in *The Two Noble Kinsmen." Shakespeare Quarterly* 38 (1987): 405–25.

Lief and Radel contend that *TNK* is characterized by a "consistent undercutting of the language of invocation," a rhetorical technique employed skillfully by both Shakespeare and Fletcher in their respective scenes. In contrast to the Elizabethan "imitation of ideal . . . patterns of behavior"—i.e., "reality on a grand . . . scale"— the "new verisimilitude" of Fletcherian tragicomedy focuses on quotidian reality and underscores "inconsistencies, discontinuities, and failure of perception." The rhetoric crafted to convey this new realism prompted the audience to respond to spectacle and language "as empirical data": the result of "rhetorical and ritualistic patterns" at odds with the experiences of the characters is "a skeptical drama that plays on the tension between reality and the attempt of characters to impose order on that reality." To illustrate how Shakespeare and Fletcher undermine "idealist mimesis and decorum" in *TNK*, the authors first examine the language of Palamon and Arcite in Fletcher's 2.2; failing to "live up to their words" once they've seen Emilia, the two kinsmen emerge as "small, absurd creatures, interesting not as they grapple with great ideas, morality, and ethics, but, rather, as they are unable to do so." Fletcher's "subversion of the idealist mimesis" in the scenes attributed to him "becomes, in Shakespeare's more able hands, a questioning of man's ability to comprehend fully his place in the cosmos"; see, for example, 1.1, 1.3, and 5.1, where audience response to the rhetoric and pageantry is qualified by Shakespeare's insinuation that both "are impotent and fail to create order." As further evidence of how the dramatists' "artifice of rhetoric ... creates a [skeptical] perspective on the action of [*TNK*], and vice versa," Lief and Radel point to the subplot, observing how the Doctor's pragmatic treatment of the Jailer's Daughter and the Schoolmaster's "sterile rhetorical figures" expose the "inadequacy" of Theseus's "abstract, ritualistic, and ethical codes." While Fletcher's dramatic gifts differ from Shakespeare's, the resulting discrepancies in the play are not as "serious" as some critics have claimed. Fletcher is "never as profound as Shakespeare," but through his "powerful manipulation of language and of subplot," he helps "to consolidate in [*TNK*] a theatrical technique that reflects a cynical and problematic world view emerging in Shakespeare's late plays and in non-Shakespearean drama of the early seventeenth century."

Lynch, Kathryn. L. "The Three Noble Kinsmen: Chaucer, Shakespeare, Fletcher." In *Images of Matter: Essays on British Literature of the Middle Ages and Renaissance*, edited by Yvonne Bruce, pp. 72–91. (Proceedings of the Eighth Citadel Conference on Literature, Charleston, South Carolina, 2002.) Newark: University of Delaware Press, 2005.

In *TNK*, Shakespeare's "uneasy emulation" of Chaucer combines with Fletcher's "revisionary engagement" with Shakespeare to produce a play that "conceives of itself ... as a collaboration between all three of these authors." While medieval writers tended to "genuflect ... in the direction of [their] sources," Shakespeare rarely did so; in his last play, *TNK*, however, he and Fletcher begin by acknowledging the play's "medieval foundation in Chaucer ... [and] continue ... to explore the meaning of that foundation by weaving the themes of emulation and authority into virtually every instant." Lynch singles out 1.2 (by Shakespeare) and 2.2 (by Fletcher) to demonstrate how each time either playwright tries to escape Chaucer's influence, "the pull of the narrative source" is felt. The Prologue's reference to the play as a child descended from Chaucer and dependent on a receptive audience (lines 15–18) suggests that collaboration "both creates the problem of legitimacy and shows the way out of it": i.e., through acknowledging and exploiting its "collaborative thematics," *TNK* may finally "rise above them." In what may be Shakespeare's valedictory to the theater, he "reveals both his nostalgia and his anxiety, allowing a glimpse both of the unfinished business he has with the past, especially with his most powerful literary father, Chaucer, and the nervousness even a strong father can experience about [the legacy he leaves to] his sons." For Lynch, Shakespeare's and Fletcher's appropriation of Chaucer in *TNK* is not a transparent or uncomplicated gesture of respect for the medieval poet but rather a "self-conscious performance of competition in several keys—political, sexual, literary, historical, sibling."

Magnusson, Lynne. "The Collapse of Shakespeare's High Style in *The Two Noble Kinsmen*." *English Studies in Canada* 13 (1987): 375–90.

Magnusson closely examines the opening and final scenes of *TNK* in order to determine the ends to which Shakespeare deploys the "ornate eloquence" that marks the many "virtuoso pieces" in his portion of the play. Her stylistic analysis (of cadence, imagery, diction, syntax, and rhetorical devices) focuses on the following passages: 1.1.65–78, 100–111, 118–34, 197–201, 202–8; 5.4.62–101, and 147–60. The "stylized, . . . strange, and over-ornate" representation of the grieving queens and the conflicted Theseus in 1.1 reflects the scene's formality and dazzling pageantry but fails to persuade us that the high style voices the speakers' innermost feelings. Instead, verbal fluency is contrived to invest a situation lacking in "compelling necessity" with serious meaning: the burial of bones did not evoke the same passion in the seventeenth century that it did in the world of Antigone; and Theseus's "dilemma" is neither problematic nor heroic in that he is not being asked to sacrifice his marriage, only to postpone it briefly. Turning to 5.4, "the stagiest climax" in Shakespeare, Magnusson argues that "gorgeous rhetoric" produces a comic effect, as evidenced by Pirithous's mock-heroic narrative of Arcite's fatal accident ("teasingly digressive" in its syntax) and Theseus's closing speech (an "empty consolation," awkward in its use of rhyme and paradox). Stylistic ornament, combined with the melodrama of a stayed execution, a death on cue, and a reconciliation "given short shrift," makes for a farcical conclusion. Close analysis of 1.1 and 5.4 demonstrates Shakespeare's use of "high style" rhetoric for contradictory purposes: first, to "conceal a failure of substance, and invite . . . serious presentation"; then, to "reveal a failure of substance, and invite . . . send-up." Speculating on the problems inherent in collaborating with Fletcher, Magnusson wonders whether the "self-exhibiting and self-consuming verbal devices of the finale may be Shakespeare's attempt to salvage at least some entertainment from a collaboration without common purpose."

Neely, Carol Thomas. "Diagnosing Women's Melancholy: Case Histories and the Jailer's Daughter's Cure in *Two Noble Kinsmen*." In *Distracted Subjects: Madness and Gender in Shakespeare and Early Modern Culture*, pp. 69–98. Ithaca: Cornell University Press, 2004.

Neely's book examines "changes in the discourse of madness" between the years 1576 and 1632. This chapter focuses on how cultural pressures "lead polemic texts to revise the Galenic tradition of deluded melancholics and create a new subdivision, female melancholy," theorized in contemporary case histories of women sufferers as a disease of the mind and genitals: "women grow deluded by desire," i.e., by their congested or disordered reproductive organs, not by witchcraft and possession. This new thinking "grow[s] out of the urgent scrutiny of women's distraction in the light of pressing needs to reassess supernaturally caused ailments as natural diseases." Neely uses the exemplars found in Andre Du Laurens's *Of melancholike diseases* (1599), Edward Jorden's *Briefe Discourse of a Disease called the Suffocation of the Mother* (1603), and Reginald Scot's *Discoverie of Witchcraft* (1584) to argue that in *TNK* (1613) Shakespeare and Fletcher "picked up and circulated" this "regendered and hence reconceptualized" theory of melancholy in the character of the Jailer's Daughter, whose growing delusion is brought on by her frustrated sexual desire for Palamon, and whose chief prescribed cure by the Doctor, namely, "coital cure," reflects the common remedy advocated in medical tracts of the period. By dramatizing the Jailer's Daughter's madness and its cure, Shakespeare and Fletcher situate women's delusions in their bodies and establish the "benefit of marriage" as therapy. When conflated with theatrical cures for deluded melancholics, the new medical remedies prescribed for women diagnosed with melancholy resulting from disordered reproductive functions "creat[ed] irresistible opportunities for stage representation and new models of female subjectivity."

Sanders, Julie. "Mixed Messages: The Aesthetics of *Two Noble Kinsmen*." In *A Companion to Shakespeare's*

Works, edited by Richard Dutton and Jean Howard, 4:445–61. Malden, Mass.: Blackwell, 2004.

Arguing that *TNK* is a product of its time, Sanders draws links between the play's generic and aesthetic structures "that commit it both to the physical playing conditions of its original performance and the political situation of 1613." She divides her argument into three parts: an analysis of the drama's five-act structure (new to Shakespeare at the time he co-wrote the play with Fletcher); a description of the architectural features of the Blackfriars theater (where *TNK* was probably first performed) and of specific spaces and places invoked and explored in the play; and a discussion of the impact on *TNK* of contemporary events (e.g., the death of Prince Henry in November 1612 followed by the wedding of Princess Elizabeth in February 1613) and of aesthetic contexts (most notably, the "dominant interest in tragicomedy . . . matched by the increased influence of the parallel genre of the masque"). Sanders describes at length the play's mastery of the possibilities inherent in a five-act structure; Act 1, for instance, "performs in microcosm the overall architectonic design of the play: wedding to funeral." She also notes an attentiveness to tragicomedy's preoccupation with margins (e.g., country settings, local concerns, women's issues, pastoral, and folklore motifs); even the play's tendency to stage major events just off-stage reflects the genre's structural bias toward margins. Observing how the physical setting of Blackfriars "encouraged . . . aesthetic links between the essentially aristocratic form of masque and the public playhouse [see, e.g., the Globe's *H8*]," Sanders turns her attention to such works as *The Masque of the Inner Temple and Gray's Inn*, *The Caversham Entertainment*, *The Lord's Masque*, and *The Coleorton Masque*. Her concern, however, is not so much with the "precise mappings of particular masques" onto *TNK* but rather with a recognition that a "nuanced notion of . . . the early Stuart masque is crucial to a proper understanding of the political as well as dramatic aesthetics of [*TNK*]." She concludes that the play is "the product of a coherent and cohesive attitude to the events of their day by two brilliant and insightful writers."

Scott, Mark W., and Sandra L. Williamson, eds. *"The Two Noble Kinsmen."* In *Shakespearean Criticism: Excerpts from the Criticism of William Shakespeare's Plays and Poetry from the First Published Appraisals to Current Evaluations,* 9:439–510. Detroit: Gale Research, 1986.

This volume presents significant passages from published criticism on *TNK*. The set of passages is introduced by a brief discussion of the "date," "text," and "sources," followed by a longer discussion of the "critical history" of the play. Each entry, beginning with Alexander Pope (1725) and ending with Paula S. Berggren (1984), is prefaced with a brief historical overview that places the excerpted document in the context of responses to the play. The thirty entries include commentary from William Warburton (1747), George Steevens (1780), Charles Lamb (1808), Samuel Taylor Coleridge (1811), William Spalding (1833), G. G. Gervinus (1849–50), Edward Dowden (1877), Algernon Charles Swinburne (1880), Theodore Spencer (1939), Mark Van Doren (1939), Kenneth Muir (1960), Clifford Leech (1962, 1966), Frank Kermode (1963), Philip Edwards (1964; see entry above), N. W. Bawcutt (1977), and F. W. Brownlow (1977). A briefly annotated bibliography of thirty-two additional items concludes the section. Subsequent volumes in the series update the criticism under the headings "Overviews," "General Studies," "Authorship Issue," "Production

Reviews," "Themes" (especially love and friendship), "Characterization," "Language and Structure," "Social Class," "Gender Roles," and "Relation to Chaucer" (see 41:289–391, 50:294–381, 58:321–78, and 70:302–45); each volume includes suggestions for further reading.

Shannon, Laurie J. "Emilia's Argument: Friendship and 'Human Title' in *Two Noble Kinsmen*." *ELH* 64 (1997): 657–82.

Whereas traditional readings of *TNK* accord with the "conventional privileged place of marriage in dramatic comedy," Shannon claims that the play offers an "astonishingly negative" view of marriage as a "brutally . . . political institution." To illustrate her thesis, she focuses on the character of Emilia, more expansive, complex, and active than her Chaucerian counterpart. In the female voice of a reasoning and self-possessed Amazon, the play not only rebuts the classical and early modern trope of ideal friendship as possible only between male equals but also offers a counterpoint to the tyranny of "coercive marriage . . . [and in the person of Theseus] tyranny in its plain political sense." Central to Emilia's role as advocate for female friendship, female proprietary space, and volitional chastity ("a homosocial bond between women" rather than simply a state of "single blessedness") are her nostalgic remembrance of the affection shared with Flavina (1.3), her present mirth in the company of her Woman (2.2), and her repeated use of a female standard to evaluate situations (see 2.5.28–30; 3.6.305–11; and 4.2.28–31). In the end, however, Theseus's imposition of marriage transforms Emilia from agent to victim: the defeat of female homoerotics, marked by a funeral rather than a wedding. Still, what makes *TNK* such an "extraordinary text" for its time is that the great figure of resistance to tyrannical power in the play is neither of the male friends but "a lady knight who revises the definitional prejudices of the male model regarding both gender and sexuality." Through Emilia, Shakespeare and Fletcher rewrite the period's characteristically masculine friendship rhetoric to suggest that female friendship is both preferable to and more lasting than the male kind.

Sinfield, Alan. "Cultural Materialists and Intertextuality: The Limits of Queer Reading in *MND* and *TNK*." *Shakespeare Survey* 56 (2003): 67–78. [The original essay is incorporated into Alan Sinfield, *Shakespeare, Authority, Sexuality: Unfinished Business in Cultural Materialism*, chapter 5 (pp. 68–85) (London: Routledge, 2006).]

Sinfield offers a queer reading of same-sex alternatives to male-female relationships in *MND* and *TNK*, two plays with strong similarities, among them the interrupted nuptials of Theseus and Hippolyta, the disruption of the affections of marriageable young people, and the festive presentations by lower-class characters. Supplying aspects of the ideological environment of *MND*, the later play accentuates the alternatives selected by each text as it "actualizes different parts of their shared field of possibilities." In *TNK*, for example, the fuller evocation of female independence by Hippolyta differs from her attitude toward marriage in *MND*; similarly, the same sex-bonding found in Emilia's nostalgic remembrance of her friendship with the late Flavina (*TNK* 1.3.57–93) contrasts with the negative view of women living together in *MND* (where Theseus threatens Hermia with "the livery of a nun . . . in shady cloister mewed" [1.1.72–73]). Ironically, at the moment when Palamon and Arcite first see Emilia and their friendship is fractured, she remains onstage talking to her waiting woman about the supe-

riority of female relationships (2.2). Although now cast
as opponents, the combative young kinsmen continue
their male bonding in that they spend more time fighting with each other than wooing Emilia. In contrast,
Lysander and Demetrius pay only occasional attention
to each other in their play. While *TNK* suggests a significant context for companionable same-sex passion,
MND implies such bonding not among the play's boys
and girls but in Titania's devotion to a votaress of her
order and in Oberon's desire for "a little changeling
boy" (2.1.123). "Read[ing] against the grain," Sinfield
suggests that a ménage à trois in *TNK* would be a more
satisfactory solution than the funeral of Arcite and the
planned wedding of Emilia and Palamon. If he were
to stage *MND*, the author would have the four lovers
resist Oberon's drugs to produce some "more interesting interpersonal combinations." Sinfield intends such
readings to provide "a critical perspective upon [the
plays'] ideological assumptions and, indeed, upon our
own."

Stewart, Alan. " 'Near Kin': The Trials of Friendship in
Two Noble Kinsmen." In *Shakespeare's Late Plays: New
Readings,* edited by Jennifer Richards, pp. 57–71. Edinburgh: Edinburgh University Press, 1999.
   Stewart argues that contrary to being a "failed
attempt at a play about idealised male friendship,
[*TNK*] is rather a play about a failed attempt at idealised male friendship." He locates the cause of this
failure in the tension between classical and chivalric
traditions of male friendship and the "realities of social
relations" in Jacobean England, especially as manifest
in a particular form of kinship: cognatic cousinage (i.e.,
the relationship of first cousins who, as the children
of sisters, share a lineage derivative from the female
side). As evidenced by the thirty-eight times they refer

to themselves in "kinship terms," Palamon and Arcite see themselves primarily as kinsmen, specifically as cousins; consequently, the best way to approach *TNK* is to think of it "as a play about the problems of kinship," not friendship. When understood in the context of a Jacobean culture that, especially among aristocratic and upper classes, continued to regard women as commodities to be exchanged between patriarchal houses, first cousins through the female line "are necessarily born into different houses, because their mothers married into different houses. This means, then, that the connection between the two cousins is not necessarily mutually beneficial." Stewart contends that the "futility" of the young men's kinship in the play is "signalled throughout . . . by a skillfully maintained figurative representation [that insistently] return[s] to figures of maternity" (e.g., 2.5.28–30; 4.2.30–31, 69–70) and to images of passive male sexuality (see the Ovidian analogies to Narcissus and Ganymede in 2.2.135–37 and 4.2.13–23, 28–35). With the cousins "firmly established as mothers' boys, the masculinity of both Palamon and Arcite is steadily chipped away." The passage at 2.2.85–93 is "one of the most passionate friendship speeches in English literature," but its sentiment is undermined by the fact that the young men are incarcerated and deprived of "their social agency": the hyperbolic promise to be each other's wife, family, and heir is immediately "shelved" once they glimpse "a way back into the real world . . . in the form of Emilia, marriage to whom will ensure not only freedom but social success in Athens." The social implications of cognatic kinship and the expedient nature of their friendship—"no more than a game to while away long hours of incarceration"—require the death of one knight (an incidental detail in Chaucer): for Palamon to win, Arcite must die. Fletcher and Shakespeare "indulge their audience in the comfortable humanist myth of *amicitia*, and the reliable codes of chivalric courtship, only to force that audience to accept the fact that ultimately these are no more than myths and codes, and that they cannot thrive together."

Thompson, Ann. *"The Two Noble Kinsmen."* In *Shakespeare's Chaucer: A Study in Literary Origins*, pp. 166–215. Liverpool: Liverpool University Press, 1978.

In her comprehensive study of Shakespeare's use of Chaucer, Thompson devotes chapter 5 to a comparative analysis of *TNK* and its primary source, Chaucer's *KT*. Thompson's scene-by-scene study confirms the "orthodox position" on the division of the play between Shakespeare and Fletcher: Acts 1 and 5 are generally assigned to Shakespeare, the middle acts (with the exception of 2.1., 3.1 and 2, and 4.3) to Fletcher. The main focus of the chapter is, in fact, "the contrast between the two dramatists . . . [who] clearly saw completely different things" in their Chaucerian source, which they "dramatized . . . in quite independent ways." The chapter concludes with a section titled "Chaucer, romance, and tragicomedy." Thompson's comparative study demonstrates that in an effort to "turn [*KT*] into a commercial tragicomedy like *Philaster*," Fletcher emphasizes situations and sensational effects at the expense of plot development and coherence of character. Shakespeare, on the other hand, approaches the source from the perspective of his final romances, which "do *not* modify accepted comic and tragic patterns in the manner of Fletcherian tragicomedy" but instead "make a more genuine claim to combine the qualities of both." The theme of sexual love's "degrading effects . . . and the jealousy which can accompany it," while present in *Cym.* and *WT*, is stronger in *TNK*. A skepticism greater than that found in *Tmp.*, an emphasis on "human impotence," the depiction of the gods as "arbitrary and controlling forces," and a consideration of "the dark side of love, . . . its cruelty, and above all its cost" make *TNK* "grimmer than the other romances": "the first of [what could have been] a new set of 'dark comedies' or 'problem plays.'" Its inconsistencies and discrepancies afford a "unique opportunity . . . to observe the many differences between [a late Shakespearean romance] and the new genre of Fletcherian tragicomedy."

Vickers, Brian. "*Henry VIII* and *The Two Noble Kinsmen* with John Fletcher." In *Shakespeare, Co-Author: A Historical Study of Five Collaborative Plays*, pp. 333–432, esp. 402–32. Oxford: Oxford University Press, 2002.

In his study of Shakespeare as coauthor of five plays (*Tit.*, *Tim.*, *Per.*, *H8*, and *TNK*), Vickers devotes chapter 6 to the Shakespeare-Fletcher collaboration responsible for *H8* and *TNK*. The designation of the latter as a collaborative effort between the two dramatists dates from the first documentary mention of the play in the Stationers' Register on April 8, 1634, and from the title page of the earliest printed edition, the 1634 Quarto, where the printer John Waterson (none of whose attributions have been thought to be false) attributes *TNK* to both playwrights. Vickers describes at length the scholarly work done through the centuries ascribing the authorship of particular scenes to Shakespeare or Fletcher; early commentators cited include George Steevens (1780), Henry Weber (1812), William Spalding (1833), Samuel Hickson (1847), and Harold Littledale (1885). From the twentieth century, Vickers considers Alfred Hart's scrutiny of Shakespeare's word formations (1934) and Paul Werstine's examination of the influence of compositors on the text (1989). As detailed in the chapter, the pattern of collaboration shows Shakespeare tackling the exposition for the main plot, beginning the subplot of the Jailer's Daughter, contributing various scenes throughout, and reserving for himself the final scene. In addition to stylistic and metrical evidence of coauthorship, Vickers notes how characterization changes when one dramatist takes over for the other: for example, in Fletcher's depiction of Palamon and Arcite, the two kinsmen, first seen as moralists with a strong sense of indignation at Theban corruption (1.2), become "two-dimensional swains" who indulge their griefs (2.2.1–59). Emilia also changes from Shakespeare's chaste virgin with a lack of interest in men to a woman with a taste for sexual innuendos when Fletcher writes her. Differences between the two playwrights' handling of the source material may derive from Shakespeare's longer experience in the theater and Fletcher's desire to adapt Chaucer's story to the pattern of tragicomedy. By giving himself the final scene, something he did not do in *H8*, Shakespeare was able to end the play on "a black note" and give it "a far more unified conclusion than had been achieved in [*H8*]."

Waith, Eugene M. "Shakespeare and Fletcher on Love and Friendship." *Shakespeare Studies* 18 (1986): 235–50.

In a close reading of individual scenes, Waith examines the conflict between love and friendship that underlies the main plot of *TNK*. His focus is on Shakespeare's and Fletcher's "shifts of emphasis" in their dramatization of the story of Palamon and Arcite, a narrative previously found in Boccaccio's *Teseida* and Chaucer's *KT*. Accepting the usual division of scenes between Shakespeare and Fletcher, Waith notes differences in their respective treatments of love and friendship but also observes a "large measure of cooperation": the play, in fact, is "better unified than is often granted." In contrast to both Boccaccio and Chaucer, Shakespeare and Fletcher make friendship central to their version of the story: in the first three scenes, generally assigned to Shakespeare, a "high value" is placed on the friendships of Theseus and Pirithous, Palamon and Arcite, and Emilia and Flavina; from their first appearance to their last, the equality of the two kinsmen (the foundation of ideal friendship in Cicero and Montaigne) is stressed; and in Act 3, both dramatists (Shakespeare in 3.1 and Fletcher in 3.3 and 3.6) play up the importance of courtesy between two friends now cast as opponents in love. "Courtesy may be only a faint echo of their friendship, but in the extreme instance of the civilized treatment of an enemy who threatens one's life it is a reminder of the high ideals on which that friendship was founded." The irony and potential for absurdity in Palamon's and Arcite's declarations of undying friendship notwithstanding, we are never meant to question the quality of their commitment to each other. *TNK*'s bias toward friendship over love is most pronounced in Act 5: see, for example, the embrace of the two kinsmen before the tournament (5.1); Emilia's compassion for Arcite on the loss of Palamon (5.3), for whom "no woman can atone"; and the "moving reassertion of the bond of friendship so nearly destroyed by love" (5.4.102–13). Unlike the Palamon in Boccaccio and Chaucer, Shakespeare's Palamon "asks for and receives Arcite's last words," thereby making clear that Emilia is won only through the loss of a friend. As befits a tragicomedy, the play concludes with plans for a wedding, but "the tone of the final lines is as somber as that of most tragedies. The predominant feeling is one of friendship lost."

Shakespeare's Life

Baldwin, T. W. *William Shakspere's Petty School*. Urbana: University of Illinois Press, 1943.

Baldwin here investigates the theory and practice of the petty school, the first level of education in Elizabethan England. He focuses on that educational system primarily as it is reflected in Shakespeare's art.

Baldwin, T. W. *William Shakspere's Small Latine and Lesse Greeke*. 2 vols. Urbana: University of Illinois Press, 1944.

Baldwin attacks the view that Shakespeare was an uneducated genius—a view that had been dominant among Shakespeareans since the eighteenth century. Instead, Baldwin shows, the educational system of Shakespeare's time would have given the playwright a strong background in the classics, and there is much in the plays that shows how Shakespeare benefited from such an education.

Beier, A. L., and Roger Finlay, eds. *London 1500–1700: The Making of the Metropolis*. New York: Longman, 1986.

Focusing on the economic and social history of early modern London, these collected essays probe aspects of metropolitan life, including "Population and Disease," "Commerce and Manufacture," and "Society and Change."

Bentley, G. E. *Shakespeare's Life: A Biographical Handbook*. New Haven: Yale University Press, 1961.

This "just-the-facts" account presents the surviving documents of Shakespeare's life against an Elizabethan background.

Chambers, E. K. *William Shakespeare: A Study of Facts and Problems*. 2 vols. Oxford: Clarendon Press, 1930.
Analyzing in great detail the scant historical data, Chambers's complex, scholarly study considers the nature of the texts in which Shakespeare's work is preserved.

Cressy, David. *Education in Tudor and Stuart England*. London: Edward Arnold, 1975.
This volume collects sixteenth-, seventeenth-, and early eighteenth-century documents detailing aspects of formal education in England, such as the curriculum, the control and organization of education, and the education of women.

Dutton, Richard. *William Shakespeare: A Literary Life*. New York: St. Martin's Press, 1989.
Not a biography in the traditional sense, Dutton's very readable work nevertheless "follows the contours of Shakespeare's life" as Dutton examines Shakespeare's career as playwright and poet, with consideration of his patrons, theatrical associations, and audience.

Honan, Park. *Shakespeare: A Life*. New York: Oxford University Press, 1998.
Honan's accessible biography focuses on the various contexts of Shakespeare's life—physical, social, political, and cultural—to place the dramatist within a lucidly described world. The biography includes detailed examinations of, for example, Stratford schooling, theatrical politics of 1590s London, and the careers of Shakespeare's associates. The author draws on a wealth of established knowledge and on interesting new research into local records and documents; he also engages in speculation about, for example, the possibilities that Shakespeare was a tutor in a Catho-

lic household in the north of England in the 1580s and that he played particular roles in his own plays, areas that reflect new, but unproven and debatable, data—though Honan is usually careful to note where a particular narrative "has not been capable of proof or disproof."

Schoenbaum, S. *William Shakespeare: A Compact Documentary Life*. New York: Oxford University Press, 1977.
This standard biography economically presents the essential documents from Shakespeare's time in an accessible narrative account of the playwright's life.

Shakespeare's Theater

Bentley, G. E. *The Profession of Player in Shakespeare's Time, 1590–1642*. Princeton: Princeton University Press, 1984.
Bentley readably sets forth a wealth of evidence about performance in Shakespeare's time, with special attention to the relations between player and company, and the business of casting, managing, and touring.

Berry, Herbert. *Shakespeare's Playhouses*. New York: AMS Press, 1987.
Berry's six essays collected here discuss (with illustrations) varying aspects of the four playhouses in which Shakespeare had a financial stake: the Theatre in Shoreditch, the Blackfriars, and the first and second Globe.

Berry, Herbert, William Ingram, and Glynne Wickham, eds. *English Professional Theatre, 1530–1660*. Cambridge: Cambridge University Press, 2000.
Wickham presents the government documents

designed to control professional players, their plays, and playing places. Ingram handles the professional actors, giving as representative a life of the actor Augustine Phillips, and discussing, among other topics, patrons, acting companies, costumes, props, playbooks, provincial playing, and child actors. Berry treats the twenty-three different London playhouses from 1560 to 1660 for which there are records, including four inns.

Cook, Ann Jennalie. *The Privileged Playgoers of Shakespeare's London*. Princeton: Princeton University Press, 1981.

Cook's work argues, on the basis of sociological, economic, and documentary evidence, that Shakespeare's audience—and the audience for English Renaissance drama generally—consisted mainly of the "privileged."

Greg, W. W. *Dramatic Documents from the Elizabethan Playhouses*. 2 vols. Oxford: Clarendon Press, 1931.

Greg itemizes and briefly describes many of the play manuscripts that survive from the period 1590 to around 1660, including, among other things, players' parts. His second volume offers facsimiles of selected manuscripts.

Gurr, Andrew. *Playgoing in Shakespeare's London*. 2nd ed. Cambridge: Cambridge University Press, 1996.

Gurr charts how the theatrical enterprise developed from its modest beginnings in the late 1560s to become a thriving institution in the 1600s. He argues that there were important changes over the period 1567–1644 in the playhouses, the audience, and the plays.

Harbage, Alfred. *Shakespeare's Audience*. New York: Columbia University Press, 1941.

Harbage investigates the fragmentary surviving evidence to interpret the size, composition, and behavior of Shakespeare's audience.

Hattaway, Michael. *Elizabethan Popular Theatre: Plays in Performance*. London: Routledge and Kegan Paul, 1982.
  Beginning with a study of the popular drama of the late Elizabethan age—a description of the stages, performance conditions, and acting of the period—this volume concludes with an analysis of five well-known plays of the 1590s, one of them (*Titus Andronicus*) by Shakespeare.

Shapiro, Michael. *Children of the Revels: The Boy Companies of Shakespeare's Time and Their Plays*. New York: Columbia University Press, 1977.
  Shapiro chronicles the history of the amateur and quasi-professional child companies that flourished in London at the end of Elizabeth's reign and the beginning of James's.

The Publication of Shakespeare's Plays

Blayney, Peter W. M. *The First Folio of Shakespeare*. Hanover, Md.: Folger, 1991.
  Blayney's accessible account of the printing and later life of the First Folio—an amply illustrated catalog to a 1991 Folger Shakespeare Library exhibition—analyzes the mechanical production of the First Folio, describing how the Folio was made, by whom and for whom, how much it cost, and its ups and downs (or, rather, downs and ups) since its printing in 1623.

Hinman, Charlton. *The Norton Facsimile: The First Folio of Shakespeare*. 2nd ed. New York: W. W. Norton, 1996.

This facsimile presents a photographic reproduction of an "ideal" copy of the First Folio of Shakespeare; Hinman attempts to represent each page in its most fully corrected state. The second edition includes an important new introduction by Peter W. M. Blayney.

Hinman, Charlton. *The Printing and Proof-Reading of the First Folio of Shakespeare*. 2 vols. Oxford: Clarendon Press, 1963.

In the most arduous study of a single book ever undertaken, Hinman attempts to reconstruct how the Shakespeare First Folio of 1623 was set into type and run off the press, sheet by sheet. He also provides almost all the known variations in readings from copy to copy.

Key to
Famous Lines and Phrases

Small winds shake him.

[*Palamon*—1.2.100]

This world's a city full of straying streets,
And death's the market-place where each one meets.

[*Third Queen*—1.5.17–18]

Men are mad things.

[*Emilia*—2.2.148]

You play the child extremely.

[*Arcite*—2.2.265]

I shall live
To knock thy brains out[.]

[*Palamon*—2.2.281–82]

Thou bringst such pelting, scurvy news continually,
Thou art not worthy life.

[*Palamon*—2.2.342–43]

To marry him is hopeless;
To be his whore is witless.

[*Jailer's Daughter*—2.4.4–5]

I'll proclaim him,
And to his face, no man.

[*Jailer's Daughter*—2.6.30–31]

A very thief in love, a chaffy lord,
Nor worth the name of villain.

[*Palamon*—3.1.43–44]

She's lost past all cure.

[*Jailer*—4.1.185]

I think she has a perturbed mind, which I cannot minister to.

[*Doctor*—4.3.61–62]

His part is played, and though it were too short,
He did it well.

[*Theseus*—5.4.123–24]

O you heavenly charmers,
What things you make of us! For what we lack
We laugh, for what we have are sorry, still
Are children in some kind.

[*Theseus*—5.4.154–57]

THE FOLGER
SHAKESPEARE LIBRARY

The world's leading center for Shakespeare studies presents
acclaimed editions of Shakespeare's plays.

For more information on Folger Shakespeare Library Editions, including
Shakespeare Set Free teaching guides, visit www.simonandschuster.com.